TROUBLEMAKERS

REBELLIOUS YOUTH IN
AN AFFLUENT SOCIETY

T. R. FYVEL

SCHOCKEN BOOKS · NEW YORK

Library of Congress Catalog Card No. 62–13142

Manufactured in the United States of America

For my daughters
HANNAH and SUSAN

Acknowledgements

Grateful acknowledgements are due to the authors and publishers for permission to quote from the following works:

Teddy Boys' Picnic, by Elizabeth Stucley (Anthony Blond).

Essays on the Welfare State, by Richard M. Titmuss (Allen & Unwin).

Social Science and Social Pathology, by Barbara Wootton (Allen & Unwin).

Borstal Boy, by Brendan Behan (Hutchinson).

The Affluent Society, by J. K. Galbraith (Hamish Hamilton).

The Young Devils, by John Townsend (Chatto & Windus).

Shooting an Elephant, by George Orwell (Secker & Warburg).

Juvenile Delinquency in Post-War Europe (The Council of Europe).

The Teenage Consumer, by Mark Abrams (London Press Exchange).

Delinquency, by Herbert E. Block and Frank T. Flynn (Random House, New York).

"What can we do about J.D.?", by Virginia P. Held (*The Reporter*, New York).

"Delinquency: the Size of the Problem", by Richard Perlman (*The Annals*, Philadelphia).

Khrushchev's Russia, by Edward Crankshaw (Penguin Books).

Contents

CONTENTS

Part Four: INTERNATIONAL

Preface

THIS is a book whose final shape is due largely to the circumstances of its composition, for what began as a study of certain kinds of disturbed young people has turned very much into a study of the society that gave them birth. This may require some explanation. My original intention in *Troublemakers* had been to write about the problems of juvenile delinquency mainly in relation to new trends in penal thought and practice. But the further I went into the subject, the more strongly I felt that the whole phenomenon of juvenile delinquency, which has been so much in the news, had to be seen from a wider viewpoint—that it could be understood only in the context of the sweeping social and cultural changes which are today transforming our Western society, as well as Soviet Russia. Conversely, while delinquency was only a marginal problem, it seemed to me that its study threw a special light on the nature of these changes. It is as an attempt—over-ambitious, perhaps—to illustrate these two themes that *Troublemakers* is presented to the reader.

It is also put forward as a book by a layman in penal matters —my previous writing has been largely on political themes— and as an informal study based on very many personal interviews and discussions in a number of countries. I need hardly add that the conclusions I have drawn, with all their shortcomings, are my own, in no way implicating my informants.

At the same time I must acknowledge my special indebtedness. I am grateful to Mr. Merfyn Turner and Mr. Hugh Klare for moral support at the outset of this work, to Mr. Hugh Lunghi and Mr. Leopold Labedz for expert advice on Soviet sources, and to Mrs. Evelyn Anderson for valuable counsel at various stages of this work. In my reading I have found Lady Wootton's recent survey of social science and social pathology an admirable compendium of current views on penology, and I am also directly indebted to the writings on British sociological themes of Richard Hoggart and Mark Abrams. In certain chapters I have drawn freely on Professor J. K. Galbraith's writings about the affluent society, though my own use of the term may well be idiosyncratic.

Some further remarks to the American reader may here be in order. *Troublemakers* is in the first place an enquiry into juvenile delinquency in Britain. While this may appear a relatively small problem to American readers, I believe that its analysis should not be without interest. At any rate, just as I have tried to show this British problem in its social setting, so for its proper evaluation I have found it necessary to go further afield. In the second half of this book, therefore, juvenile delinquency in Britain is compared and contrasted with the same phenomenon in the more bourgeois countries of Continental Europe, in the United States, and in a different setting in the Soviet Union. The chapters on trends in the United States should therefore be read as a comparative British view of a rather disturbing American problem—as a picture of how this problem looks when viewed (I hope, with some understanding) from across the Atlantic.

Lastly, a brief personal note. Readers may remark that I introduce my chapters on the United States with some passages by George Orwell, and these represent in a sense one real starting point. In 1947, when I was working on a London weekly for which Orwell wrote, there came across my desk a new edition of John Habberton's one-time American best-seller, *Helen's Babies,* which both Orwell and I discovered we had read as boys. It was as the outcome of our nostalgic discussion that Orwell (who had never visited America) wrote one of his most perceptive essays, *Riding Down to Bangor,* in which he compared children's books of the earlier United States with some of the far from innocent reading matter produced today. Orwell's thoughts in this essay, in turn, were still among the strands in my mind when years later I turned to the problem of troubled youth in the United States. As for my acquaintance with it, this is based in part on reading and discussion, and in part on an extensive study trip through the United States which a generous American institution enabled me to take.

All in all, therefore, I should like *Troublemakers* to be regarded as a book by a political writer on a subject new to him, but which he found increasingly compelling; a book which, in addition to figures, theory and quotations, seeks to present the middle-aged author himself as, in various parts of the world, he gazed wonderingly around at the problems of the young, with but one certainty in mind—that we are living in a time of revolutionary social change of which we should take note.

London, December 1961   T. R. F.

Glossary

An explanation of some British administrative, penal, and educational terms may be helpful. A "Committee of Inquiry", on which laymen and officials serve together, is a favorite British Government means of dealing with a problem, either to shelve it or, more rarely, to produce a report which serves as a social landmark. A statement of Government policy in connection with such a report is often called a "White Paper". The "Home Office" is the British department of state which deals with penal matters. In the case of juveniles, its functions extend to some of those covered in the United States by the Department of Health, Education, and Welfare. In 1961, the Home Office had been presided over for some years by a well known Conservative Party leader, Mr. R. A. Butler.

British court procedure is scarcely touched upon in this volume. The British Probation Service, while differing in detail, is in principle similar to that of the United States. As for the official British age categories for young offenders, those from 8 to 17 go before juvenile courts (where, incidentally, their names may not be revealed by the press). The corrective institutions to which they may be sent are called "Approved Schools", corresponding, with differences, to American reform or training schools. Offenders between 17 and 21 are classed as "young adults". They go before ordinary courts, and can be sent to residential corrective institutions called "Borstals", for which there is no one precise equivalent in the United States. The majority of Borstals are open institutions without bolts or bars.

In education, the "Public Schools" occasionally referred to are of course not what their name suggests, but Britain's historic and expensive private schools, mostly boarding schools. With various other fee-paying establishments, the Public Schools make up the private sector of the divided British educational system, and their pupils do not enter much into the story as here told. However, contrary to what is often believed abroad, some 80-90 per cent of British children attend what are wholly, or in effect, free state schools. This British state school system is, however, in turn divided in its structure (and these divisions are the subject of much current debate). All children attend the same state school till the age of 11. Then they take a test, popularly known as the "eleven-plus test", to decide their future. About one quarter pass on to what by historic British tradition are called "Grammar Schools". They can attend these, though not all do, up to the age of 18 to 19, that is, at the most up to university entrance on a state scholarship; at this point their level would be roughly that of second-year American college students. The other three-quarters of state school pupils go on to "Secondary Modern Schools", which most of them leave once they have completed compulsory school attendance after their 15th birthday. There are also some new, large schools attended by all grades of state secondary school pupils. They are called "Comprehensive Schools", but are still comparatively rare. It will be seen, therefore, that the British state educational system is more sharply divided than public education in the United States—there is no real equivalent to the United States High School—and this division forms part of the background to the story which follows.

Part One
INTRODUCTION

CHAPTER I

From a View to a Theory

INTO THE WILDERNESS

IN the late 'fifties (it may seem portentous to begin with an opening like this, but that is how the period remains in my mind) I often used to watch a London street-scene which seemed to have its special significance.

I was then living in a top-floor maisonette in an area near a London park round which much slum clearance was in progress, and for a while the windows of my back room provided a wide-open view of a new public housing estate—locally simply known as "the Estate", already a sprawling conglomeration dominating the district, but still expanding steadily. There were times when I felt that this vista reflected the precise spirit of the age: the bold aims of modern architecture watered down by the anonymity of local government. The big blocks of flats, seven to eleven stories high, embodied the early ambitions of the post-war welfare state; against the background of surrounding slums they looked clean and functional, yet with all the thought that had gone into them they somehow failed to look attractive.

There was too much asphalt; the entrances and hallways had a cramped look; there was an impression of just so much provided in accommodation and no more. Still, I knew from all my contacts that, apart from the normal complaints about high rents, practically all the families who had moved into the flats from the demolished surroundings considered themselves fortunate enough. The big buildings certainly teemed with life; laundry hung above the small, concrete balconies; especially towards evening the sounds of commercial television or the Light Programme seemed to drift from everywhere through windows, doors and ceilings. Quite a few cars stood parked on the surrounding concrete, mostly small and bought second-hand, but lovingly tended and increasing in number almost week by week. In fact, general opinion had it that with all their much-discussed defects, such as the high rents and lack of soundproof walls, the flats provided their London working-class occupiers with better homes than the majority had known before.

With one fairly notable exception—the adolescents, the teenagers living in the flats, who spent a good deal of their time in hanging about the stairs and courtyards. And, for some years, each Saturday and Sunday, towards dusk, I used to witness a curious procession. From my distant window I could see the small, dark figures of boys and half-grown youths drifting off in twos or threes or larger groups, and all of them, it seemed to me, wearing the identical Teddy boy suits. All of them, as if drawn by a magnet, also made off in the same direction, towards the main streets beyond the big railway stations, an untidy area of converging streets and crowded traffic, of shops, cinemas, public-houses and bright lights, aesthetically a God-awful wilderness, but to the boys obviously representing life with a capital L.

I sometimes thought that one could see the social wasteland through which they wandered in actual visual terms. North of the Estate lay row upon row of squat nineteenth-century slum streets, with bomb gaps of fifteen years before still showing, an area mostly condemned and waiting only for demolition. So it should be, one felt, yet for many of the youths from the Estate these grimy houses had been originally their parents' homes. Now they stood condemned and so were harshly degraded, like a whole way of life to be put out of mind, together with memories of worn doorsteps, dark passages, mother at the sink and father shirt-sleeved in the kitchen with his newspaper—a whole world of working-class childhood memories now shattered. On its other side, the Estate was bordered by a network of crescents and terraces which up to the 'thirties had been a solid upper-middle-class neighbourhood, a focus for the whole district. Now the tall terrace houses stood subdivided, stucco was peeling from porticoes and façades, untidy cards marked the bells at the front doors; from this vista, too, all its former social authority had fled. So it had from the two local churches, whose dull angularity suggested only the dead aspirations of the Victorian era.

Between these areas, as a replacement crammed with new life and expanding all the time, stood the Estate itself. But I felt it represented another question mark. Though the lines of the flats were clean and straight—their main asset—those blocks which were half a dozen years old already seemed to reflect a certain weariness of the spirit. Perhaps it was that skimpy detail spoke of the accountancy of remote public bodies; the entrances and stairways had already the neglected air of a place not loved; the whole impression was of too much public anonymity, of a space-saving set of buildings for those lucky enough to get in, but which proclaimed no satisfying new way of community life.

Not, anyway, to the young. For them, as was clear, the one source of satisfaction they understood perfectly lay in the crowded high streets beyond the big stations. It did not matter that in its back streets this was a dispiriting region of blank warehouses, untidy street-markets and sleazy lodging-houses. In the main streets, at any rate, the young felt surrounded by a full tide of confident life. The confidence of the age was reflected in the ultra-modern layout of the chain stores; in shop windows crammed with radios, television sets, record-players, streamlined tape-recorders and musical instruments; in others offering modern furniture to make any young couple happy at only so much down and so much per week. Confident commercial voices addressed the young from newspaper headlines, cinema posters and perhaps most insistently from the skilfully designed glossy pop-record covers: here were Presley, Sinatra, Steele and Wilde, expressing sentiments of love, anguish and desire, and explicitly for you, if you were young. Here, too, was the neighbourhood pleasure ground: the plush cinemas, the modernized dance-halls, the pubs with a singing trade, the late-night cafés with juke-boxes blaring and girls to be talked to at the tables. For many of the boys from the Estate, this London, offering its pleasures freely to those with money, spoke with the only voice of authority that mattered. The importance of their homes had dwindled; work meant little. Their one emphatic link with society lay through its entertainments, from treble-chance pool to the week's Top Ten: these they understood and clung to. One could gather this from the boys themselves or the leaders of the struggling local youth clubs where on occasion they drifted in and out.

It was also not hard to see the basic defects of their link with the new culture of the streets. It was not so much because the latter was primitive, but because in the 1950s it had become so many degrees more commercialized and deceptive and artificial, so that it seemed dangerously easy for young minds cut off from other influences to see all society in terms of caricature: that is, a society where newspapers were concerned solely with sex, sensation and betting, where television dealt only in violence and get-rich-quick quiz programmes and the popular film was a gangster film; a life of recurring boredom where nothing mattered but money and the smart thing at all times was to give as little as you could for as much as you could get; in short, as they saw it, a distorted materialist society without purpose. On this soil, luxuriant visions could flourish, where fact and fancy were apt to mingle:

> Ordinarily we'd just stand at the coffee-stall at the corner—some of the blokes would stand there until 2 or 3 in the morning—but some nights we'd all pile into a taxi and drive down to the west, you know, Greek Street and Charing Cross Road. There's cafés there and hot dives. We'd go there looking for mysteries—that's what we call the girls—or some fellow had a job, that'd be thievin', picking up a few easy pounds. No, it wouldn't be what you'd call real crime. One time a bloke offered us £5 to beat a fellow up but we never did anything: it was a Greek offered us the money and we didn't like him. We'd try to pick up prostitutes after they had finished work. They didn't mind taking a young Ted home for the night. We'd pick up some of the club hostesses too. Beautiful girls they were, and they'd come home with a young bloke if they liked him. We didn't have to pay, there was no money in it at all.

But the fanciful flight from boredom could also lead too smoothly to violence.

> No, we don't have so many fights any more. We used to have them, with knives too. Well, it was the excitement! I've seen our blokes heave a fellow they didn't even know through a plate-glass window—I tell you I couldn't stop laughing. I remember one time six of us went to get one of the Blacks; I didn't know what he'd done but anyway he was a Spade, but then the coppers chased us but we all chucked our knives away as we ran and when they searched us they found nothing. When they finished we all got into a taxi and went down west. We just didn't care: it was the excitement, different from going every night to the pictures where nothing ever happens. One time we used to go regularly to the Angel where there's a lot of cafés and we

aimed to start trouble with the Greeks and Turks, start a punch-up. They're Cypriots, you know, grease monkeys we used to call them—our chaps all hated them.

The young man who freely confided these fancies to me was a good-looking young café regular, dandified in dress, who not long after was up before the Court and on his way to Borstal for a spell of re-education at the State's expense.

HOOLIGANS OR CRIMINALS?

"We can no longer think of generations in traditional terms," said a recent UNESCO report.[1] "Interests and activities are today changing so fast that sets of young people not more than seven or eight years apart in age may be as far apart in their thinking and behaviour as the generations formerly were." This swiftness of change is itself significant. Just as about fifty years ago, when the young followers of Shaw and Wells set fire to the Victorian lumber-room, so today, in the nuclear age, youth has evidently turned sharply from the outlook of its elders, less perhaps in actual beliefs than in its whole way of thinking and feeling, which is even more important. The secession has found one expression in the writings of what have been vulgarly but not inaccurately described as "angry young men". Another reaction, increasingly felt by the authorities in many countries, has been a wave of intensified youthful lawlessness, expressed both in mob hooliganism and, more seriously, in a rise in the figures of youthful crimes and notably crimes of violence.

As far as Britain is concerned, British juvenile crime figures have shown one of the steepest increases of all, and the chief point is that they have risen against a background of steadily expanding welfare services—as Mr Butler put it sorrowfully, the rise came "after years of the most massive social and educational reform for a century". This rise has already dispelled some traditional views. A generation ago it was still widely held that even if poverty was only one cause of crime, the delinquency figures would at least roughly follow the curve of economic dislocation and unemployment, but this link has clearly been severed. Economically the

[1] Issued by UNESCO Youth Institute, Munich, April 1959.

years from 1953 to 1960 were a phase of distinct progress. They were years of full employment, higher wages and rising mass consumption, especially on the part of the young. The years 1955-1960 saw well over a million new houses built—by 1960 a quarter of the population was living in council houses or flats; they saw around a million new cars on the roads, and several million more television sets in the front parlours. That is, the massive movement of the British working classes away from their former drab slums into a new suburban council estate life with its novel gadgets and respectability, continued apace. Nor was the expansion of State education and child care and other welfare services noticeably halted. Above all, the replacement of old primary and secondary schools by new schools housed in beautifully designed modern buildings was steadily continued, even though there was quite a way to go before the replacement would be complete. Yet the figures of juvenile crime did not go down during these years, as had been hopefully predicted before at the end of the war-time hangover. On the contrary, after an initial drop the statisticians' curve showed a sharp and alarming upward turn.

The following figures tell the story.

Male offenders convicted of an indictable offence (England and Wales):

Year	14-17 age-group	17-21 age-group
1938	11,645	10,131
1955	13,517	11,269
1956	15,029	13,425
1957	18,149	16,962
1958	21,628	21,232
1959	23,059	30,086

Percentually, this meant that in 1959 just over two per cent. of youths in both age-groups were convicted of an indictable offence. The figures of those convicted for breaking and entering tell a similar story:

Age-group	1938	1956	1957	1958	1959
14-17	2,770	3,895	5,000	6,931	7,125
17-21	1,396	3,051	3,934	5,513	5,474

Similarly, the figures of those convicted for offences of violence against the person.

Age-group	1938	1956	1957	1958	1959
14-17	80	461	576	787	985
17-21	163	1,248	1,635	2,084	2,366

These figures appeared to surprise even the most experienced social and penal workers. For example, the unforeseen increase in delinquency in the male 17-21 age-groups was reflected by an equivalent rise in the Borstal population which went up from 2,800 at the beginning of 1956 to 4,500 at the end of 1958. Unprecedented measures had to be taken to absorb this new clientéle, and Mr Butler's White Paper of January 1959 accordingly introduced the biggest prison-building programme for young adult offenders for many years, including plans for the building of eight new Borstals, together with eight new Detention Centres, designed to administer "a short sharp shock".

These figures of actual law-breaking are only part of the post-war story. Equally noticeable was the appearance among a section of working-class youth of a more intensified gang life, characterized by a hostility towards authority in every form which could flare into violence upon a trivial cause. Coupled with it went a sort of stylized warfare between the gangs themselves, especially those wearing exaggerated Teddy boy suits, and a fashion for carrying improvised offensive weapons. In fact, if one regarded only the outward picture, a disturbing dichotomy seemed to be at work. As British working-class youth was becoming more urbane, as more modern schools and housing estates went up, so more boys seemed to drift into the new gang warfare and to walk about carrying flick-knives or such things as bicycle chains "for defence". Defence against whom? The wave of unrest reached one climax in such large-scale disturbances as the 1958 race riots in Nottingham and Notting Hill, which were largely started by working-class adolescents, which outraged public opinion in Britain and abroad and brought the Law down heavily on the offenders through the resurrected concept of "causing an affray", used for the first time for many decades. Not long after, early in 1959, the charge of "causing an affray" was used again after two large gang fights at dance halls in which two young men were stabbed to death, one of them a policeman.

These events of 1958-59 seemed to represent a definite climax in the wave of youthful violence. Well before this, however, as far as the popular press was concerned, juvenile delinquency had for the first time in Britain become elevated to the status of a national problem. Usually the focus was on the Teddy boys. Popular press reports picked for their headline value tend usually to be exaggerated, yet there was an insistent similarity about most Teddy boy stories. The following are items from cuttings which I kept at random from the newspapers of one year—scores of others of the same nature might have been quoted:

Liverpool. One hundred detectives were searching Liverpool dance-halls last night in the hunt for a 20-year-old Teddy boy gang who attacked 18-year-old G. W. outside a dance-hall late on Saturday. W. was knocked out and kicked as he lay on the roadway. A passing car accidentally ran over him and late last night his condition in hospital was said to be "still critical".

Nottingham. Singing, shouting and swinging bicycle chains and straps, 70 Nottingham Teddy boys swarmed into a Derbyshire double-decker village bus and ordered the driver "to get a move on". He did—straight to Sandiacre police station, where police officers who had been waiting as part of a pre-arranged plan leaped aboard. They had been planning for this chance to break up the rowdyism and hooliganism by a city gang reported from little outlying places each week-end.

London. A London policeman was coshed and injured by four Teddy boys last night when he asked them to move on while they were making a disturbance outside a public-house in Vauxhall. Early today the police officer was reported in hospital with suspected skull fracture.

Wallington, Surrey. The fighting equipment of a Teddy boy gang was set on a table in Court yesterday. In front of the magistrates were: two heavy belts; a weighted cane; a sheath knife; two flick-knives; three lengths of chain, two attached to handles; two bottles and three stilettos. They had been collected by police in a coffee-bar opposite Wallington Town Hall "after a concerted effort by one group to go out and beat up a rival gang".

Norwich. During the closing performance last night of the oldest cinema in Norwich, gangs of Teddy boys and their girl-friends protested against the closing. They tore seats from their fastenings and wrecked the screen. The manager said it seemed as if the attack was planned.

London. A girl and a number of youths were injured in the biggest gang fight in London for years between two 100-strong Teddy boy gangs in Euston last night. The two gangs clashed outside a Cypriot-owned club shortly before midnight. Some carried knives, others razors, some broken bottles. People watching from their windows said that before the police arrived some of the wounded had been carried off by their supporters.

Popular press publicity should be treated with caution. Even where the facts quoted are correct, they can be selectively sensationalized, and the Teds happened to be a convenient subject. (A Yorkshire youth club leader told me how, after a disturbance on his premises, he was badgered by a bevy of reporters to admit that the destruction had been caused by youths with tight trousers and elaborate hair-styles, though for once this was not the case; this report appeared, all the same.) Yet was the popular press so wrong? The reports of the incidents I have quoted have their undeniable cumulative effect. They make it hard to resist the conclusion that there was something new afoot among a section of British youth, a new and considerable wave of unrest of which the Teddy boy movement was only one expression.

A SUBURBAN MILIEU

This argument was also put to me by a senior social worker of many years' experience in youth work, who gave me a picture of what he was up against in one of the outer London areas, a prosperous place of new factory and housing development, but also distinguished for one of the highest juvenile adolescent crime rates. This is the gist of what he told me:

I no longer know what to think except that we have somehow lost our sense of proportion. Society has been changing under our noses. In our youth work I feel like telling our people every day: "The social conventions you are clinging on to have become irrelevant." What we offer the youngsters in our clubs, the whole spirit of it, they know is wrong for them. Even our mixed clubs are still directed towards our old middle-class culture with all its sharp little distinctions.

They, the young people around here, live already in a much more primitive society, where income differences no longer matter, especially because among young people in general there is now money in biggish quantities. As soon as young people start work and tend to make money, they drift away from the clubs. They think they can fit into society better on their own, but evidence shows that many don't find this a very happy process.

Why should this be? I wish I knew. You sometimes get the feeling there is more than the ordinary mental sickness among those born in 1937-42. It was all tied up with evacuation, the absence of the fathers and all that. You might say there has been a bulge of indiscipline travelling up just as there has been a bulge in the birth rate, but this indiscipline has become a new way of life. In any case our whole type of society is itself changing. It is every day becoming more technical and more atomized. Family life is becoming very much emptied of content—I find the ties of family are often very weak among the middle-teen generation.

I notice this particularly in the type of lad of 17 to 19 who, after what he pays for his board at home, has about four pounds a week or more of money to spend on himself. Many such lads seem to me to have lost the capacity for friendship and they feel basically isolated. Their affability conceals it—but they are bored nearly all the time. To escape from this, they always want to do something different and daring, to get into a fight, "to have a giggle", smash up something, to go joy-riding. As this is their aim, all persons in authority are resented and rancour against the police is very strong, but these lads themselves have created the situation where they claim with some justification that "the police are down on boys in tight trousers" and they are treated as second-class citizens. A study of the life of these lads would need new terms. For instance, the dominant new social group is what is called the clique. The basis of the clique is purely territorial. The clique and its territory make up what I call the milieu, which holds the members together. There is a clique not far from here which must number about two hundred of both sexes, yet the way it is composed appears to be quite accidental. There was no foresight whatsoever in the way its groupings came about.

One young man, a keen member of the clique, told me that his close acquaintances within the clique are about 12 young men and 8 girls. Side by side with these he has about 80 more distant acquaintances; another hundred or so young people are in loose association with these—the majority being between the ages of 17 and 22. "Their lot", as they term it, has a territory where strangers are regarded with distaste. The two local cinemas are part of the furnishings of this territory. A dance-hall and jazz-club are also regarded as "theirs". Among the cafés, they lay claim to two of them. Pubs are not usually part of the milieu: the lads in the clique are not habitual drinkers. Other similar groups with territories exist in a complete ring right round us, from Central London all the way out into the countryside.

The *territory* is the real home for a member of the clique: his own home is merely the place where he sleeps. If a club or youth centre is in the area, it is either theirs or else they will have none of it, "theirs" meaning that they should be allowed to use it as they wish. Quite a lot of boys and girls, too, travel up and down by train to get to the territory . . . they are disturbed at the loss of contact with the milieu for even one night a week. One boy whose family had moved into a suburban council estate was most upset. "There's nobody living up there." The girls who are part of the milieu are met in cafés where the lads talk to them. For a start the relationship may be platonic but before long the girl would be attached to one of the lads and respected as such. In any case, once girls are members of the clique they are looked after, given coffee, taken to the pictures, and it is understood that they are guarded against any attentions by outsiders.

The week of the clique in which my young man was a member had a definite routine which was quite interesting:

Monday night. To the pictures with a male clique, paying about 4s. (or nothing). Appropriate cafés are called at first, to meet, then a return in a large body to one of the cafés, and the organization of some amount of betting (I have a suspicion certain other activities might also be discussed on this occasion, but the less said the better). This routine was rigidly maintained: "When you're going steady, even if the girl is in the café, well, you'd be kind to her, but it's understood that Monday you're out with the fellows."

Tuesday night. In the milieu, usually purely male with just coffee or a soft drink. Expenditure—one shilling.

Wednesday night. Jazz-club with a crowd, meeting girls—three to five shillings.

Thursday night. On the coffee-bar grape-vine—about two shillings.

Friday night. Jazz-club plus real drinks—about ten to fifteen shillings.

Saturday night. The real do: to the ballroom in the High Street with girls, sometimes without—twenty-five to thirty shillings.

Sunday night. To pictures with girl and others from clique, later to cafés—about ten shillings.

That is the basic structure of the week, but the milieu also has bigger occasions. A milieu get-together is organized by word of mouth on a progressive basis. The telephone is the normal way of communication. It is also taken for granted that motor transport is always available. Many lads have cars or motor-bikes, or else there is enough money to hire cars. As an example: the lads from the clique decided a few weeks ago to invade the N. territory for a "punch-up", a spot of trouble. It was also agreed on this occasion not to carry actual weapons. That was at 8.5 p.m. around here. By 8.20 p.m. a second troup from further up north had been fully organized to join them. At 9 p.m. there were over 50 boys and girls in N., milling round the café belonging to another group. Newspaper reports put it at even double the number. This shows the speed of the grape-vine.

As for week-end trips, it was habitual for these to blow up out of nothing. As the impulse took them, half a dozen on motor-bikes or else up to a dozen piled into a couple of cars would drive down to Brighton or Eastbourne. If they had no girls with them they would try to pick up girls down there. A fight might blow up; it would die down. Then they came back.

Sometimes it was a big occasion. Last Bank Holiday a trip to Margate was arranged on the Sunday. My young man was treasurer. The charge was calculated at twelve shillings and when I saw him he had already received money from ninety participants—he had fifty-four pounds in his wallet. The whole thing was done on the grape-vine. Word was given out that the trip would start by coach at 9 on Sunday morning and everyone would be back at 2 a.m., girls and fellows together. My young man had booked two 45-seater coaches at twenty pounds apiece; he had also ordered crates of beer. The money that was over in the end was divided up and returned. All this was done without notation—the milieu is organized on a non-literary basis. Everything was based on trust and memory. At Margate they split up into groups; they sat on the beach; later on they moved about the town "to have a laugh" (get into mischief). Three of them were actually taken in charge by the police which was thought a big lark, but the rest got back safely if late: that was their day.

I'm the last one to worry about high spirits, but if asked what is wrong with the life of the clique, I should say it is this—that it's always a primitive life, it's rootless and neurotic, it leaves these young people unsatisfied and so they are pushed to go too far and get themselves into trouble. To me it is also like the end of a process of disintegration. When I look back on my own boyhood, it seems to me that around 1910 to 1925 most working-class lads and girls still moved in a milieu which was centred on a place of worship. There were other links too, like going to the same school, but the dominant one was the religious centre. Then came the impact of the first War, then the depression, breaking this up. Still, I remember how in about 1931 I myself was part of a close milieu of perhaps a hundred young people, based on school acquaintance, contacts at youth clubs and contacts through religious bodies (though these last were becoming rare). It was based on links of common interests and friendships—it was not a territorial milieu, like that of the clique.

For me, the visible and rather alarming change which has come about is this shrinkage from circles of genuine friendship to the more neurotic, shifting and primitive society of the clique. Nowadays you may find a great deal of solidarity—in the framework of the clique this expresses itself in temporary loyalty, but not real friendship . . . nor even in any firm neighbourhood focus in the old style. A vicar recently opened a local coffee-bar. The mob moved in, made it part of the milieu, created some trouble and that was the end of it. It was simply swallowed up in this search for a dramatic, neurotic way of life.

I know that most boys and girls in these parts are getting a far better education than they've ever had before; lots of them are doing fine things, they're busy as can be. But there is also the other side, the shifting life of the clique. You take an area like this: up to about 1948 the neighbourhood youth clubs were making progress, but since then they have steadily gone down. The reason? To my mind, 1948 has always been like a watershed. It was the year when the separation through the 11-plus exam. really began to work. Since working-class talent is now drained away, what is left is a sort of leadership of local boys who at the same time vaguely know that they are second-class citizens. They feel declassed and don't quite know who and where they are, and try to work out their own social pattern. That's why they cohere, even when like the clique they have nothing to cohere around.

I know that all young people tend to fall into associations of their own. But theirs is modified, indeed dominated, by a territorial milieu in which a youth club is only part of the furniture—that's the depressing difference and the measure of our failure.

Old slums or new industrial suburb: the wave of youthful unrest seems in some of its characteristics much the same. And there is further justification for describing this unrest exemplified by the Teddy boys as a "wave" because the British experience has been far from unique. Since 1950 an increase in juvenile delinquency and gang life has occurred in a sufficient number of countries to arouse attention as an international problem.

CHAPTER II

The Teddy Boy International

THE SIMULTANEOUS OUTBREAKS

THE argument that the Teddy boy movement and the increase of lawlessness among British youth represent something new, a new "wave" in delinquency, arising from a specific combination of contemporary social conditions, is strengthened if one looks at the international scene. Reports of youthful disturbances similar to those in Britain have come from a number of countries; mostly they are countries which are technically and industrially advanced (although there are also interesting stories from others, like the report from Greece that local Teddy boys, called by this name, had engaged in the pastime of throwing yoghourt in people's faces and as punishment had their heads shaved, evidently a successful deterrent). Especially during the last few years, it was not hard to find newspaper reports of disturbances to match those quoted for Britain; in the first place from the United States, where the public has been shocked by such startling revelations as that in a single year about 5 per cent. of American children get into trouble with the police or the courts, and that youngsters under 21 constitute over half those arrested for car thefts and robbery.

Daytona Beach, Florida. Nearly 4,000 car enthusiasts in their teens fought police and firemen for five hours today in riots which began when police ordered a group of youngsters to stop making acceleration tests on a main street. The youngsters slashed tyres of cars, smashed shop windows and tore down advertisements before armed police dispersed them.

New York. New violence flared yesterday among packs of unruly teenagers stalking the streets of New York. The newest outbreak, in more than a week of tenement jungle warfare that has claimed four lives and caused several critical injuries, occurred in Brooklyn. Two men were shot by a gang that ambushed them with a shotgun blast of birdshot as they left a restaurant. The victims of the unprovoked attack were taken to a hospital for treatment of painful injuries. The shooting came only a few hours after police prevented an all-out gang battle in the Bronx between members of the Scorpion and Fordham Baldies gangs, made up of both white and Negro boys. Detectives moved in on the boys in a park. They arrested 13 youths and seized an assortment of lethal weapons. New York City officials scheduled a meeting with State Youth Commission officials today to determine whether state help is needed to combat the teenage crime wave.

Or to turn to Europe, the following reports from Germany, Austria, France and Sweden are typical of many which could have been quoted:

Duisburg, Germany. Thirty-three young people were arrested yesterday after a night in which hundreds of excited people had milled in the streets, smashing street lights, damaging private cars and starting free fights. The disturbance, which reached the proportion of a minor riot, followed similar incidents in Hamburg, Frankfurt and Brunswick. A police spokesman said that hardly a day seemed to pass without reports of some pitched but aimless battles between young rowdies and members of the public, the police or the new armed forces.

Vienna. The Halbstarken—the leather-jacketed "Teddy Boy" gangs of Western Germany—have spread to Austria, and the steady increase in teenage delinquency in the country is alarming the Austrian people. Nearly every day in the past few months police have reported at least one clash between the *Halbstarken* gangs in Vienna. Police patrols have had to be increased in many Vienna districts to keep down violence. Criminal activity by teenagers has trebled compared with pre-war. The Vienna police are taking concerted action to put down gangs. They comb out regularly the public-houses and coffee-houses where the gangs have been known to meet.

Paris, July 1959. 26 adolescents between 14 and 20 years arrested and detained; clubs, bicycle chains, and buckled belts and similar weapons confiscated by the police. This was the balance sheet of an expedition organized last night in the 15th Arrondissement by a band of "blousons noirs" (blackjackets). For several months the police had watched a band of young ruffians from the Saint-Lambert quarter, who had been indulging in public violence. Last night, about a hundred boys from this band, all dressed in leather jackets and blue jeans, gathered in an organized force at a street crossing for a battle with a rival band from Vanves. As the latter did not turn up, the "blousons noirs" began to smash up a café. The arrival of the police started off a wild pursuit amidst the traffic. . . .

Stockholm. Gang criminality had hitherto been of minor importance in Sweden. Since 1958, however, several youthful gangs in the real sense of the word have been exposed, most of them in Stockholm. These gangs are mostly made up of youngsters in the age-group 13-18 years, mostly from the same city block, who terrorize other young people as well as adults. . . . They are ruthless towards one of their own who does not conform to the behaviour pattern of the gang. Their weapons include stilettos, air guns and bicycle chains. In October 1958 one such gang caused a sensation when the members brutally beat up a boy in the very centre of Stockholm for having broken with the gang. . . .

Such reports from Sweden, with its tradition of neutrality, its high living standard and enlightened welfare institutions, have attracted special attention because the lawlessness of the young rioters has been on a surprising scale. And, just to show that not only capitalist countries are involved, the following story from the Soviet newspaper *Moskovsky Komsomolyeti* (22nd January 1959) shows that conditions in Leningrad parks are at times not so altogether different from those in Central Park, New York:

Moscow. It is a shocking event that through lack of proper foresight, a Moscow youth has been stabbed to death by eight hooligans in a Leningrad park. Our seventeen-year-old Comrade Vadim Trainin of Moscow had gone to Leningrad early this month on a vacation. While there he contacted the Young Communist League headquarters and asked to go on patrol with one of their squads whose task it is to aid the militia in keeping order in the city. Together with two other boys and three girls, Trainin was put into a squad which was assigned to patrol duty in the city's Lenin Park.

In the park, the squad was set upon by a hooligan gang and it appears that the two other boys and the three girls abandoned young Trainin who was thereupon stabbed to death.

In this needless tragedy, it must be said that the Leningrad

Young Communist League has evidently treated this killing with an unjustifiable lightmindedness. We find it essential that the perpetrators of this crime should pay the fitting penalty. We further recommend that all Young Communist squads on patrol duty should be of adequate size and should include young people able to handle trouble.

There is, in fact, evidence that what the Communist press calls "hooliganism" is a serious problem in the Soviet Union and the East European satellite states. In Communist Poland this is openly admitted. How large the problem is in the Soviet Union is not easy to say. However, the censored Soviet press only admits defects in Soviet life when they have reached major proportions, so that when Soviet newspapers in 1958 complained about drunkenness and hooliganism among the youth in cities like Moscow, Leningrad, Tiflis, Odessa, Rostov and Sverdlovsk, it is fair to conclude that delinquency had become a major headache for the Soviet authorities.

To turn to Asia, consistent reports from post-war Japan tell of insubordination at high schools or in the streets in American style and almost on American scale. Figures quoted in alarmed articles in the Japanese press reveal that, as compared with 1938, the number of Japanese youngsters, including students, picked up on charges of vandalism, truancy and drunkenness had increased just about tenfold. All in all, therefore, the evidence seems to be that there is a new spirit of lawlessness abroad among modern youth which has found organized and violent expression in a number of advanced industrial countries.

A NEW PHENOMENON?

Does all this amount to a new social phenomenon, to be studied as such? I think it does, even though some of those working in the field argue that when one considers individual cases, there is nothing new in the pattern of delinquency, which is by now well documented. A common individual starting-point is insecurity in childhood, due to a broken home or bad family background. A child from such a home, feeling emotionally insecure and unloved, rejects rather than leaves his home. School to such a youngster often appears a mere meaningless accompaniment of the home which has failed him; the one prospect of security, esteem and status seems to lie in the street gang and defiance of society: and this often is the start of delinquency. This established pattern, it is said, has in no way changed, except in such detail as the fashion for exaggerated costume. Secondly, it has also been argued that the whole delinquency problem is not as large and general as commonly made out. The official statistics of the United States, for instance, so as to avoid racial distinction, fail to reveal what a large proportion of juvenile crime is concentrated among ethnic groups like Negroes or Puerto Rican immigrants, living under squalid conditions of discrimination which must encourage crime.

Thirdly, there is of course the war. In Europe, the children born in 1939-45 are the adolescents of today. In Britain, case studies have traced some adolescent lawlessness back to the effect of wartime dislocation on children—the bombing of British cities, the disruption of family life through evacuation, the prolonged absence of millions of fathers. Germany, of course, suffered still more. In view of the large number of young Germans who have grown up as orphans or with only one parent, the surprising thing is not the level of German juvenile crime and rowdiness but that there is not more of it. The same could be said of Japan. The unruliness of Japanese students must have its roots at least in part in the disturbance of the war, reinforced by the shocks of defeat, the atom bombs and surrender. Again, in countries like Russia and Poland, military and civilian loss of life was far greater than anything experienced in the West. The effects on the minds of young children must have been catastrophic and it is therefore not surprising if under the gloss of Communist repression and censorship, these effects have been working themselves out through such phenomena as widespread adolescent delinquency.

All these arguments carry some weight, yet they cannot really explain the international wave of youthful unrest—they certainly cannot explain it away. For one thing, the delinquency figures in many countries are simply too large. In Britain, for example, they are much higher than they should be in view of the progress in social welfare on every side. It seems also clear that the aftermath of the war can be only a very partial explanation of the unrest. Neutral Sweden, to quote only one instance, has after all been beset by this same problem. In the United States, again, the figure of young people convicted has risen so regularly year by year—by now uninterruptedly for eleven years—and the lawlessness has been spreading from the big cities into the small towns and suburbia—that, whatever one may think of war aftermath, the phenomenon must be connected with current developments in American society, as indeed it very obviously is.

Furthermore, the recent rise in delinquency has some very special features. In most countries it has occurred in conditions of rising material welfare, which has caused some German experts to give it the name of *die Wohlfahrtskriminalitaet*—"welfare criminality". Again, in a general reading of reports, from other countries as well as from Britain, the new youthful violence seems to have become curiously stylized, linked with a special gang life and special fashions. Not all those who dressed in Teddy boy style or in the style of the *Halbstarken* in Germany and Austria were actual delinquents, perhaps indeed not more than a fraction. Nevertheless, the spirit of rebellion denoted by the costume and the rise in youthful criminality have noticeably gone together. And they have gone together rather viciously. In the United States, public opinion has been roused by the fully-fledged gangsterism recently displayed by juvenile street gangs. What brought Britain's Teddy boys their international publicity was not merely their eccentric dress and trend towards violence—in earlier days there was plenty of violence in industrial England—but their cult of amorality and the brutality with which they have set upon out-numbered victims. (Again, without stressing it too far, we can bring a parallel from behind the Iron Curtain. When Soviet newspapers in 1959 carried renewed articles against "young criminals and bandits" and threatened the death penalty for those caught with flick-knives, it indicated that the Soviet authorities faced a similar problem of youthful amorality.)

Apart from such violent crime, and to go back to youthful lawlessness in the wider sense, it is also significant that in various countries new names have simultaneously been coined for these young offenders who are readily identifiable by their provocative dress and attitude. In the United States they have been called "Rebels without cause", a name which sums up the movement. In Britain, the Edwardian dress associated with the rowdiness gave rise to the name "Teddy boys", which survived the costume.

In Western Germany and Austria, the similar gangs of pro-vocatively dressed adolescent rowdies have been called the *Halbstarken*, the "half-strong". In Sweden, trouble-makers were referred to as the *Skinnknutte* or "leather-jackets", a name originally for gangs of youths obsessed by a craze for motor-cycle racing in the streets. France similarly has her *blousons noirs*, or "black jackets". The Japanese, elegant as ever, have coined the name *taiyozoku*, or "children of the sun", for their new groups of anti-social youth. The Australians, more briefly, have termed theirs "bodgies". And it is instructive that Soviet abuse has been directed not only at the lowly mass of hooligans but also at the *stilyagi*, or "style boys", a type of defiant, educated Soviet youths whose elaborate hair-styles, draped jackets and crêpe soles, as well as their addiction to jazz, show that in spite of censorship they have tried to model themselves on the Teddy boy international.

What does it all amount to? I found myself asking this question one night in Hamburg when by chance I happened to be a spectator of one of the *Halbstarken* mass outbursts. The immediate pretext for it had been a concert by the rock and roll experts Bill Haley and his Comets. Earlier concerts by Bill Haley in West Berlin and Essen had already led to mass teenage riots and vandal-ism, and so it happened in Hamburg. When I came on the scene, a crowd of two thousand adolescent boys and girls, who earlier had stopped the recital and smashed chairs and windows in the hall, was still milling in a dense mob in the square outside. They seemed in a frenzy, yelling insults and in some cases fighting squads of baffled policemen, who were trying to clear the streets, at first good-naturedly, but in the end, amidst rising tempers, found it necessary to disperse hysterical youngsters by use of tear-gas. The whole spectacle was baffling. Germany in a not so recent past had seen riots over mass unemployment; later, the political mob violence of the Nazis, but this was quite different. These German teenagers were living in a dull, prosperous Germany; they looked healthy and well-dressed—so what lay behind their excited frenzy, their anger, their trivial rebellion without a cause?

Or, for that matter, what lay behind the violence of the American street gangs or that of the Teddy boys? Or what was the reason for the striking rise in juvenile crime in the 'fifties in so many advanced countries? Adding it all up, it seemed hard to doubt that there was something afoot, that there were some aspects of our materialistic, mechanized twentieth-century society—something in the way of life, in the break-up of traditional authority, in the values of the news in the headlines, which encouraged widespread youthful cynicism in general and rather violent delinquency in particular. It is against this wider background of the unrest of a generation that I think the Teddy boy should be viewed. However, in each country this unrest has also taken on its own characteristic cultural forms.

Part Two
REPORTAGE

CHAPTER III

From the Shallows

WHAT follows is a self-portrait of Ron, a rather troubled and troublesome youth, which I obtained in an interview. Occasionally one meets a case history which reflects a number of the themes discussed in this book—Ron's story seemed to me one of them. Apart from necessary changes for fictionalizing, I have given it as reconstructed from my notes, if not in Ron's precise words, at least in an attempt to catch something near enough his flat monotone. If certain fanciful details are derived probably from the imagination of this young citizen of the welfare state rather than from fact, this, I think, makes them no less significant.

Q. You haven't always lived here at the Elephant, have you?
A. I only came here when I was about 13. Before that we lived down Croydon way, my father and my mum, that's my real mother, and me. My father, he's a Master Printer. We used to have a nice house and a garden. He left my mother when I was 8; I was an only son. My mother died when I was 12. That was a terrible shock to me and I went to live with my grandmother who had a tobacconist's shop, over at Brixton. Then I found out my father had married again and was living here at the Elephant, and he and my stepmother, they came and said it'd be better if I lived with them.
Q. Did you like that idea?
A. I didn't think much about it. But I had a grudge against my father because he told my stepmother they could expect trouble because I was a bad lot.
Q. Now what gave him cause to say that?
A. Well, when I was 10—I was still with my mother then—I was sent to Approved School and my father knew all about it. It, was for breaking and entering a shop. It wasn't a shop, really, it was a warehouse for fruit. There were three of us, we were just kids, and at that time we were mad about oranges and we went to get some. When we got to the warehouse, I found

money lying on the counter in front of me, so I took it. We took tobacco, cigarettes and money. There were some of these soap-box trollies about and we loaded one full of fruit and were wheeling it out when one of us knocked over an alarm clock. Two detectives caught us and took us to the police station. I remember my mother cried in Court and broke down when they said I was to go to Approved School, and I cried, too.

Q. If they sent you away, surely you must have been in trouble before?

A. Yes, I'd done a lot of playing truant, going swimming mostly. When I was at junior school I was hardly ever at school. I'd go swimming in the river. There were about six of us; we'd play on the sewage farm, playing in the trucks. My mother used to get regular summonses. They put me away at Stamford House, that's a remand home, but after I was there three weeks they sent me home again. It wasn't so bad, I wasn't frightened, it seemed easy—I'd say now it didn't frighten me enough, 'cos I went on truanting. I didn't like school, because they said I was backward; well, I was at reading. I just couldn't be bothered. I admit I'm sorry now—since I left school, I've practised reading, the posters on the station. I'm not so good at it even now. My mother? I admit she spoiled me, I had all the money I wanted given to me, and the toys; she used to have toys made for me. When I was ten I was sent to that Approved School I was telling you about. That was in Hampshire. I had to do scrubbing and work on the farm and in the fields. It was strict but not so bad; I quite liked it. Sometimes they were too strict, but other times I'd say it was like a holiday camp.

When I came back, I was 11, and I'd say I was changed all right. I had to live with my grandmother because my mother was working in a hospital, it was a living-in job, but she always visited me. I was quite happy living with my grandmother. I always make friends easy—people take a liking to me because I'm always ready to help somebody out. Then, when I was 12, my mother died. Yes, I was terribly upset. I broke down; I had to be sent to a convalescent home at Southend.

Q. You were 12 then—what happened after that?

A. I went back to my grannie, but when my father said I should live with them I said I would—I thought, let my family help me. He was in the print, but my mother, my stepmother, that is, she had a dry-cleaner's place; she had the money in the family. When I moved I went to this Secondary Modern School in the Borough. It was a bit of a rough place—if you want to know about the Teds, that's where I first met them.

For about six months, I think, things went pretty smooth, and then, all of a sudden, my father didn't want me hang up a wedding photo of him and my mother—my real mother. He said she was dead and all that was done with, he didn't want it, so one day I found the photo gone. My stepmother said she didn't know anything about it, so I put it down to my father. He said he didn't know where it was, but I never believed him. I had a grudge against him—that's when I started stealing. I said to him: "You didn't want the photo 'cos you left her. Still, she was better to me than you two ever will be." So I started stealing a bit from the dry-cleaner's downstairs and my parents—that's my father and my stepmother—they sent me away to boarding school. What sort? Well, it was a special sort of school. It was quite small but it was a private school, you had to pay—all the boys came from decent families.

I stayed there till I was about 16. I was happy there, everything was going nicely. But I used to steal a bit from the masters' rooms. All the time I used to say to myself that I shouldn't do it, but I was never found out. Lessons? I didn't like it at first when they said I was backward; it was only that I couldn't put my mind to it. I said, "I'll prove it to you that I'm not backward," and for one term I put my mind to it and I was top of the class. (?) One thing I remember—it makes me laugh. There was that master living there with his wife and daughter and one time I used to slip out of the dormitory every evening and go to that girl and come back early in the morning. She was about 17, but she knew a lot. I always found girls easy to get; I could always persuade them to give me what I want. She wrote to me quite a few times afterwards, I never bothered to answer. After a time, I didn't like the school so much. My parents, they wanted me to be a gentleman. I say they went too far, one way and another. So they took me away when I was about 16.

[Some fantasy seemed to have crept into these memories.]

Q. And what happened then?

A. Well, I was at home again and after a time I got myself a job in the building. My parents wanted me to give it up, it wasn't good enough, and so one day I said, "Right, I'm leaving." I got myself a room near the Elephant and I started going down the Walworth Road. One night, in a café down the Walworth Road—it was a Greek caff—I saw the Greek what owned it hit a young bloke just because he was sitting on the corner of a table. So I said: "If you hit him again I'm going to bring the boys and you'll get your caff smashed up." Mind you, I got nothing against foreigners—I just don't like to see a white man hit, I mean a Greek hit a chap of my own nationality. With that, this Greek picked up a chair, and I hit him. The Greeks started coming at me and this other bloke and me, we smashed up the windows and we were fighting with bottles. They made a case of it at the Borough Court, but we denied everything and we got away with it.

Well, when this other bloke got home, he told his mates there's a fellow just come down the Walworth Road, a terrific puncher, and I met their mates and I went to dance halls and had a few fights. After getting myself well known I met a girl, a nice respectable girl, and she kept me out of trouble. She didn't like the way I was living, she knew I was very hot-tempered, so I didn't let her know when I was out with the boys.

After about six, nine months of fighting and getting known, a bloke said to me: "Charlie is coming out of prison tomorrow. He's a hard nut from the other side, a ponce." Well, we went to meet him and I liked him and gave him some money. I started going over West with him and stopped the building work. We used to go to dives where there was all the prostitutes hanging about. Charlie had two girls; they gave him all their money, and he gave me some. I saw blokes were making a lot of easy money, thievin' and poncing. After I'd been going some months—I was 18 then—I found a girl who took a liking to me and started to live with me. She used to walk alongside the Strand, soliciting.

Q. Did you have any feelings about that?

A. Me? No. Girls—I've had intercourse with thousands of girls.(?) What I didn't like was people talking. They'd say: "Here comes Ron the Ponce." Respectable girls didn't like it, they wouldn't go out with you. This girl, this prostitute—they don't call it "prostitute", they'd say "I'm soliciting"—this girl used to take fellows in a taxi. There's drivers in the West that do it, they take 10s. a time. The driver stops the taxi in a side street and goes for a walk, it only takes about five minutes. Some of the blokes give a lot of money; the Yanks, they got no idea of English money; when they're new they think a fiver's the same as a pound note. They don't get the real thing. This girl I was with, she was on the game for sixteen months, she had the real thing only three times. These girls, they know how to move their legs so a fellow doesn't know: they got a way of fixing things so a fellow thinks he's having it naturally when he isn't.

Well, I was with this girl all the time. Sometimes she'd make twenty pounds a night and she'd give it to me. If you're a ponce, the girl is like a wife. They want you more or less to be like a husband to them. She gives you the money and if you're kind you buy her clothes and things and protect her. Funnily enough, this girl came from a very nice family in Croydon. We visited them, making out as if we were going steady. We spent the money on smokes, suits, juke-boxes, plenty of things. We had a flat in the Old Kent Road with a bedroom, a front room, a kitchenette. I was with the girl all the time. I used to smoke a lot; I'd spend a fiver a day on juke-boxes and cafés. (?) The girl went over West and I used to watch. If a policeman comes, you walk up and say, "I've been waiting here for you for hours," and he can't do a thing. Of course if he doesn't believe you and he thinks you're poncing, you can get six months.

Well, after some time I got fed up; I was bored with all this night life and I packed it in and went back to the building. I was 19 now and getting full rate, about £10 a week clear. Well, after a time, this other girl of mine, I made a clean breast to her and said I was sorry and she forgave me and we went steady again. She was a sales girl in a dress shop and things were going fine and one week-end I stayed with her family. Well, not long after, one day I got the sack, and so I got the hump. I went to the hairdresser with the girl and while I was waiting I got hold of the heater and turned it hot. She was screaming, but I wouldn't turn it off—dunno why—didn't think it was doing her harm, but it burnt half her hair off. I still don't know why I did it. Well, she wouldn't speak to me, so late that night I was outside the Brick and then I walked along with my mate and two other blokes to the coffee-stall at the Elephant. I thought, this is as far as I go, and was just going home when two girls came along. I said to one of the blokes: "I bet they're on the game over the other side—they must have quite a bit of money," and he said: "Thinking of taking it?" Well, we got talking and bought them cups of tea, and then we said to one of the girls we'd walk her home, just to protect her. Well, just before we got to the Borough we pretended some rough fellows were coming and ran with her down an alley—just to rob her, you understand. My mate, he started kissing her, and he took her bag. The next thing one of the other blokes who was with us was practically trying to rape her. Me and my mate started to run and saw he wasn't with us and the girl was screaming. So we went back and had to pull him off her. We ran down Long Lane and went to the coffee-stall when three squad cars came up. We hadn't a chance. They pulled us into the police station where there were twelve detectives and the girl was there and the only one she remembered and recognized was me, 'cos I was wearing a tie with a girl painted on at that time. The coppers started beating one of the other two blokes and we thought we might as well tell the truth. Next day at the Borough Magistrate's Court they remanded us for a week at Brixton.

Q. Well—was that a shock?

A. I'll say it was. I may sometimes pretend I'm a big fellow, but I don't mind saying, that week I cried my eyes out. I couldn't eat any food—I had to sew mailbags—I thought I'd go potty. When we got back to Court, they dropped the charge of rape, it was just robbery with violence. It turned out the girl was a hairdresser! We said we mistook her, we thought she was a prostitute, and that helped us a bit. Anyway, the others got off with a fine but I got sent back to Brixton to see if I was suitable for Borstal training.

I used to cry a lot. After a few days I was made workshop orderly. I wrote to my girl but I didn't hear from her. I thought it was because of the row at the hairdresser, but later on she told me she'd been round to my father and he said she ought to leave me because I was a bad lot, I'd always be in prison, she'd better pack me up. I was in Brixton a whole month. I used to get down on my knees and pray I'd be let off. At the end of the month when I got back into Court they said the Probation Officer gave me a good reference and they'd give me a last chance—so I was free. My girl had a new flat down the New Kent Road and I went there, but she said it was all finished.

Q. So you were on your own again?

A. Yes, from then on I went with the Boys. I'd play dice and billiards with them, play the juke-boxes, picking up jobs. That went on till the middle of last year, when I thought all this was getting me nowhere.

The Boys? Well, our clique we could be about 100, 150. Once we went over to the East End, there were 200 of us in cars and lorries and vans; we went to fight against the Greeks and the Turkish down in the Commercial Road. It was a terrific punch-up. Only a few people got pulled in.

Ordinary way, of course, there weren't so many. Our clique, we'd meet in billiard halls, we'd play dice. For instance we might go to the Greek caff and play the juke-box, me and a few mates, and one of us might say, "Let's go over to Camberwell and have a punch-up." So we'd all go to a caff down that way, and one of us would say, "Anyone here thinks he's a hard nut?" and then we'd bring out the Boys and there'd be a fight. Or else we'd try to get somebody out of a dance-hall. We used to stand and look for a bit of bother, you know, someone'd look at us cheeky and we'd get him outside.

Q. What about the fighting—how did you set about it?

A. Well, it'd start with fists like, and then somebody'd get rough. We used bottles and chains and hammers. I never got hurt, not serious, and never caught, either. Some did. There's Tommy, he's inside now, and Sid, he's been in the last six months, he had to have thirteen stitches. Or we'd try to fight the Blacks. We used to shout at them in the street "You black bastards" to try to provoke them, to beat them up, like. Over Brixton way, we'd try to stop them getting off buses, to frighten them. We'd often go for the Blacks, we don't like them round here, we hate them. No, never met any Jewish boys, don't remember any fights with Jews. Greeks and Turks we used to beat up—smash up the caffs. The police? No, they weren't exactly afraid of us. Some, like the old Inspector bloke round here, he'd come into a caff and say "Cut it out" and we'd go out. But the ordinary copper, well, if he was alone he'd walk past and look at us and not say anything. Of course some were brave, they'd walk straight up to us; we liked them for that. Course it all isn't what it used to be. The fighting is dying down round the Elephant; over the other side, too. The fellows are all 21 now, or 22. There isn't a new lot yet. Couple of years' time, I think it'll be rough again.

Q. Did you yourself like fighting?

A. Ever since I was a little kid I wanted to make people be frightened of me, I was determined to make my name. That's why I liked fighting. I don't want to boast, but all that time I only lost one fight. I'm pretty strong, but you've got to have it up here, you got to be fast, it's the quickness. I'd come in and they'd think I was going to hit them and I'd butt them with my head. You got to guard against kicks. Why do we kick a bloke when he's down? Well, gives him something to remember. But don't get me wrong, I'm not crazy. All along I had the ambition to be somebody. I never had the chance to be somebody—I said to myself I couldn't be a film star or a runner—so I wanted to be somebody by being a boxer, and then when I missed the chance through that accident—well, there was fighting.

Q. What about the clothes?

A. I'd say I had six suits, cost about £20 each.

Q. Where did the Boys get all that money?

A. Ah, that'd be telling, but some made hundreds of pounds.

One time I had a special suit of satin, with 14-inch drainpipes, 4 buttons, draped; I'd wear a Slim Jim and creepers. Whole outfit cost about £35. Some of the Boys used to have their hair permed. Don't see anything wrong with it. A girl wants her hair to look nice, why shouldn't a fellow? That's what gets me about ordinary people. The moment you've got your hair done up and wear a Slim Jim, they think you're a freak, a Teddy boy.

Q. What about your clique?

A. Our clique? They were mostly drivers, in the building, packers, in the meat market, some of them just loafers—you had to have money for it. But they'd always lend you a few bob. That's what I say, they were not like ordinary people, not snobbish. They had a lot more decency; they'd always put you up. If they had the money they'd share absolutely. Once a couple of buck Irishmen beat me up and got away with a lot of money. My mates said they'd look for them if it took a year. When you're with the Boys they stick by you. When you're inside, they send you things. They're pretty good, they'll come to see if you're in Court, and they're always willing to be witnesses; they'll take the risk of bearing witness; they're a good lot, they stick to each other.

That's why I say, it's the ordinary public that causes the trouble. If we walk into a café they'd say: "Sorry, we don't want none of you in here"; they'd say we're Teddy boys and they're afraid of trouble. And all the time you're just perfectly normal—it makes me wild when people stare and laugh at me. No one is going to look at the Boys and laugh and get away with it. Don't get me wrong; we don't take any notice of ordinary people or old people. If they do nothing, we don't interfere. But when a bloke gives me a look and he doesn't like the way I dress and perhaps he says, "Cor, what a sight," well, I swing at him.

I tell you: ordinary people, they're supposed to be so high and mighty, like having a lot of money; what I'd say is, "You think you have everything and we Teddy boys have nothing; you think we're simple; well, we could have it twice as good as you if we tried!"

Q. All right—but how did you get out of it all?

A. It was this way, the middle of last year. There were those letters and photos this girl had sent me when I was inside. I'd left them in a room and the landlord, he was an Irish fellow, he didn't want to give them to me. He said I should go to the police, he knew nothing. I went to the police, but they said they could do nothing about it. It made me wild, because I tell you, I worshipped that girl. So I went to the Irishman and I kicked his door open. We had a fight, me and him and his wife, she was screaming. I hit him with a chair and kicked him and I went on smashing the furniture. A few days later they picked me up on a charge of GBH—you know, Grievous Bodily Harm—they said I broke the Irishman's arm. Well, I was on three years' probation so it looked bad, but the Irish fellow, the police knew he was queer, and that helped me. They said I'd made a lot of progress; the Magistrate said I was lucky not to be going for five years, but he'd give me a final chance, and I got a £10 fine. But I'd had a fright. I told the probation officer I wanted somewhere to live that was different, like when I was at home, and he told me to come here to the old Reverend's House. There was four of us young fellows staying there, it was like a family; I was there six months. I'd say its through that I learned there's more in life than just hooliganism. I got a job now, in a warehouse. I went back for a bit to my parents, but I wouldn't stay. They wanted me to dress different, not to wear tight trousers. I worked hard in the warehouse, but they didn't think I'd changed, they wanted me to be in by eleven every night, so I packed it in.

I've got a room now, but I still come here to the Reverend's place once a week, and things are different. I've met a girl, I'm going with her now, going steady. She's a decent girl. I want to get married next year. In the warehouse it's hard work; I make about ten pounds a week, take home clear. I wouldn't say I don't go out with the Boys now and then, but not much. I want to do something better. What I want to say is this: I'm older now, I want to have a sense of responsibility, I want someone I can love and look after and make a home. It's funny, this girl, she lives at Peckham and several times when I've missed the last bus I've walked home to the Borough. I like walking at night. I had that Swiss watch then and for something to do I used to time myself—see how fast I could make it from her home to mine.

So far, society had not made Ron's uncertain uphill struggle easy for him.

CHAPTER IV

The Fashion from the Elephant

BUT FIRST FROM MAYFAIR

THE young man interviewed in the previous chapter could be described as a fairly typical Teddy boy. The more I thought about the confused ideas filling his mind and those of similar youths I talked to, the more it seemed to me that the Teddy boy movement could be seen as throwing light on two developments in English social life of the 'fifties. The first was the struggle of the bottom layer of young unskilled workers for social emancipation, for a place which should be their own by right within the new classless mass culture. The second development was the growth of a new type of violence which seemed to be associated with this drive.

To start with the positive side. If we want to regard the Teddy boy movement as a symptom of proletarian rebellion, a piece of defiant flag-flying, then it is interesting to note that the actual post-war Edwardian fashion was from the start a symbol of revolt, but on two extremely separate social levels. The first proletarian Teds made their appearance in the early 'fifties in such tough London areas as the Elephant and Lambeth, but these areas are also not far from the West End, and for the earlier origin of the fashion one has to go across the Thames to post-war Mayfair and Soho.

It was soon after the end of the war that debutantes' escorts and similar youthful men about town were first seen in the West End wearing well-cut Edwardian suits which recalled those worn by their grandfathers in the great Imperial age. The fashion had in the first instance been launched by the Savile Row tailors in an attempt to regain the leadership in men's styles lost during the war, but there was more in it than that. The fashion was from the beginning a symbol of slightly pretentious revolt, even on an English upper-class level. The young dandies who after the war strolled through the West End, wearing longer jackets, tighter trousers, curled bowler hats, with their hair worn at exaggerated length and carefully brushed, were also making a proclamation. Their fashion was an announcement that the war with its uniformed heroes and general drabness was now over and done with, that it had become a bore and now a new era of youth had begun. The revolt was directed alike against the despised social levelling brought in by the Labour Government and the new mass culture from America. In short, the upper-class Edwardian fashion proclaimed the idea that belonging to the English upper class was still something unique in the world and so to be emphasized by a special style of dress.

On this level of the top young people, the post-war Edwardian fashion did not last long; partly because the spirit of its assertion was too contrived. After all, the circumstances of British power in the Edwardian era were gone for good, and Mayfair, too, was now no longer an aristocratic preserve but simply a fashionable business centre. Another reason was that the fashion had too quickly spread to the wrong people. A friend, a sociologist, told me that he came to this conclusion already in 1950 when he met a party of young men in a suburban train who were obviously young city clerks, but were dressed in curled bowlers, fancy waistcoats and tight trousers and talking to each other in carefully rounded phrases as though to the aristocratic manner born. By this time the true upper-class Edwardianism was already practically over. Savile Row and Bond Street were shying away from anything except suitable vestiges of the fashion, and they did so all the faster because in the meantime the Edwardian style in its full bloom had utterly unexpectedly transported itself across the Thames to working-class South London, that is, in terms of class, to enemy territory.

On this other side of the River—and of the class barrier—the Edwardian style was also a symbol of social revolt, but one which was not generally recognized. It was certainly not easy to see this at the time. To the public eye, the first thorough-going proletarian Teddy boys, standing about at the Elephant or in the streets of Southwark in their full regalia, looked at first like music-hall caricatures. At the same time, their aggressive anti-social attitude was baffling and alarming; there was something distinctly un-pleasant and dangerous about these young men. The first public reaction towards them was therefore one of derision mingled with growing hostility. Indeed, no group of young people in modern England has found itself the target of quite such concentrated dislike. Perhaps the early Teds merited this, but what was not understood—I think this is clear in retrospect—was the significance of their strange movement. For first of all there was clearly something catching and attractive to a large section of working-class youth in this particular amalgam of dandyism and gang life. From its birthplace in South London the Teddy boy fashion spread, in fact very quickly, to other parts of working-class London and soon to many parts of the provinces. Secondly, as the sartorial Teddy boy fashion spread, its exaggerations were also spontaneously reduced. In the guise of the "Italian style" it became eventually the smart walking-out wear, with Continental touches, for a majority of English working-class boys. And this signified a breach in class tradition: for the first time, English working-class boys had not merely imitated an upper-class fashion, but developed it independently into their own dandyism. This came later, but because the fashion trend illustrated these considerable changes in British working-class life, it is worth looking in detail at its strange pioneers, the original Teddy boys, long since superseded.

THE FIRST OF THE FEW

From all accounts, the first Teds who introduced the fashion south of Waterloo and Vauxhall were a pretty rough lot. In terms of age-groups they still had their links with the older cloth-capped gangs which in earlier years had dominated areas like the Elephant, keeping the police on the run and razors in their pockets. A social worker from the Elephant area told me, "As I recall it, the local Teddy boy fashion in its first bloom had few law-abiding members. It was definitely the 'submerged tenth' who popularized the new clothes. They were the groups who were not respectable, not socially acceptable." A young man who was briefly in one of the earliest gangs described its members as almost entirely unskilled workers or just drifters. "They were market porters, bricklayers, a lot of van boys, all in jobs that didn't offer much—'labourers' could cover the lot." Some of them were out of work but had their own methods of keeping up. "They just went in for thieving. Many of the Teds thought nothing of it: they call it having a bit of business. I remember how they'd always try to bring in words they didn't know the meaning of, like calling somebody they didn't like 'bombastic'."

At the same time, given the ingrown conservatism of any English working-class community and its opposition to dandyism or any hint of effeminacy, it must have taken a special boldness for the first Teddy boys of South London to swagger along their drab streets in their exaggerated outfits. How had the style managed to cross the River? It could hardly have come straight from Savile Row. The general explanation is that it reached South London via Soho. It was a new post-war development that young manual labourers from South London, especially those who had seen military service, went far more readily than before for their evening's entertainment to "the other side", that is, the West End, the square mile of large cinemas and little clubs, jazz haunts and juke-box cafés, which around Soho abut on theatreland and fashionable restaurants. It was in Soho that the Elephant Boys were said to have encountered the new fashion of dressing eccentrically, through meetings either with young Mayfair Edwardians or the latter's Soho imitators. Anyhow, the novel fact was that they picked up the fashion and imitated it, perhaps because its look appealed to them, but probably also because its exaggeration corresponded to something in their own outlook, a nagging dissatisfaction, a compelling demand to draw attention to themselves.

A further interesting point was that they not only took the Edwardian style back with them across the River, but fashioned it into a new dandyism of their own, perhaps grotesquely stylized yet even so not to be written off entirely as an aesthetic failure. As a London dress-designer once said to me while we watched a group of Teddy boys who stood about in typically languid poses in a dance-hall: "You know, the effect only just fails to be attractive!" These particular lads, however, might have been described as already of the second or third generation of Teds. In the first generation, this look of near-attractiveness was less apparent as they swaggered through their streets. For one thing they were still proletarians: their faces did not go with the dandified clothes; they had not yet that smoother post-war look of the new generation of English working-class boys accustomed to a moneyed life. For another thing, as determined innovators the first Teds carried the eccentricity of their garb to an extreme which had an effect of masquerade.

Reading from top to bottom, this early Teddy boy costume, which became the delight of cartoonists and photographers, went something as follows. In the hair-styles the influence was American and plainly acquired from "the pictures". The basic elements were mostly aggressive sideboards, with masses of hair at the back and a fuzzy shock of it above the brow. Early individual styles were the Tony Curtis, distinguished by a jutting wave over the forehead; the so-called D.A.—very soigné and combed together at the back; in the Boston, the back of the neck was by contrast closely shaved; most extreme of the early styles was probably the Mohican, involving a fiercely shaved skull. But whatever the variations, these hair-styles were an immensely important part of the new fashion. They were a source of particular pride and attention to their wearers and were acquired by appointments with special barbers, which involved the use of dryers and hair-nets and cost between 7s. 6d. and 15s. for a setting, a considerable outlay for young wage-earners. Quite clearly they played a special rôle in a cult which in its other aspects put stress on violent masculinity, and psychologists can no doubt explain their meaning.

Among the clothes it was the jacket of the suit which came nearest to true "Edwardian". It was very long and fully draped, usually black, though light colours were also permitted; with a single button in front with extra pockets and flaps and, in the case of those who could afford it, topped by a velvet collar. The shirts were usually white. One popular kind was called a "Billy Eckstein shirt", with a long fly-over collar worn frequently with a black knotted string tie or a "Slim Jim". Waistcoats were usually plain, though particularly opulent Teddy boys displayed some flowery showpieces. The Edwardian trousers were tight fitting and narrow and called "strides". Socks again could be ornate, and with them, initially, went heavy shoes with round toe-caps, or so-called "creepers" with thick crêpe soles. A whole outfit might cost upwards of £20, of which the suit itself might come to £14. This was considerably less than such smart clothes cost a few years later, but then in the first days of the Teddy boys, cash and credit for clothes were not as easily come by as towards the end of the 'fifties.

In the cloth-capped gangs preceding those of the Teds, a few girls had mingled with the members, and it is worth mentioning that for a brief period a number of girls tried to dress up in conformity with their Teddy boy friends. The recognized style of the Teddy girl included a grotesquely tight skirt, hair worn in pony-tail, and the carrying of an extra long umbrella which presumably could be used as a weapon. But this feminine intervention was no more than a brief flicker: women's fashions don't arise from below. Moreover, it appeared to be of the essence of the Teddy boy cult that its members were more interested in each other and in their group life than in girls. And this was a novel touch. As Mr Hugh Latymer wrote with insight at the time,[1] the first Edwardian personality which emerged in the process of adjustment to the clothes was startling in a working-class environment in that the pose was of solemn formality: "In cafés, public-houses or milk-bars which Teddy boys favour, there is no singing on Saturday nights. The boys sit posed in groups, conscious of arranged hair, creased 'drains', they laugh at the group butt (usually the worst-dressed member of the party) and drink intently. Girls sit together, waiting to be picked up by somebody, but terribly correct about it all."

This formality could also be noted in the dance-hall where the early Teds did not deign to dance—this was before the invention of rock and roll—or only in a condescending manner. The fashion was that of a vague shuffle, accompanied by dead-pan facial expression and monosyllabic speech. This lassitude was, of course, only a surface affectation. If girls were scorned as real companions, they were very much in the Teddy boys' minds as objects and as prey. In fact, one could say that this whole dressing up in groups by young unskilled wage-earners was only a means of furthering the usual aim of such young men—the nightly prowl for girls. And, just as the sartorial fashion was like a romantically stylized assertion of being important, "being somebody", so the primitive romanticism which inspired the clothes was applied to the night life too. The result was the organization of Teddy boys in gangs, some quite large, to defend territories defined as "theirs"; or,

[1] *The Observer*, 19th June 1955.

when the mood came, to raid those of other gangs for girls. In this way the police and public around 1953 and 1954 first became aware of a new type of Teddy boy disorder in the late night hours. This disorder was also formalized, rather like a ragged fantasy of warfare. A bus conductor told me that in a certain public-house at the end of his run which was something of a frontier post, he could on Saturday nights see huddled groups from different gangs watching each other like cats, or in the words of the old song, "Tread on the tail of my coat."

In fact, before long the Teddy boys seemed to have created a little world of their own—a sub-culture with its own laws of dress, behaviour and territory, in which they strutted about, looked challengingly at outsiders, chased girls, occasionally fought each other and planned the occasional larceny. There were perhaps a few thousand of them in inner London, and in its peculiarly organized form the cult went on for a few years. On the whole, it was a primitive performance. The early Teddy boys were working-class youths with a grudge against society and an itch to assert themselves—this was the new element—but mostly they were just young toughs on the road to nowhere. As a result, the rebellion was one without core. The elaborate dress might be intended as a defiant declaration of status, but even that was spurious. There were perhaps moments when the romance of Teddy boy gang life seemed to become real. There was perhaps some satisfaction in the obsessive banding together, in wreaking vengeance against anyone who disparaged the uniform; in adopting a threatening attitude in public places; in leading an indiscriminate sex life; in baiting such victims as café owners and bus conductors, in defiance of the police and being in on the knowledge of local crime. But as this did not help the Teddy boys to get on as their adolescence passed, and did not bring them new status, with all the dressing up and the gang organization, most of them in actual fact led a dreary life. A young man who had belonged to one of these first gangs in East London until he went for his national service into the Navy gave me the following picture of its life, put down here from my notes in the form of question and answer:

Q. Where did they hang out?
A. They used to collect at Arcades or in a caff. The pictures, too.

They were always going there. In the afternoons they'd bump their way in without paying; evenings too, and Sundays. Then they'd go back to a café and sit there till closing time.

Q. What did they do with their time?

A. Sometimes they picked up girls. There was a place they used to call the "kitchen". Five or six fellas would go in and watch each other perform. The girls? They were just about the lowest, the scrapins.

Some Friday or Saturday night, perhaps, they'd get into a car—there was always a car—and go down West.

In the cafés there was always talk about what they'd call "business". Everybody'd know; I used to, myself. It didn't pay to miss anything because you had got to be topical in conversation . . . it was like a message going through everything. The fellows would know all about the fighting; it was a sort of broadcast: there might be a fight, so all meet at the so and so place, because you'd want to go in with a nice team.

The fighting? They didn't carry knives much: it was usually lumps of wood or bottles.

Girls? There never were any girls in the gangs. Fellows had girls, but they didn't mix . . . they didn't mix fighting and girls.

Q. Otherwise . . .

A. It was sport, mostly. Some fellows went in for boxing and weightlifting and swimming . . . a bit of football would creep into it. The fellows would play in their suits every Wednesday in the Park. . . . It'd be without a referee, about 15 a side, pretty rough.

They used to make jokes. When a mob got on a bus, they'd play the conductor up. They'd all say someone else was paying. One time I saw about 40 fellows all flag a taxi, then everybody'd say it was somebody else.

Q. And what happened to these original Teds?

A. Some were put away. Borstal, quite a lot went to. What happened to most of the others was exactly what happened to ordinary people in ordinary life—mixing with the opposite sex and sooner or later they'd go steady and they'd end up pushing a pram. When I got back from the Navy I found the top men married and settled down, to my amazement. Fresh fighters had taken over, but I thought they were not as tough as the old 'uns—they'd been a rough mob. . . .

Viewed in cold retrospect, the story sounds dismal. Most of the early Teddy boy groups probably led much the same unconstructive life. Driven on by boredom, by the need for spending money or just by anger against society, a good many of them landed up in the dock and went on to Borstal or prison, and that was the end. And yet—and this is important—the early Teds also started something. If it brought little good to the individual gang members, their collective revolt had consequences. Through the mere fact that they maintained their stylized dress and gang life for several years, regardless of what society thought or the jeers they encountered, they showed that the winds of change were blowing through the British slums—in a way they helped to hasten a social break-through. For example, the fashion they inaugurated had by the middle 'fifties spread through the greater part of Britain. To be sure, it was also changing, it was no longer quite *their* fashion. Even so, it had been the early Teddy boys who, as crude innovators, had first established the British working-class youth's right to his own dandyism.

The achievement was all the more remarkable, because by background the early Teddy boys came largely from the "submerged tenth" of working-class life, that is, from a group of whose whole existence the English upper and middle classes were not so long ago hardly aware. In fact, at the risk of being a little fanciful one might say that, rather later than the Irish and Indians and at the same time as the Africans, the Teddy boys of London were staging their own little anti-colonial revolt against inferior social status.

WINDS OF CHANGE

True, this revolt was a ragged and confused little affair, yet observers on the spot could also sense the social change it illustrated. The point was, for example, emphasized to me by the Rev. Douglas Griffiths of Friendship House, a Methodist Community Centre, in what was not so long ago darkest Lambeth. At this Centre, Mr Griffiths in 1951 launched a successful youth club for boys, many of whom were alleged to be "unclubbable" or had police records. As he has described it, from this vantage-point he could clearly observe the social advance from the old-style toughs to the newer Teds—one might say from the first to the second wave of post-war youth in this London area, where nineteenth-century slums were being pulled down and new council flats being put up:

The gangs of young people who invaded Friendship House in its first days were still in the old tradition. The boys mostly wore rough sports coats and cloth caps and carried razors. Quarrels came more from rivalries between gangs than about girls. It usually took us six weeks to persuade them to leave their razors behind and to awaken some degree of Club loyalty in them. Language was bad, contraceptives were found about the corridors, discipline was difficult.

Two or three years later the type of gang in the Youth Club seemed to change rather abruptly. In February 1954 we were invaded by the first large gang of Edwardian boys and girls, and they were followed by other similar groups. These gangs were noticeably larger in membership than was the case with the earlier ones. At that time I used to know personally of gangs in London numbering in one case 150 and in many cases 50 or more. Their members appeared without noticeable standards, except for an almost obsessional loyalty towards each other. Yet they were no longer as one-track in their minds as their predecessors. To be sure, girls were hanging round these Edwardians in large numbers, getting the age-old kick out of being fought for. But on the whole, with these newcomers, sex tended to predominate less than with the earlier gangs. As an interest it had to compete above all with their sartorial self-concern, which was not without its advantage.

I thought then and still think that the so-called Edwardian dress which started in Savile Row was not the red herring which it appeared to some critics. It was a rather pathetic attempt to find significance by lads searching for something. But everyone has the right to be someone, and the special way of dressing which is considered a virtue in a Guards Officer or even a Chelsea artist ought not to be counted a vice in a modern working-class lad.

To give another parallel, as the Teddy Boys faded out, they

were succeeded in the public eye by the Beatniks, also dressed-up youthful rebels, only this time middle class.

It is also worth noting that if aesthetically the Teddy boy fashion had its grotesque sides, there were also times when the dandyism could even look engaging: it all depended how one looked at it. I remember thinking this in 1958 during a visit to Sheffield, which then sartorially seemed at the stage London had reached in 1954. In the mornings I could see whistling young boys stride out gaily against a background of smoke-stacks, challenging the world with bright scarlet shirts worn under their jackets. At night I saw a group of them in a small café, wearing striped maroon-and-black and green-and-black silk shirts and standing about with dead-pan expressions on their faces below their shocks of hair. It was all still pretty well off-beat, but with a little sympathy one could also sense the confused revolt against the drabness of industrial England around them which was involved in this dressing up.

Another point which showed that the fashion involved a distinct social emancipation was the fact that it not only persisted without guidance from above, but, as it spread, underwent changes as definite as those imposed elsewhere by M. Dior and his colleagues.

For example, when the extreme Teddy boy style went out in London in 1955, it was followed by that of the Drapes, or Drape Boys, which represented the first moderation in eccentricity. The jackets in the new style were still draped and long, but without velvet collars and with not so many pockets; trousers remained narrow, but were now worn with ordinary shoes. Experimentation was also on the increase. Writing in *The Observer* in 1955, Hugh Latymer found that a Teddy boy had taken his suit from the pages of *Man about Town*, choosing the coat from one page, the waistcoat from another and adding facings of his own design. A Deptford tailor said that some of his male clients would describe to him something they had seen in the West End, while their girl companions would come in with the pages of *Vogue*.

A little later came the brief interlude of the Bohemians, or Bo's or Boees, another small pointer to the current social revolution. By this time, skiffle music had swept into English youth life and in other circles the vogue for both traditional and modernist jazz had spread pretty wide. Viewed against this setting, the Bohemian style represented an experiment by the Teds to cross another

frontier, not a particularly successful attempt, but interesting all
the same. For instance, my young informant from London, E.,
gave me this view:

It was about 1955 you got the skiffle crowd and the traditional
jazz people coming into the cafés. They dressed like artists—we
always called them Boees—and some of the fellows, van-boys,
labourers and the like, dressed the same way, too. They used to
put on pullovers and duffle coats like the Boees and tried to mix
in a bit, but it didn't work: there was always segregation between
them and the Boees. I personally didn't go for it. The traditional
jazz people seemed to me a sweaty crowd who didn't mind
wearing dirty old pullovers. Maybe they weren't unclean under-
neath, but they gave that impression. One thing you've got to
say for the Teds—they knew how to look after their persons.

At least the Bohemian interlude showed that the Teds no longer
considered themselves entirely cut off from the world of Gully
Jimson, which clearly had a certain fascination for them.

Next among the fashion influences came the well-known Italian
style which took quite a long while to establish itself, but, when it
did so, denoted a new and decisive social advance. For unlike
the Teddy boy fashion, which had been the mildly challenging
wear of a small set of pathetically grotesque dandies, the Italian
style was of a kind which could be, and was, taken up by steadily
increasing numbers of working-class boys. The main components
of the style were short jackets, fully draped at the back and at first
often broadly striped on the Italian pattern. The trousers were
narrow; shirts could be coloured as well as white and cuffs and
handkerchiefs were prominently shown. The new shoes were
finely pointed on the Italian model and in London called Pickers
or Pointers. With this went the elaborate but now shorter and
rather attractive hair-styles which had also come into fashion
among students on the Continent: the James Dean, the Marlon
Brando, the Crew Cut, the Crop. . . . Although it had evolved out
of the Teddy boy fashion, the far less eccentric and provocative
Italian style marked a social transformation in the life of English
working-class boys. As my social worker from the Elephant put it,
the Italian style was no mere "anti-style", one for outlaws. Quite
the contrary. It was worn by boys who liked smarter clothing for

its own sake and who were socially much more acceptable. Indeed, among the working class it was considered the proper style of the more sophisticated and intelligent boys who cared for the way they dressed, whereas the Teddy boys had predominantly belonged to the extremer elements, those who didn't want to be integrated.

In other words, the pioneers who opened the way had, as so often, been superseded. (It would be interesting to know what has happened to the original Teds—most of them are by now probably very ordinary married men, apart from the minority who tumbled over into criminality.) Fashion has not stood still, and within the Italian style there have been attempts to introduce variants. There was the "College Boy", which went with crew cuts and jackets of extra broad stripes. A hybrid with other and "arty" echoes was the "Modernist"; its mark was still shorter haircuts and woolly coloured shirts worn without a tie. Another model, taken from yet another social sphere, was the "Prince of Wales Check", a prominent light grey, checked tweed suit, for a short time very much in popular fashion. However, these were minor variations: the salient fact was that by 1957-58 the exaggerations in young working-class wear had been overcome. The Italian style, but less and less rigidly formalized, had become the normal walking-out wear. In other words, the great change in the fashion-consciousness of contemporary working-class youth which had started with the Teddy boys had now reached its objective, and one could make some interesting observations about this development.

First, there is the fact that the style arrived at was international. What was novel was that English working-class youths had now discovered Europe and were ready, indeed eager, to know what was being worn by young people on the Continent.

This is quite striking: the fashions of French and Italian students are much closer to those seen at, say, South London youth clubs than to those in English university halls.) Furthermore, well-dressed working-class youths had also broken through into the week-end informality of colourful jeans and modern sports clothes, away from their former week-end awkwardness of either rolled-up shirt-sleeves or stiff Sunday best. In this particular they had actually fallen into line with English upper-middle-class habits—but this also for the first time. These fashion changes were of course important less in themselves than in what they reflected, namely the steadily increasing economic affluence and social emancipation of working-class youth throughout the 1950s. My young informant from London, E., who as a teenager had been among the early Teddy boys, found when he came out of the Navy in 1958 that his area was still a tough working-class "manor", yet the whole atmosphere had subtly changed:

> The gangs were definitely smaller. For one thing the pin-table arcades where the fellows used to hang out had mostly disappeared. And a good thing, too. They had been depressing places, dirty and moribund.
>
> The fellows in the gangs were different, too. Where early on it had only been about 2 out of 10, now 5 out of 10 of all boys were dress-conscious. I noticed flick-knives had come in much more, but I still think most of the fellows carried them only out of bravado. Mostly they happened to know someone who knew how to use a knife genuinely, who'd got a name for it, so all the others would back him up.
>
> The big change was, the average fellow had more money— you had to have more money now to be in the swim. Things cost more but there was a lot more cash about. For one thing, all the chief gangs now had fellows with cars and motor-bikes. The special motor-bike mob who wore black leather jackets thought of themselves as the top lot; they met by themselves in their own pub. In general, the fellows now met not only in cafés but in dance-halls and saloon-bars, and the older ones had started drinking again. You could go to all kinds of clubs—that was new, too—and there were lots of parties. Some of the fellows had record-players and you'd have a party going on all Sunday, with fellows and girls and drink and dozens of records.

That is, even in the dead-end districts of London there had been radical social change. Boys and youths working in unskilled jobs were no longer loutish, but searching to take part in, well, ordinary mid-twentieth-century city life. This was the positive side of the social revolt whose flag had been raised by the Teddy boys half a dozen years earlier. But as some of the accounts I have quoted show, the movement had also gone round strange corners, to produce other results denoting not progress but regression.

CHAPTER V

The Destructive Element

THE CULT OF VIOLENCE

THERE were some very obviously unpleasant sides to the Teddy boy movement. From the start, it was mixed up with a rather ugly streak of violence and a general hostility towards society which often overlapped with actual criminality.

Perhaps this was also not immediately recognized. On his first appearance, the London Teddy boy with his strange Edwardian regalia, his wild shock of hair, dead-pan expression and cigarette dangling wearily from his lips, seemed just another eccentric proletarian figure thrown up by the post-war age, a fit successor to the spiv in the cartoonist's column. It took a little time before he was also recognized as an ominous character, drawing his inspiration from American gangster films as well as Edwardian fashion plates. However, as the gangs of Teddy boys spread outwards to the London suburbs, this unpleasant side of the phenomenon impressed itself fairly forcibly on the public mind.

There were a number of reports of Teddy boys causing wanton damage to cafés. Incidents occurred where pedestrians were terrorized in the streets. Frequently, youths not belonging to a gang were beaten up; the typical Teddy boy assault seemed to be in odds of five or six against one. At the same time the police authorities in certain areas became aware of an increase in thefts and burglaries and the evidence indicated that some of these operations at least were being planned in the cafés and other hangouts where the Teddy boys gathered.

In fact, in certain Teddy boy circles, complete disregard for the law seemed to have become an accepted feature of a new sub-culture. This statement needs qualification. The majority of the youths who on leaving school bought the Teddy boy uniform and tried to become junior members of a gang were not delinquents and had probably no intention of engaging in more than a spot of brawling and collective bravado. But because the original Teddy boys had come from the "submerged tenth", there was an overlap between their movement and the criminal world. As the police saw it, in each large Teddy boy gang, in each regularly frequented café, there were usually some hardened young characters with police and prison records to be found, and there was also something in the whole atmosphere of deliberate defiance cultivated by the Teddy boy movement which made it easier for this minority to establish their authority.

The extent to which the Teddy boy groups were mixed up with criminality probably varied greatly with the district. A probation officer in the North London area who had witnessed the arrival of the very first Teddy boy gangs in his district and later saw quite a few of their members in the dock and among his clientele, told me that he had recognized them from the start as a danger which ought to be stamped out, or at any rate stamped on. The danger of the movement, in his view, was that it brought together two distinct anti-social attitudes. The first was simply that of the usual adolescent rebellion, although he thought the Teddy boys represented a concentration of lads whose antagonism against teachers, employers and the State was quite abnormally tense. However, the second attitude which the Teddy boys had also made their own was the outlook of the typical criminal area where lawbreaking was part of ordinary life and the police were always the enemy. By associating the spirit of adolescent rebellion with criminal traditions, by giving it the glamour of a special uniform and gang life, the Teddy boys were in fact spreading this criminal area outlook far beyond its usual confines, and therein lay the danger. Young boys in his district had joined the gangs simply because they appeared romantic. The collective cynicism and the uniform offered psychological security and status. It seemed daring and exciting to sit in a café where the conversation amongst older youths ran on who was a good man with a knife and how much the boys had got away with in the latest case of breaking and entering. But before long one youngster after another appeared in Court, sometimes on charges which resulted in their being sent away, and many of these were boys who, but for the attraction of the Teddy boy fashion, might never have joined such company. In fact, said this probation officer, the connection between the spread of Teddy boy culture and that of criminality seemed to him pretty direct, at least in the sector of London he knew. As soon as the large gangs had staked out their territories, his case load began to lengthen and so did the number of local lads sent off to Borstal and Detention Centres. Some lads were in this way started off on criminal careers for which they had not been by temperament predestined: they had simply been sucked towards crime by this sinister fashion and not been clever in getting away with it.

Since the first Teddy boys were drawn largely from the more lawless areas of London, this overlap with criminality was in a way explicable. An aspect of the movement that caused rather more surprise was its cult of violence—a rather novel type of violence. There was a peculiar viciousness in the Teddy boy assaults on each other and on outsiders. The violence seemed to blend bullying gangster methods with an irrational touchiness. Observers often felt that a sense of basic insecurity was revealed both by the swagger of the gang and their code of an imagined insult which had not merely to be revenged by force, but viciously revenged. This addiction to violence which seemed quite senseless was one long puzzle presented by the Teddy boys, and there was also another. It was not difficult to see that this particular sort of gang life had its attraction for certain unstable types of youths. The question was why the number of such youths who felt a need for gang life should suddenly have increased so much. One explanation accepted by many observers was that the adolescents of the early 'fifties represented a generation which had suffered unduly from childhood disturbance during the war, and so threw up an unusual proportion of psychologically disturbed teenage boys and girls.

How much weight to give this factor is not easy to say, but the explanation of some extra degree of instability in the make-up of this adolescent generation would also account for some other features of the Teddy boy cult. For instance, it could be argued that the combination of obsessive violence and obsessive interest in personal adornment betrayed not only a social but a sexual unsureness among the gang members in general. It was certainly the case that in the inner Teddy boy circles homosexualism was regarded as one of the ubiquitous facts of life. A shrewd Irish observer who had knocked around with the London Teddy boys for some years gave me his view that if one picked any hundred of them, especially from those who had been to prison, seventy-five would have had some homosexual experience, some of them, as he said, "just for cash, some out of curiosity, the majority out of sheer boredom". Still, to equate the Teddy boy gang life with a sudden increase of an overt homosexual streak on a certain level of British society is probably too simple and direct an explanation. Indeed, outward appearance might suggest the contrary. For the majority of gang members, the monotonous nightly prowl for girls (if necessary prostitutes would do) was the ultimate aim of their activity. But it could also be argued that this promiscuity was in itself the sign of a continuous need to demonstrate a masculinity which was felt to be threatened without such demonstration.

A similar interpretation of a sexual twist in the make-up of the Teddy boys could be ascribed to their excessive interest in their own and each other's clothes and hair-styles, such as the habit of the early Teddy boys of having their hair permanently waved. The interesting stock answer given by Teddy boy dandies to enquiring journalists about this usually was: "If the girls do it and make themselves look nice, why shouldn't we?" My Irish informant was sure that this revealed a basic effeminacy and nothing else:

> If you look into the motive you will find it was largely jealousy —jealousy of the girls for being the centre of attention. They just couldn't stand not having it all to themselves. If you had listened to these Teds as I did when they stood about in dance-halls, all you would hear about was clothes and style. One would say: "I paid seventeen guineas for this suit at so-and-so's", and the other, "I paid this new Jew tailor nineteen guineas for mine". They could talk literally for hours about styles and cut and prices, the way you usually only hear women talk. But even if they all weren't effeminate, though I know some of them were, the main thing with these Teds was that they had to out-shine the way the girls were dressed by the way they themselves were dressed. The Teddy boy himself was always the person who had to stand out.

This whole notion of a streak of intensified psychological disturbance, derived from war-time dislocation, but which made itself felt belatedly in a certain adolescent age-group, is speculative, but it could go some way to explain various characteristics of the Teddy boy cult, such as the need for obsessive gang loyalty, the importance of the uniform as a symbol of "belonging", i.e. having security and status, and also the tendency to react with senseless violence to apparently trivial provocation. If it is accepted that many of the Teddy boys were disturbed adolescents who were always impelled to prove their manhood, then to them their violence was not senseless. As they felt about it, such a thing as a disparaging remark about their appearance, even if only made jokingly, was not trivial but an attack upon their very *raison d'être*, upon their insecure manhood, and to be reacted to as such.

During the first phase of the large Edwardian gangs one of the ways in which they signalled their presence was, indeed, through outbreaks of fighting triggered off by some quite disproportionately small cause. But if the notion that the flare-up of violence in the early 'fifties was the expression of a particularly disturbed generation, a delayed effect of the war, makes some sense, it is still only a part of the explanation. There is also the question why this type of violent reaction should have perpetuated itself so that it became simply part of the social climate of the late 1950s. In this perpetuation some other factors were surely at work which will be discussed in subsequent chapters. At this point it may be enough to say that the tradition which the Teddy boys bequeathed to their adolescent successors was that group violence could be part of ordinary street life and that by a special new sub-cultural code it was in order for them to take the law into their own hands. If a certain youth was objectionable to a gang, it was both possible and the expected thing to ambush him and teach him a lesson, and if cleverly organized, this could be done almost with impunity. Even after the original large gangs had disintegrated and the nervous tension which had been part of the original Teddy boy life had quietened down, the tradition of reacting violently to an alleged insult survived, as illustrated for instance by the following report (with names omitted) of a case of assault in a Thames-side suburb, a favourite gathering place of the second and third generation of Teddy boys.

A gang of Teddy boys flung a man through a quarter-inch thick plate-glass window of a shop in X High Street during the night, after attacking him and beating him almost unconscious. The man, Mr B, aged 38, was taken by ambulance to hospital where stitches had to be inserted in wounds in his head, right leg and back. Mr B was on his way home after a darts' match.

He had just left a friend's car in the High Street when the gang stopped him. This is how he described the attack:

"The Teddy boys were shouting and pushing each other. I went to walk past them when one of them asked me if I was swearing at them. I told him, 'I've not said anything to you, cocky', meaning 'cock' in a friendly manner. He said to me: 'Call me mate, not cocky', and then took a vicious lunge at me. The whole gang then jumped at me and I went through the window. I must have been almost unconscious. I can only just remember crawling out of the window and then being kicked."

Mr B's friends in the car and two other men saw the attack. They ran to help Mr B, but the gang had scattered before they reached him.

After which, if any of the high-spirited youths were identified or arrested, they ran the risk of sentences ranging from conditional discharge to being sent to Borstal or Detention Centre. Only rarely were prison sentences imposed, for the authorities had the good sense to know that few consequences would be more dangerous than to expose such disturbed youths to the company of seasoned criminals. It was more reasonable to hope that they would within a few years grow out of this adolescent gang life, either through the break of military service or in some other way, and get married and settle down as ordinary citizens, which indeed mostly happened—but not always, and this was the important point.

It was in 1954 or thereabouts that the authorities noted that the tide had changed and juvenile crime, which for some years had been subsiding from the post-war peak, had again taken a sudden sharp upward turn. More than that, the Teddy boy movement was unmistakably linked with this rise. Odd as it seemed, these strange young citizens of the welfare state, with their shocks of hair, draped jackets and expressions of weary disdain, were more than a cartoonist's delight. At the very least they had become a major nuisance factor and were gradually becoming more than that.

In the popular press, enough reports of such violence were coming in to add up to a general new heading of "Teddy Boy Stories". In London, traditional trouble-spot areas in the East End, around the Caledonian Road, the Old Kent Road and Wandsworth Road, were becoming the scene of night-time fights and disturbances in which quite regularly large mobs of rowdy youths were involved. Impromptu weapons were used, stabbings occurred, and as a rule police squads had to be rushed to the spots to break up fights—their arrival was usually the signal for the participants to scatter. Enterprising reporters managed to ferret out that some of these disturbances had been Teddy boy gang fights on a territorial basis of one area against the other, and produced stories how Teddy boy gangs up to a hundred strong had been mobilized for a "punch-up" involving coshes, bottles and knives; mostly it was only the threat of knives, but in some wilder clashes they were actually flashed and used.

Nor did the gangs only fight each other. Cafés were damaged in actions of revenge against their proprietors, especially against Cypriots. For a certain period, bus conductors on late-night routes were molested, and in one or two cases beaten up and left badly injured by Teddy boys who vanished into the night. Another disturbing trend was the violent hostility of Teddy boys against certain youth clubs, which became the target for recurring raids and vandalism. Because of running disturbances, well-established institutions were forced to make new regulations barring youths in Teddy boy clothing. Some smaller clubs had to be temporarily shut down. Club leaders, in interviews, confessed themselves at a loss how to cope. There was a new senseless exaggeration in the violence. It was no longer a mere matter of fights—the kicking of victims on the ground had now also become accepted procedure.

The Teddy boy movement was also spreading outwards from the centre of London. Dressed-up youths who congregated at week-ends in large gangs were creating new trouble spots in outer suburbs like Kingston, Croydon, Barking and Finchley. Other centres of congregation were open spaces like Blackheath and Clapham Common. Gangs also made a nuisance of themselves on the Saturday night trains to Brighton and Southend. Similar reports came from the provinces. Among cities which became centres of Teddy boy life were Birmingham, Nottingham, Liverpool and Bristol. Another development was that the movement appeared to be attracting boys at a younger age. Schoolmasters in secondary modern schools in London working-class areas complained that some of their boys were losing interest in school life at the age of 13 and 14 because their minds were already stuffed with wild tales about the doings of Teddy boys in their district, the romantic café life, the tooling up and the battles, and their whole attention was already fixed on the acquisition of suitable outfits for themselves and the day when they might join as cadet members of the gangs. In fact, the impression which a foreign correspondent in London might have got from his reading of the British press in, say, 1955-56, was that the Teddy boys and their violence were already a small but significant and alarming part of English life.

SEEING THE PROBLEM IN SCALE

This was probably seeing the problem in false scale. England was, and remains, a relatively law-abiding country. Even at the peak of the movement, the number of Teddy boys in the Greater London area did not exceed a top figure of 30,000 (some observers thought it only half or a third of this figure), and most of these spent probably most of their time in boredom rather than activity. Nevertheless, the net result of their arrival was that lawlessness was going up. In spite of the change from unemployment to welfare state, Britain was more lawless in 1955 than 1935, and above all among juveniles and young adults this lawlessness showed some definite new features.

It was becoming clear that, within not more than two or three years, the primitive gang life of the "submerged tenth" had under the impact of the Teddy boy movement become more organized and sophisticated. The street corner was going out and superseded by the café as the centre of the new "anti" groups. Secondly, the Teddy boy fashions undoubtedly gave these groups an added cohesion. Some social workers saw this very early on as a new danger. A probation officer in a Midland town told me that at first he could not make up his mind whether the expensive suits suddenly sported by his local lads did more harm than good. He thought they gave expression to the artistic sense of the boys, which was to the good. At the same time the exaggeration of the dress had set people against them. "They've worked up a feeling that they are being unjustly chivvied and laughed at. So they are driven in on themselves, into a few cafés of their own, and their sense of being against society is all the time kept going and intensified."

A third difference between this crime wave and preceding ones was that the 1950s were an age of mass publicity. The Teddy boys were therefore not only news in the press, on television and radio, but they *knew* that they were news. Many social workers felt this was one of their main troubles. An example was the publicity given to the wave of rock-and-roll riots in British cinemas in 1955. These began at the Trocadero Cinema at the Elephant, where a mob of young people broke up a performance of a rock-and-roll film featuring some well-known virtuosos. To the accompaniment of delirious yells and shouts, seats were torn out, attendants molested and the performance brought to an end. A social worker from the area told me that after these first riots at the Elephant he was not surprised to see them repeated elsewhere. Anyone could see that the excitement and sense of destruction were fed by publicity. The gangs felt that such behaviour was almost expected of them. "You had the feeling that they had read all about themselves in the papers—actually, quite a few of my boys had already had personal contact with the press, and one could see that they were affected: they began to behave more defiantly, to show off, to be 'big-heads', to become what they thought the public wanted them to be—cosh boys, Teddy boys. It was as if they were being sucked into violence by something bigger than themselves."

In other words, press publicity itself sharpened the lines of conflict between society and Teddy boys. The cinema riots, which were repeated in a number of forms, were in themselves no profound event. Another incident, however, which illustrated to the public how far these fantasies of a spurious youthful gangster life had spread in England was the so-called Clapham Common murder case of 1954.

This took place on Clapham Common, on a peaceful summer evening, at a spot where a band was playing. The audience sat listening on park chairs while some young people were dancing on the concrete. Lounging on the seats were four youths called Ryan, Beckley, Chandler and Carter, aged 17 to 19, who sat smoking with their feet up on the chairs. This evidently annoyed another youth, a 16-year-old shop assistant called Coleman, who, together with his girl-friend, was trying to get through the row of seats. There was an altercation about their not making room for him; a few words and insults were exchanged. During this, Beckley suddenly noticed that Coleman's "gang", who had an unpleasant reputation in the neighbourhood, were standing in force not far away, with some girls among them, and he suggested to his friends they had best get away. With the music still playing, the four youths therefore strolled away towards the edge of the Common, but the gang, including some of the girls, followed them ominously. As the four tried to run, the gang closed in and a savage fight began.

Such a spot of trouble could occur very ordinarily wherever boys and girls in rival groups were congregated. However, the new traits illustrated in this incident were the neurotic concentration on points of gang insult, the complete disregard of surroundings and bystanders, and the deadly use of knives, all part of the gang life fantasy in the imagination of these youngsters. Miss Elizabeth Stucley, who at the time ran a youth club for troublesome boys in this area, has reconstructed the incident in her book,[1] and one cannot do better than quote her account of what followed:

It was a violent, silent attack. Wordless, they went for each other, with their fists, kicking. Two boys held Beckley while a third kicked his head. The girls fell back. Someone in the scrimmage shouted: "Get out your knives!" They had small flick-knives that could be palmed.

Ryan was stabbed in the shoulder, and seeing how his friends were outnumbered, he ran away. Beckley and Chandler also started to run. They pelted across the grass with their assailants at their heels. By now they were all panting, muddy and bruised, perhaps bleeding a little.

The larger gang was hot in pursuit. As Miss Stucley says, the bystanders probably thought it a mere game.

As Beckley and Chandler came gasping to the road, they saw with relief that a bus had stopped by the traffic lights. They darted across the road, leapt on board, thankful to have found sanctuary. The lights changed, the bus went on.

The other boys, having seen what happened, had altered course. They were still filled with the fury of battle. They ran, cutting the corner, to the next bus stop, the one near my house.

Elizabeth Stucley, *Running a Youth Club in London*. Blond, 1958.

It is a request stop, and unfortunately someone must have rung the bell. Beckley and Chandler were still on the platform when the other boys sprang on them, dragging them and the conductor into the road. The fight began again, more violently than ever. The passengers were at first staggered by this attack, then two men leapt out and tried to stop the fight, to help the conductor, but by then Beckley was mortally wounded. He lay on the pavement, propped against the wall, the blood gushing from the stab in the aorta vein. Chandler with a stab in his stomach, had got back into the bus. The assailants had fled.

It was, of course, not long before they were picked up. The strongest evidence for the killing pointed at one boy, who had been known for carrying a knife in his schooldays. After running away he had been heard to say how he had got rid of the knife, but later that evening he demonstrated at a coffee stall how he had used the blade—an action typical of the dream-life Teddy boy bravado. He also informed his 17-year-old girl-friend that if she spoke to the police, he would get somebody to hurt her. At any rate, five boys were arrested, and two of them were charged with murder at the Old Bailey. One was acquitted of the murder, but sent to prison with the other boys for common assault. The other, after a re-trial, was found guilty, his sentence being commuted to imprisonment. Miss Stucley concluded:

> When this boy heard the verdict, he said: "I am not guilty of murder, sir." I think he probably spoke the truth. When you know the boys as I got to know them, it was so easy to understand how Beckley came to be killed. The foolish, pointless quarrel about nothing, the savage onslaught in which the boys became drunk with their own violence, the herd hatred that made them hound the miserable Beckley to death, I saw these emotions in embryo over and over again. There, but for the grace of God, went any pack of undisciplined, unoccupied boys. They might not be murderers in their hearts, but they were all liable to violence.

Yes, but why? What had society done to these boys to set off this spirit of violence? Miss Stucley was not the only one to ask such questions.

While at first they had been treated as a joke or curiosity, a new and understandable development of the late 'fifties was a sharp public reaction against the Teddy boys and their aura of violence. In the worst-affected areas they were barred from cafés, cinemas and certain public-houses. Dance-halls imposed rigid rules about dress and behaviour permitted on the floor. In some parts of the country the legal authorities also reacted forcibly. The probation officer from a Midland town, whom I have quoted earlier, told me that it was in 1956-57 that he and his colleagues felt suddenly that they were up against something new in juvenile lawlessness. With the spread of Teddy boy cafés and "big ideas" imported from London, they felt they were moving towards the sort of situation which existed in some American cities, where the juvenile gang leader held the field as a successful opposite number to the probation officer. This development demanded counter-measures before it got out of hand. My informant put it something like this:

We had to show both the leaders and their followers that crime was not an automatic passport to probation, and so we recommended that certain characters we had had our eye on should at the first chance be packed straight off to Borstal, even without previous convictions against them. This not only gave a sharp shock to the young gentlemen themselves, but it also had the salutary effect of stunning everybody else in the gangs and so giving us in the probation service the necessary breathing space to get on with our individual case work. These sentences were quite a departure, but we felt it was the only way. The thing we had to do was to strike sufficiently quickly, to get at the cynical, anti-authority, couldn't-care-less elements whose motto was "What have I got to lose?", to sort these out and hit them in a way to demonstrate that they had plenty to lose.

At the same time, as far as the general public was concerned, the causes of the whole phenomenon seemed to remain inexplicable; wasn't incomparably more being done for the education and welfare of young people than ever before? It was not surprising that the late 'fifties also saw the start of that inconclusive public debate about the morals of the young generation which is still in progress. On the one hand, some fairly strong charges were made against the young, and by implication against their teachers, and repeated from Westminster, from the Bench and in editorial columns. The attacks were apt to be rather sweeping, singling out not only the Teddy boys but the generally obnoxious way of dress and behaviour of a large section of youth. Blame for these shortcomings was laid on lack of parental authority, on too much easy money, on pampering by the welfare state, the general decline in morals and so forth. On the other hand, it was noticeable that almost all teachers and social workers in actual touch with the young strongly rejected these general charges against youth as ill-informed and prejudiced. After all, what were the many-coloured clothes but a challenge cocked at a dull and materialist society? One of the most experienced youth workers in Britain, Dr Josephine Macalister Brew, protested in her book *Youth and Youth Groups* against what she considered an unprecedented degree of ignorant prejudice against the whole young generation, based on exaggerated reports of isolated incidents[1]:

> Young people have never been under more heavy fire; their manners, their spending habits, their love of modern dancing and modern music, have all been the subject of abuse, and for the first time in the history of this country a section of the community has not been able to dress as it pleased without virulent attacks and suspicion. In spite of the fact that the *rise in delinquency consequent on the war years has been halted*, the relatively few cases of unquestionably violent gang behaviour have been magnified out of all proportion to their incidence.

The italics in the above quotation are mine. It was very natural to make this misjudgment. Without the slightest doubt, the general social and educational standards of British youth were rising year by year. The parallel phenomenon of rising lawlessness and violence followed a little later in the 'fifties, but was unfortunately equally real. Far from being halted, the upward trend in the juvenile crime rate persisted steadily. In 1955, the total of those found guilty of indictable offences in the male 17-21 age-group in England and Wales numbered 11,269. In 1956 they were 13,425; in 1957, 16,962; in 1958, 21,322, and in 1959 stood at well over double the 1938 total. The number of youths in this age-group

[1] J. Macalister Brew, *Youth and Youth Groups*. Faber, 1957.

convicted for violence against the person showed an equal rise from 745 in 1954 to 1,595 in 1957, and 2,051 in 1958—in 1938 the figure of such convictions had stood at 147.

By 1958 this new development was also apparent to the legal authorities. For example, in London and the Home Counties one magistrate after the other made comment on the fact that the criminal minority among young people had become noticeably both larger and more criminal. Noting that crime in Berkshire had in the course of two years gone up by a third, the Chief Constable of that rural county said (9.4.58) that the average age of those responsible for burglary and other breaking-in offences was under 20. At Wokingham, the Chairman of the Magistrates said (19.3.58): "I have no hesitation in saying that the children of this part of the county are guilty of more serious crimes than the adults. The juvenile crimes I have had to judge are more like a calendar at the Old Bailey." As Chairman of Quarter Sessions in neighbouring Bucks, Lord Birkett said (15.4.58): "There are thirty-six prisoners and of these there are no less than twenty-two who are 21 and under: among these, one is 19, two are 18, seven are 17 and five are only 16. Everyone reviews such a state of affairs with a profound taste of dissatisfaction, in these days when so much is done for the care and protection of the young." The Chairman of Middlesex Quarter Sessions, Sir Ewan Montague, Q.C., said a few days later (24.4.58) that the proportion of young offenders who had just come before him was quite appalling: of 89 cases of dishonesty on the calendar, no fewer than 44 of the defendants—or one-half—were under 20. One youth had the almost inconceivable record of eleven previous convictions at the age of 20, a second, six previous convictions at 18, and a third already four at 16 years.

THE THIRD WAVE

If these absolute figures were not really so large, they were all the same unmistakably indicative. What they showed, when broken down, was that among a fairly large minority of youths, criminality was quite steadily becoming not less but more wide-spread. In 1953-55 this minority had been dominated by the very large gangs of Teddy boys. Now this was much less the case, but the trouble had not been halted. Quite the contrary. For instance, as the Rev. Douglas Griffiths put it to me, of the three distinct waves of adolescents organized in gangs, whom he had seen in his experience of youth work in the dead-end areas of London, the third wave was the most troublesome. The first wave, as already mentioned, had been that of the old cloth-cap gangs of tough razor boys in the years immediately after the war. Next came the Teddy boys, washed and spruced up, strangely and expensively dressed up, moving about in large gangs, lawless and dangerous in their way, yet driven on by recognizable social urges and ambitions.

By 1955-56, however, the height of the Teddy boy cult was passed, certainly in London. The very word "Teddy Boy" had become a term of derision. "Teds", "a mob of Teds" was the more common description. The new wave of adolescents who now took the stage were more sophisticated; they went about in much smaller, more purposeful gangs; their special clothes in the Italian style were not particularly formalized; but among those who tended towards criminality the lack of any standards or restraints had become, if anything, even more marked.

In Mr Griffiths' view, this deterioration was in a paradoxical way even linked with the break-up of the original Teddy boy fashion of distinctive clothes and very large gangs. The change, as he saw it, was roughly in the following terms.

The Teddy boys in their early large gangs, at the height of the vogue, had a fierce sense of being an outcast community. They cultivated this sense, they depended on it. The revolt certainly went with violent behaviour directed against society, but was also marked by a primitive romanticism; it had its *esprit de corps* and depended on the rigid loyalties of members towards each other. However, when large numbers of boys took up the fashion so that it was no longer easy to tell who was a true Teddy boy and who was not, the Teddy boys themselves were no longer a community "which stood up against society in loneliness". As the wearers of the garb became more numerous, the ties that bound them together were loosened. The original gang spirit and cohesion was lost, and the large groups broke up into smaller groups linked by definite aims.

According to Mr Griffiths, this had its negative results. The anti-social attitude cultivated by the Teddy boys remained; what was lost was the sense of outcast pride and fair play that had existed alongside. The Teddy boys had, for instance, possessed their own code of conduct and been obsessively loyal to each other. The new larger community of smaller gangs had few such scruples. As Mr Griffiths saw them, many of the members of these gangs,

lived in a social situation in which conscience or ethics played no reasonable part. They had therefore even less inhibitions against violence to overcome. While some of the Teddy boys I knew had often been notable for tenderness towards children and gentleness towards old people, their successors in the smaller gangs showed no such saving grace.

According to Mr Griffiths, this total lack of standards was the context in which one should see the increasing tendency of young gangsters to attack and rob women and old people. True, the actual perpetrators of these crimes were few in number; but they expressed the steady coarsening of the spirit in certain areas of London which, Mr Griffiths felt, was a feature of the years from 1956 to 1960.

At this point one can perhaps draw a rough balance sheet between the opposed features of the Teddy boy movement. On the positive side, the Teds could be seen as forerunners of a larger movement for the sartorial and social emancipation of working-class youth, in which they were soon left far behind. On the negative side, they had introduced an element of violent lawlessness to which in their own lives they tried to give romantic formal rules. With their decline, these limitations dropped away, but the general heritage of violence remained. Events in the second half of 1958 were to bring dramatic proof of this.

CHAPTER VI

A Political Event

THE TEDDY BOYS AND NOTTING HILL

THE influx into Britain in the 'fifties of about a hundred thousand Coloured West Indian immigrants created a total British Coloured community of not more than twice that number, not really very large, but the immigration clearly had a very strong emotional impact on popular feelings. The British working classes (as observers from abroad have always assured us) are remarkably law-abiding, philistine, good-natured and tolerant. They are also deeply conservative, insular, and suspicious of foreigners and foreign ways. In the case of the West Indians these suspicions were heightened by the difference in colour with all that this implied; still, the first hostility against the West Indians followed much the same lines as English working-class reaction on earlier occasions against the immigration of Jews into the East End, or against Polish and Irish immigrants after the war. The main charges bandied against the Coloured newcomers was that they competed unfairly for jobs and houses; they had dirty habits and were given to overcrowding and general immorality, that they made a lucrative business out of prostitution. There is no need here to go into the subject in detail. As on previous occasions, the charges were true of an isolated few of the newcomers, but as far as the great majority of Coloured immigrants was concerned they were mythological and untrue, however firmly the mythology was believed in by landladies, mothers of adolescent daughters, people waiting on the housing list, or people who were unemployed. In the rather drab areas of London and some provincial cities, where the West Indians became concentrated enough to be noticeable as neighbours and in the life of the streets, there were, however, factors which made the West Indian immigration a touchier problem than the arrival of previous immigrants.

First, because the newcomers were Coloured. Secondly, because the British working classes, themselves on the move, had become much more vocal in their demands for adequate housing and

employment. The third difference was that by the time the West
Indians arrived, the Teddy boys were also on the scene and had
become more and more accustomed to take the law into their own
hands. The issue of colour prejudice was suitable for this purpose
because it was so highly charged with emotion. In my own conversations I found this one subject on which a section of the London
working class was pretty much of one opinion. For example, one
young ex-Teddy boy, who in other respects was particularly
critical of his old associates, surprised me because on the subject
of the West Indians he spoke like all the others:

> I don't hold with injuring people, but mind you, I think the
> Spades have brought most of it on themselves. For one thing,
> they have no consideration for others. They are moving in all
> the time, buying up property and evicting people. Some of these
> people had sons and naturally they didn't like this. Another
> thing, you can't ever reason with a Spade. I know one man who
> has been to Court five times—he had a black landlord who was
> trying to push him out of the house, and this black fellow told
> the most fantastic lies, it was no good going to Court, so in the
> end the man's son got a few of his friends and they paid the
> fellow out.

And in this spirit another incident was chalked up. In 1958,
a number of social workers gave warning that troubles might be
expected. The first big clash occurred, however, rather unexpectedly not in London but in Nottingham. On a Saturday
night, in the St Anne's Well area of Nottingham, fighting broke
out between white and Coloured youths in which improvised
weapons such as bottles were freely used. The clash spread quickly
as at first hundreds of people, and then thousands, crowded into
the area and turned the disturbance into a confused riot which
went on for some hours before order was restored by the police,
aided by firemen playing their hoses. By then, a large number of
people had been injured, a good many arrests were made, and for
the first time the emotional headline "Race Riots in Britain"
appeared in the British press.

The incident itself was bad enough, but more serious still was
the revelation of the fury displayed by this particular Nottingham
mob against the Coloured men and women, and also against the

police. The newspapers largely blamed the Teddy boys for this. The *Manchester Guardian* (25.8.58) quoted a Nottingham café owner as saying that there had for a long time been bad blood in the area between West Indians and Teddy boys. "As you know, some Negroes live off white women and a lot of Teddy boys would like to. It's as simple as that. This time, instead of fighting with a rival gang, the Teddy boys picked on the Coloured men." The special correspondent of the *Observer* (31.8.58) drew an alarming picture of prevailing colour prejudice in the Midlands, compounded of sexual and economic fears, and pointed out that Nottingham was a city of more white women than men: "That white women should welcome the company of coloured men is therefore not surprising, although it is annoying to the Teddy boy element."

There were rumours that the fighting would be resumed on the following Saturday. What in fact happened was that large crowds of Nottingham youths, bent on revenge against the Coloured, were stopped and dispersed by strong forces of police mobilized for this purpose. In the ensuing mêlée, individual police constables were assaulted with a fury and evident encouragement from the crowd which came as a shock to the authorities. At the subsequent Court proceedings, the Presiding Magistrate left no doubt of the serious views taken of this. He said that such lawlessness which made the Colour question an excuse for riots was not going to be tolerated in Nottingham. Not only heavy fines but a number of sharp prison sentences were imposed on those charged.

This ended the Nottingham disturbances. But there was tension in other areas too. For example, the *Manchester Guardian* (27.8.58) warned that in the West London area incidents had been increasing and gangs of Teddy boys were said to be cruising the streets at week-ends looking for isolated Africans and West Indians to attack.

There was hardly time to act on this warning. The next eruption came only a few days later in the Notting Hill area, one of the typical neglected areas in the inner belt of London between the business centre and the suburbs, a drab district of shifting population, surviving slums and racketeering landlords, where a large number of West Indians had settled and Teddy boys were apt to roam the streets in big gangs. In spite of everything written about it, the motives behind the opening incident of the riots were never quite explained. It appears that on the night of 31st August a group of nine working-class youths got together in order to launch a deliberate physical attack against Coloured residents in the Notting Hill area. They were between 16 and 21 years of age—six of them were only 17; all were in unskilled work, but earning quite good wages. There was something curiously accidental about their coming together and their expedition. One of them had a friend who had been knifed by a Coloured man, and they had a vague idea of exacting revenge for this and also for the Nottingham disturbances. Yet two of the youths only met the rest by chance on the evening concerned and agreed at the last moment to come along. What they then did was the following. They armed themselves with coshes and iron staves and went walking through the streets of Notting Hill. When they met an isolated Coloured pedestrian they rushed at him and beat him up in a frenzy, without the slightest provocation. They did this in five cases. Two of the victims managed to get away, three others were left lying senseless and bleeding on the pavement—it turned out to be fortunate for the youths concerned that no one was killed, as might easily have been the case.

The disturbances which followed this extraordinary attack were well documented by the press. The expedition of these nine youths was the spark which set off three nights of sporadic rioting between White and Coloured in the Notting Hill area. Coloured men and women in the area and also in some cases white women living with Coloured men were chased through the streets and assaulted. The West Indians naturally reacted and the police had to break up a number of fights in which knives, chains and broken bottles were used. After the first night, the scene in fact became very ugly. Reinforcements of white youths from many parts of London converged on Notting Hill, where they came up against large squads of police. They stood about in sullen groups, shouting insults, jeering at and threatening West Indians who were being escorted by the police. Repeatedly the police had to use their truncheons to hold back excited crowds; a number of constables were injured by white youths, of whom many were arrested. By the second and third night, not only the London press but foreign correspondents and television cameras were on the spot to report the strange scene. London had seen nothing like it for many years.

"It comes as a shock", wrote the *Manchester Guardian* (2.9.58), "to hear the ugly phrase 'lynch him' on English lips in an English city." Another feature which attracted attention was that groups of youths who were stopped from pursuing Coloured men seemed to turn on the police with exactly the same fury.

By the fourth evening, the Metropolitan Police was on the scene in full force, and order, if not peace, was restored in Notting Hill. By this time many people had been injured, some seriously, although fortunately there was no actual loss of life. Scores of arrests had been made, mostly of young men of the ages between 16 and 21. The outbreak had also become a major scandal—more than that, an international incident. The story of "race riots in London" had for several days been headline news in the world press. For a short time it seemed to be questioned whether it was not dangerous for a Coloured Commonwealth citizen to live in London. From the island of Jamaica, stunned by the news, the Chief Minister, Mr Norman Manley, flew to London to consult with the British Government. He told his fellow-countrymen that he had come to bring them moral support, and visited the Notting Hill area. The Home Secretary, Mr Butler, found it necessary to issue a statement (4.9.58) saying that the race riots in Nottingham and Notting Hill had been fully reported to the Prime Minister. The Government was determined to maintain law and order with the utmost strictness, he said, nor would it let itself be deflected by violence from the time-honoured practice to allow free entry to immigrants from Commonwealth and other countries.

Few people doubted this, just as few doubted that within a short time Notting Hill would return to normal. However, the damage was done. In staging the race riots, the Teddy boys had given notice that their lawlessness had gone beyond being only the concern of the Courts and of social workers. In producing an incident which had probably a subtle psychological effect on the whole relationship between Britain and parts of the Commonwealth, they had put themselves on the political map with a vengeance.

THE PUBLIC RECKONING

This social change was also acknowledged in the fact that, to cope with the new scale of Teddy boy lawlessness, the authorities had revived the long dormant charge of "causing a common affray". Presently, the nine young men who had started off the organized attack against Coloured people found themselves on trial on this charge at the Old Bailey. The trial ended with a historic summing up by Mr Justice Salmon. Telling the nine young men that they were an insignificant group who had brought shame upon their district and filled the nation with horror and disgust, Mr Justice Salmon went on:

> Everyone, irrespective of the colour of their skin, is entitled to walk through our streets with their heads erect and free from fear. That is a right which these Courts will always unfailingly uphold.

These were ringing words, flashed to every corner of the globe, which did much to restore British credit abroad. Mr Justice Salmon also left no doubt that he intended to pass sizeable penalties which should discourage repetition of these outrages. In passing sentence he declared that he had borne in mind that the defendants were all young, without previous convictions, and luckily for them their victims had recovered. But for this he would have imposed heavier sentences. As it was, each of the accused was sentenced to four years' imprisonment, and he wanted them, and any who might follow their example in staging assaults, to understand that such crimes could not be tolerated and would inevitably meet in the Courts with stern punishment.

The element of deterrence in these prison sentences imposed on adolescents was emphasized by Lord Justice Denning in a House of Lords debate early in 1959. Lord Denning said that a point which a judge had to consider was the impact of a sentence on the community. In the case of the nine young men and in view of their youth, Lord Denning said[1]:

> Had it been a question of deterrence only, one would have thought of a Borstal training for the older ones and maybe a detention centre for the 17-year-olds. They were all from good homes, all of good character; none of them would have done anything singly, but they were carried away because one of their comrades had previously been cut with a knife. But the

[1] *Hansard*, 8th April 1959.

sentence of the Judge was on each and all of them four years'
imprisonment, at the age of 17. And the country approved. The
conscience of the community was aroused by white youths
attacking black. The Judge in his sentence expressed in words
the horror, indignation and disgust of the people . . . occasionally
there should be severity—one might almost say extreme
severity—for the good of all.

This was the case for inflicting severe sentences for the sake of
law and order and also to safeguard the reputation of Britain in the
Commonwealth. From this standpoint the sentences at the Old
Bailey had their undoubted effect in keeping things quiet in
Notting Hill. Yet beyond this there was a strange reluctance to
enquire into the underlying causes of the attack. Mr Justice
Salmon's summing up was in this sense characteristic—indeed, it
makes curious reading. Addressing the young men in the dock,
he said that the object of their assault had been to instil stark terror
and inflict as much pain and grievous injury as they could. They
had attacked law-abiding citizens without any shadow of an
excuse or provocation, indeed, knowing nothing about them
except that their skin happened to be of a colour of which they
apparently did not approve. This was an appalling action. Mr
Justice Salmon then went on:

> As far as the law is concerned you are entitled to think what
> you like, however foul your thoughts; to feel what you like,
> however brutal and debased your emotions; to say what you
> like, providing you do not infringe the rights of others or imperil
> the Queen's peace; but once you translate your dark thoughts
> and brutal feelings into savage acts such as these, the law will be
> swift to punish you and protect your victims.

As a definition of the separate responsibilities of the Law and of
society, this will do, yet the odd emphasis of these words leaves
the basic question unanswered. After all, what were the ideas, the
emotions, which in the year 1958 swayed the minds of nine
apparently ordinary London working-class adolescents so that
they took coshes and iron bars and began to beat Coloured people
senseless, apparently without thought of the consequences?
    Outside of a court of law, this was surely the main question, and
it remains something of a puzzle. All one could say was that two

distinct factors were involved. Ignorant race hatred was one, of course, but only one. The other cause was the spread of the Teddy boy sub-culture, within which gang warfare, the carrying of weapons and the use of violence were regarded among a certain section of adolescents as "legitimate". It is interesting that in the view of the police in West London, the riots were more of an example of hooliganism carried to an extreme than of a deep racial clash. The local youths, said one police authority, had merely made the Coloured population the latest target for the sort of acts of violence which they had for some time been perpetrating against café proprietors, other gangs and each other. This might be just a little simplified, but the leader of a youth club, to which several of the nine young men at the Old Bailey had belonged, also told me how much, he thought, sheer accident had played its part in the affair:

It all happened on the night the club wasn't open. Not knowing what to do with themselves, the idea came to them to have a go at the Spades. Yet if they hadn't been at a loose end that night they might never have started. At the club you might have said they were the sort of boys who wouldn't say boo to a goose, but once the excitement started they were swept away by it. When these sort of boys are at a loose end they'll take up any activity to break the boredom. A fight with a neighbouring gang would ordinarily do the trick, only a neighbouring gang isn't so easily recognized. Coloured people are, so on that evening they decided to beat them up—and the rest followed.

Evidence that the Colour question was only one expression, if a dangerous one, of new habits of violence among a section of youth was also soon provided from other parts. Before the shock of the sentences at the Old Bailey had been completely absorbed, the charge of "causing a common affray" was used again twice in succession in cases of ordinary gang warfare, that is, only involving white victims.

MORE ANGRY YOUNG MEN

The first of these affrays was remarkable for the surroundings in which it was staged, namely on a quiet Council Estate of little suburban houses and gardens in East Barking. In Woodward Road on this estate, the Barking Council had recently built a small community centre called Woodward Hall, to be used for dances, concerts and other functions. Tuesday evenings, for instance, were given over to a popular weekly Rock 'n' Roll session. At the beginning of 1959 it was noticed that these dances were being invaded by "outsiders", that is, adolescents belonging to rival motorized gangs from Dagenham and Canning Town, and seven stewards were appointed to keep order.

On the night of 24th February there was talk of trouble between the two gangs, but the dance went on as usual. Among the 200 young people on the floor who had paid 2s. to rock and roll to records was Alan Johnson, a good-looking young ex-sailor from Canning Town, who had not long before taken on a shore job as upholsterer on becoming engaged to a 17-year-old girl. Half-way through the evening, when the organizer of the dance, himself a young man of only 22, was changing a record, he saw a solid group of young men push suddenly and menacingly into the hall. Before he could gather the stewards, fighting started.

The invaders were the Dagenham boys, bent on planned revenge against their Canning Town rivals for some previous trouble. Most of them were unarmed, intending no more than a "punch-up", but among those who carried weapons there was one particular 19-year-old Dagenham labourer, who carried a sheath-knife he had bought that day for a shilling. As the invaders burst on to the dance floor, they went in film gangster fashion from one male dancer to the next, asking where he came from. Any one saying "Canning Town" was at once set upon. Within a few moments, and before the stewards could intervene, the whole floor was turned into a wild mêlée of fighting in which the combatants hurled chairs and snatched up bottles, while women ran screaming from the hall.

By ill chance, among the first asked for his identity was Alan Johnson. He did live in Canning Town, but did not know it was dangerous to admit it. It was said he did not even know of the gang feud. So, when asked, he replied "Canning Town", and was immediately hit in the face. He tried to fight back and was then stabbed in the stomach by an assailant from the Dagenham gang and he fell bleeding to the floor.

While the dance organizer was in his office frantically telephoning for the police, the running fight moved from the hall into the street, where around fifty young men from Dagenham and Canning Town were now swept up into a frenzied brawl in which they wielded wooden bars they had snatched up, broken chair legs and bottles. Householders in quiet Woodward Road, attracted to doors and windows by the noise and the shrieks of women, could not believe their eyes. The improbable spectacle ended suddenly as police cars roared up and the combatants, brought abruptly to their senses, disappeared into the night. Inside Woodward Hall, young Alan Johnson had in the meanwhile died before the ambulance arrived. He had three stab wounds, one of them through the heart.

The next day there was a deathly hush in Woodward Road as a large number of police conducted investigations, and tracker dogs were used to search for the fatal knife. This did not take long because the Dagenham youth, obviously shaken by Johnson's death, came forward to give himself up. Altogether, it was not difficult to reconstruct the way this gang fight had started. The charge of causing a common affray was used again, and a number of young men were given varying prison sentences. The Dagenham youth was tried separately in June 1959 at the Old Bailey on a charge of murder. In his defence he did not deny having taken part in the fight or the possession of the knife, but claimed he had only stabbed Johnson once and not caused his death. His evidence was also extraordinarily revealing of the way in which young gang members regarded "weapons". According to him, he was not the first to attack, and he saw Johnson move his hand towards his pocket and he thought he might have a knife. The questions then went on:

> *Counsel:* He never took anything out of his pocket, did he?
> *Defendant:* I do not think so.
> So when he was coming towards you he was still unarmed?—I did not know that.
> Seeing he was still unarmed, you stabbed him in the stomach? —Yes.
> Are you saying to the jury it was necessary for your self-defence to inflict that wound?—Yes.
> Although he was unarmed?—Yes.

Found guilty of murder, the young assailant was, at the age of 19, under the Homicide Act of 1957, sentenced to imprisonment for life, the only sentence, the judge said, which the law allowed him to pass.

In view of his youth, there is little doubt that he will not actually remain in prison for life. However, in the second case where the affray charge was brought forward after a gang fight involving a death by violence, the killer was executed.

This was the notorious Marwood case which, before its tragic and squalid close, evoked motions in Parliament, an editorial in *The Times* and ugly disorders outside Pentonville prison. The youthful gang fight from which the affray charge arose occurred at a Dancing Academy in the Seven Sisters Road in Holloway, an area where such goings-on were more to be expected than in suburban Barking. The affair started with an altercation and a dreary feud between two local characters, one Budd and one Dean, both 19 years old, and both attended by followers. On the night of 11th December 1958 the two sets turned up at the Dancing Academy in force, well armed for emergencies. When a number of youths from each side were later in the dock on an "affray" charge, the prosecution brought into Court a collection of weapons including, among others, six choppers, a plasterer's hammer, a bayonet blade, an air pistol, various chisels and knives. The principals very nearly came to blows inside the Academy, but had the caution to let themselves be separated, but as various youths left angrily by the door, scuffles broke out and a brief but violent fight arose on the pavement. Into it, two young men were drawn to their death.

The first was a young police constable, Raymond Summers, athletic, 23 years old, engaged to be married. Seeing the fighting and commotion on the pavement, he waded into it and was trying to arrest one of the fighters when a knife was stuck into his back. The man who had wielded it was Ronald Marwood, an odd and puzzling character. By occupation a skilled scaffolder, 24 years of age, married and earning well, Marwood was really too old to be knocking about with gangs of brawling 19-year-old adolescents. Nor had he any kind of police record. But he was known in the neighbourhood as an oddly withdrawn character, a heavy drinker, a "hard" man with whom it was wise to avoid trouble, and one who carried a knife. On that night he had been celebrating his wedding anniversary and was afloat in beer. What possessed him to plunge into the fray was never made quite clear, but at any rate, once mixed up in it, he drew his knife and plunged it into the back of P.C. Summers, who fell down dead on the spot. The sight of a uniformed policeman lying dead on his face in a London street, a rare enough spectacle, proved sobering and the combatants fled.

The events which followed took much the same course as in the Barking incident. The "affray" charge was used again and a number of youths, including followers of both Budd and Dean, received fines and prison sentences. Marwood had gone into hiding in the home of a friend, but as the search closed in he gave himself up. In doing so he made a statement in which he admitted stabbing Constable Summers. At his trial at the Old Bailey on a murder charge, he withdrew the statement, but, largely on the strength of it, he was found guilty. Under the 1957 Homicide Act, which the Conservative Government had brought in as a compromise after the House of Lords had rejected a bill for abolition of the death penalty, death by hanging was retained as penalty for certain types of murder, such as murder of a policeman, of a prison warder by a convict, murder with robbery, murder by shooting or bombing, and some others. As the killer of a policeman on duty, Marwood was therefore sentenced to be hanged.

Since the Parliamentary controversy over the abolition of the death penalty was still fresh in the public conscience, this sentence was likely to be controversial, and in fact it aroused a wave of protest on several grounds: because the verdict seemed to rest solely on Marwood's confession, because he had a clean record and because he had been involved in the "affray" when under the influence of drink. Appeals for his reprieve came from many sides. A petition by clergymen in his district received thousands of signatures. In the Commons, a motion by that leading abolitionist, Mr Sydney Silverman, M.P., linking Marwood's reprieve with the abolition of the death penalty, was supported by 150 Labour members. It was countered by a Conservative back-benchers' motion by Mr Cyril Osborne, M.P., calling on the contrary for widened application of the death penalty for murder. The atmosphere surrounding the case and sentence was made even more repellent by the attitude of a section of the London press.

Since public pressure on Mr Butler for a reprieve was considerable, while at the same time it was fairly clear that there were no
grounds on which it would be granted, several London newspapers
scented the chance of a drama—and went full out to exploit it.
Emotions were kept going by headlines like MARWOOD TO DIE or
MARWOOD'S LAST HOURS; reporters swarmed to interview the
relatives of victim and killer; no journalese detail was spared in
arousing a synthetic and morbid emotion. As a result, wild and
macabre crowd scenes took place at the announced hour of
execution outside Pentonville Prison, where for several minutes
mounted police were surrounded by a swarm of kicking, cursing
men and women held back from the prison gates. The press was
there to the last. It could be noticed that press photographers were
particularly intent on snapping Teddy boy types, while, for
example, an hour after the event a London evening paper screamed
in a headline right across the page in the largest type it possessed:
RIOT AT THE JAIL AS MARWOOD DIES. It was also noticed that foreign
correspondents and television cameras were again on the spot,
commenting with astonishment on a raggedly savage spectacle
that, as was said, seemed like a Hogarth scene come to life. *The
Times*, in an editorial on the following day, protested angrily both
against the whipping up of feeling and attempts to put political
pressure on the Home Secretary by mass agitation. "The Home
Secretary, a man whose whole political life is witness to his own
kindly humanity, was faced with a decision as onerous to make as
any that the responsibility of office has ever placed on his predecessors. His ordeal should not be made even more cruel than in
any case it must be."

All in all, it could be said that when the rival followers of 19-
year-old John Budd and Peter Dean arrived at the Dance Academy
in the Seven Sisters' Road on that December night, properly
tooled up for action, they started events which had far-reaching
consequences.

After a day or so the Marwood case was of course dead news.
But a few weeks later came a rather ominous incident when a
young West Indian carpenter, Kelso Cochrane, was killed in
Notting Hill, according to first reports by a gang of white youths
who stabbed him to death. The police quickly clamped down on
this alleged evidence as unproven, but in the meantime the wires

had already flashed news of another race incident to the West Indies. . . .

In conclusion. Everything has to be seen in proportion; these highly publicized cases were of course only isolated incidents in British life. All the same, by the spring of 1959 it could no longer be denied that certain parts of London at night were dominated by a new spirit of insecurity. If the total number of crimes of violence was nothing like as dramatic as headlines suggested, still, the number was going up year by year. There were other signs of the current trend.

In April 1959 a Private Member's bill was discussed in the Commons to prohibit the sale of flick-knives. That enterprising national institution, the *Daily Mirror*, was running its own campaign for the voluntary surrender of weapons by youthful members of gangs. After a week the newspaper's office had received hundreds of items ranging from army revolvers to home-made weapons fit for a do-it-yourself age. At the same time the Home Secretary admitted to his deep regret that in 1959, just as in 1952, there were still 6,000 men sleeping three to a cell in Britain's antiquated prisons, the reason being that the additional accommodation built during those seven years had been entirely swallowed up by the increase in the number of inmates.

The overall number of people in British prisons and Borstal institutions was still only 26,000. Though this was an all-time record, it could perhaps be said that organized crime in Britain was still not the major social problem it was in certain other countries. But it looked on the way to becoming such a problem. At any rate, by 1959 it was also apparent that British public opinion had woken up to the existence of an alarming streak of violence among a section of youth; that is, to the strange problem of the Teddy boy society in its midst.

CHAPTER VII

Teds and Café Society

PAST AND PRESENT

IN a sense, the new state of insecurity appeared like a historic regression. The remarkably law-abiding character of twentieth-century English life had often been commented on. Looking back in 1940 on an era which he felt was ending, George Orwell wrote: "Perhaps the most marked characteristic of English civilization is its gentleness. You notice it the instant you set foot on English soil. It is a land where the bus conductors are good-tempered and the policemen carry no revolvers."[1] Orwell associated this gentle quality of the common English people with their deep-rooted dislike of militarism and war and their extraordinary respect for legality, the general belief in "the Law" as something above the State and the individual. "Everyone takes it for granted that the law, such as it is, will be respected, and feels a sense of outrage when it is not. Remarks like 'They can't run me in; I haven't done anything wrong', or 'They can't do that; it's against the law' are part of the atmosphere of England."

This picture of the law-abiding England of pre-1940 was one which most foreign visitors carried away with them. Today the picture has already a somewhat dated look, but to be quite accurate, it was never a complete picture. Even the gangs of Notting Hill and Holloway had their immediate predecessors. The Industrial Revolution came to Britain much earlier than to the rest of Europe. Its impact was harsher and it left behind a heritage of historic slums and of some primitive gang life, which lingered into the inter-war years. If London had its Hoxton Terrors, provincial cities had their equivalent. In the steel town of Sheffield, particularly badly affected by the depression, cloth-capped gangs with hundreds of members, such as the Mooney Boys and the Garvin Gang, haunted the drab streets of the Park, Crofts and Norfolk Bridge districts of the city, defying the police and rendering the districts unsafe for several years. The razor

[1] George Orwell, *The Lion and the Unicorn*. Secker & Warburg, 1940.

gangs of Glasgow were as notorious as that city's tenement areas, and equally a product of economic depression. Well-known early gangs like the Redskins, the Black Hand and the Beehives were recruited from the great army of unemployed created in Glasgow by the economic crisis after the First World War. These Glasgow gangs familiarized the broken beer-bottle as a fearsome and feared weapon in public-house and dance hall brawls and proved difficult to put down because witnesses were too terrified to give evidence, and the Glasgow police system had some salient weaknesses. An additional element of political and religious strife came to Glasgow gang life in the 'thirties when the two most notorious rival gangs were the Roman Catholic "Norman Conquerors" and the "Billy Boys", who were William of Orange Protestants.

For a time these later gangs engaged in a regular sort of warfare of organized public marches and territorial raids, which is described in the autobiography of that versatile police officer, Sir Percy Sillitoe.[1] As he tells the story, a favourite weapon used in fighting was a heavy pick-shaft. Both gangs also used hatchets, swords and sharpened bicycle chains habitually, and these were conveyed to the scene of their battles by their queens, or women members, who concealed them under their clothes. (However, if this picture of Glasgow's inter-war gang life sounds not only colourful but also pretty fearful, one need only look at the statistics of the very few casualties to see that it was never remotely like that of Chicago.) Sir Percy Sillitoe had already put down the Sheffield gangs when he took office as Chief Constable of Glasgow in 1935, where he succeeded equally within a fairly short time in dealing with the Glasgow gangs by instituting special flying squads of picked police trained in physical combat. By the time the real war came in 1939, the Glasgow gangs had been broken up and reduced to scattered remnants (incidentally, as one might expect, some of their leaders went immediately into the Forces and made good soldiers).

If the Teddy boys of Notting Hill and South London therefore had their predecessors, the studies of Sir Percy Sillitoe and others also reveal the difference between the two periods. The older gangs were basically a product of poverty, of mass unemployment and degraded slum life like that of Glasgow. The gang leaders were not

[1] Sir Percy Sillitoe, *Cloak Without Dagger*. Cassell, 1955.

adolescents but older men, who were often also notorious criminals. The gangs were strictly confined to certain areas; their ascendancy rested on primitive brute force, and an intelligently directed opposing force of picked and aggressive police officers was therefore enough to shatter their ranks. On the other hand, the Teddy boys of today are adolescents rather than adults, and represent a widespread new way of life found throughout the country. Or one might put the difference as follows. While the cloth-capped pre-war gangs of Sheffield and Glasgow were a survival from a cruder past and could be dealt with as such, the Teddy boy gangs—and this is the disturbing point—are a direct product of today, a by-product of a new economic revolution which has put spending money on a scale not known before into the pockets of working-class boys and girls. Spread as it is throughout the country, the Teddy boy society seems like a distinct, recognizable little stratum of society.

The pages which follow include some personal impressions of this society. They are based on conversations with youngsters involved in this life and with social workers in contact with them. The conclusions are not meant to be expert and exhaustive. They are, in fact, "impressionist", and my excuse in putting them forward is that in a field where so little is documented even an outsider's views may be of value. Perhaps it should also be stressed that the descriptions apply to a period when the Teddy boy fashion developed by the early large gangs had already receded. What I am writing about is the present society of the smaller gangs who have followed the Teds. However, since the words "Teddy boy" and "Ted" have become general currency, it seems convenient to go on using them.

THE TEDS AND BOREDOM

A good start for any study of the Teddy boy society is its habitat, the café, or caff. The spread of café life among working-class boys and girls has surely been among the more interesting developments of the post-war years, and it has also been spontaneous. Whether one looks in on such a café in London, a small country town or seaside resort, the impression is much the same. The usual picture is of a long room with a counter for the sale of coffee, soft drinks and snacks, and tables placed close to each other. Young men, all dressed up, will look challengingly at the intruder, the girls appearing less certain of themselves. A new and shiny juke-box will usually be giving forth its sounds. If the décor is contemporary, this adds to the popularity of the establishment. In fact, an atmosphere of garish gaiety, warm coffee steam, contemporary décor and the noise of the juke-box seems to have become for many young people an antidote against the emptiness of their lives. And why not? Here I come to a subject on which I have some very personal views, namely the pall of boredom which has for so long hung over much of English social life and especially the lack of social amenities for young people in working-class areas.

Adolescence is a time of life when young people feel uncertain and expectant, driven on by urges they do not fully understand; when they feel the need for gregariousness and for places where they can come together informally, to meet the opposite sex, to drift, to experiment, to feel their own way towards adult life, and this without supervision from their elders. Urbanized industrial society is in general deficient in providing such opportunity, but I think that in England (up to about 1950) this shortcoming was more noticeable than anywhere else.

I may be prejudiced on this point, because my own childhood years were spent in less class-conscious and puritan parts of Europe. However, I have remained impressed by this peculiar English social deficiency whenever I returned from a trip abroad and again saw that familiar English sight of groups of working-class youths standing about at dusk at the street corners, looking repressed, bored, sullen and at a loss. Yet the question which always bothered me was what else there was for them to do? The social life of an English provincial town had no focal point equivalent to the Mediterranean piazza or promenade, the Continental café, or even to such an unpretentious meeting place as the American corner drugstore. I always felt that after dark the average English town had a dead and shuttered look found nowhere else to quite the same degree; for the bored lads at the street corner there was probably no choice but to spend the evening at an isolated milk-bar, coffee-stall or pin-table arcade, or else once again at the pictures. To be sure, there were pubs, but it is probably time that the brewers' legend of the public-house as a modern community centre was done away with. By today the majority of public-houses have become little more than commercialized outlets for a few multi-million brewery combines,[1] while the State has also stepped in to make the consumption of beer and spirits a highly taxed pastime. The pub was also not a place to which a young man ordinarily took his girl. But then, where else? In some districts, though not all, there might be a club, but this usually demanded the special effort of joining in some activity. For the majority who did not want to make this effort, there was often nowhere to go but the anonymity of the local cinema with its latest American film, or else the dark back alley.

The reasons for this gap in English social life are no doubt of long standing. The foremost to my mind is the historic class division of England into two nations which has enabled the middle classes to look after their own leisure time (the English, after all, invented the secluded middle-class garden suburb), while anything in crude or commercial entertainment was thought good enough for the working class. A second evident cause was the persistent hangover of the Industrial Revolution in working-class life, that look of an uncouth past which still clings to the chip shop, the coffee-stall and the spit-and-sawdust corner pub. Yet another cause was English puritanism, that tight-lipped sabbatarian outlook which has given the English street picture on a Sunday that unique air of everything closed, while newspapers providing surrogate fantasy are sold at the corner. And this of course points to a fourth cause, the sheer size and financial strength of the British mass entertainment industry.

There is no need to dwell much on these historic tendencies. What matters is the outcome—that for working-class boys and girls there were probably fewer rendezvous places and simple entertainments available in England than in most other countries, and the resultant great boredom. I think this boredom reached a particularly advanced pitch in the 'thirties and 'forties. Motoring through England on a Sunday afternoon, seeing the couples supine and making love on the grass in public parks, watching long queues of young people standing in broad daylight outside a local Odeon or Granada, waiting dully for opening time, I have

[1] This may be exaggerated, but the trend is certainly in this direction.

often felt that this sense of boredom within a commercialized society was like a deep injury inflicted on the English working class by its rulers. It was not surprising that the English crime rate should rise to a steep weekly peak at 4 p.m. on a Sunday afternoon.

Nor have things changed so much even now. Anyone who wants to see puritanism and commercialism combined at their worst need only take a walk in the West End of London on a Sunday evening, say down Tottenham Court Road and then along the sleazy pavements of Charing Cross Road and Shaftesbury Avenue to the delusive journey's end of Piccadilly Circus. The sight he is likely to encounter will be like a study in frustration. All the way along, our observer will meet crowds of people walking in an aimless and, by all appearances, joyless promenade. He will see no theatres open and almost no restaurants where people can sit and relax. All that will be open will be a few milk-bars, some pin-table arcades, a good many pubs, of course, and also the cinemas; but even these, taken together, can only provide entertainment for a fraction of the crowds who have been attracted, so that most of the people in the streets seem to be simply walking past advertisements and shop windows in search for a sociability that just is not there, and if our observer looks carefully he will see this lack clearly reflected in the vague and discontented expressions around him.

THE JUKE-BOX CAFÉ

The last ten years have seen a fairly vigorous attack against this void on the part of the young generation. This has expressed itself in a variety of new ways; for instance, in the fact that working-class boys and girls now go in growing numbers on holidays abroad; in the persistent teenage demand for a new urbanity which has produced the luxuriously equipped Mecca dance-halls, and caused youth clubs to be rebuilt with attractive canteens; in such spontaneous movements as skiffle and rock 'n' roll; and, above all, in the spread of the young people's café and of its superior variant, the espresso-bar.

The drift of the young generation from pub to café reflects a considerable change in habits. Youths of today who believe themselves mature at 16 or 17 are put off by licensing restrictions and the fact that they cannot take their girls to public bars. In most pubs they are not welcome in groups and the pub is not the place for their kind of noise, which is connected with the world of juke-boxes and "pop" records. On the other hand, the average little café answers their demands. The price of coffee is cheap, there may be music, and above all the ordinary café is a small enough place for a group of young people to be able to regard it as "theirs". "When a bloke goes to the same café every night, well, I mean he's known—he's somebody." A group of tough 16- and 17-year-old London youngsters (with already quite a few police records among them) told me what they would regard as their ideal for life after dark: to have a choice of several cafés in their own neigh-bourhood, which would be nice and cheerful places, modern in decoration, with tables for those who wanted to sit, and room enough for others to dance, and which would stay open till midnight!

Needless to say, this ideal is not found very often; in the case of these particular boys there was actually not a single late-evening café open in their area. One reason is that it is hard to make such places pay. It may well be that the English working-class young have staked their demand for café life rather too late in the day. In an age of advertising and large-scale entertainment of every kind, the running of a small café purely for the entertainment of young people has already become a doubtful proposition in many localities. In many places one finds that the young complain that there are not enough cafés open after dark, while the proprietors maintain that there is no economic demand to justify them.

Within these limits, however, a working-class café life has developed in several distinct forms. The most common is the development of the original rough working men's "caff", which provided cheap, simple hot midday meals and has now extended its hours to provide coffee and juke-box music to the young. Of other forms, the less successful is probably the milk-bar or soda-fountain in a newly built-up area. Through a peculiar English lack of skill in this trade, this has never achieved the efficiency of the American drugstore counter. A more successful development is that of the espresso-bar, whose popularity has its cultural significance. While the sophisticated may deride espresso-bar glamour, to the majority of British working-class youth this glamour, which goes with the "Italian style" in clothes and films, seems precisely part of that modern life they want to aspire to. In some parts of London most of the cafés catering for the young are today run by Cypriots bent on making them paying propositions.

Another decisive import from abroad has been the American juke-box. This instrument is, of course, the product of a large entertainment industry, and as soon as one speaks of the juke-box one is involved in an argument of pros and cons. To the refined middle-class ear, the raucous sound of an infernal machine blaring out something like "Jailhouse Rock" at deafening volume in a small, confined space, i.e. a small café crowded with overdressed Teddy boys and their girl friends, may seem like a good idea of hell. And yet, and yet. . . . Talking to those in touch with these young people, I have always felt that there is a good deal to be said for the juke-box. First of all, it has made the café a place to which girls can come on their own. The music provides justification; they can sit and nod to the rhythm as they sip their coffee without appearing too obviously waiting to be picked up. Conversely, the juke-box enables the boys to express their personalities at sixpence a time through the individual choice of records. Moreover, behind the loud noise the youngsters genuinely respond to the catchy rhythm. As against this, the voices from the juke-box speak in American or pseudo-American accents, and therefore incessantly conjure up a world of fantasy which to the listeners must remain unreal, and at its worst the din may merely help to kill time in an hypnotic way. As one graduate from the Teddy boy society confessed to me, while the juke-box was playing "the fellows don't have to think, they don't have to talk, they can just sit there with a dazed expression".

While all this is true, it does seem to me that the positive side perhaps outweighs the other. For its adolescent habituées, the juke-box café or espresso-bar with music does satisfy the need for a rendezvous and social life after dark which is so strongly felt. Often it is an obsessive need. For many youngsters their most vivid link with contemporary culture is through the lyrics of "pop" music. The juke-box café, especially if featuring the Top Twenty, fits with this emotional attitude. To the Teddy boys of today and their girl-friends, it is like a magnet, drawing them evening after evening to its lights and music, a primitive substitute for the Continental café and wine, women and song.

In practice, cafés with permits to keep open in the evenings are found irregularly in urban areas because some local councils have given such permission, while others, who felt that this night life resulted in disorderly behaviour, have restricted the hours severely. In practice, again, every urban locality has at least one establishment which has become known as the centre of night life and a meeting point of working-class young bloods. Rather fewer localities have a choice of different cafés, such as for instance one extensive London area where one evening I was shown the rounds by a young ex-Teddy boy—let me call him Len. Len was a tall and elegant young man. For some years he had been one of The Boys and had twice appeared in Court on charges of fighting. He now admitted he had been lucky not to end up in Wandsworth or Pentonville. Now that he was older, he felt also more sophisticated. When we met, he had just been to see the film of "Farewell to Arms"—he pointed out that it was taken from a book by a man called Hemingway and had impressed him more than the ordinary run of films. Len was now also bent on respectability, but on one or two evenings a week the old urge still drove him to put on one of his dozen or so smart suits and go on the café round. The following are notes jotted down of my own impression.

Café 1

According to Len, a decent place, the best in the whole district. Len came here when he felt flush. One could sit outside, he said, as in France. The establishment surprised me in its setting. More restaurant than café, it had a small garden with a few tables and pleasant décor. We had a reasonable meal of soup, a small piece of steak with fried egg, and coffee, for about seven shillings per head. As a visitor from another generation, I was struck by the classlessness; in my time such a restaurant could not have had working-class customers. We were not far from a college of music and a corner was occupied by young people with instruments. They were duffle-coated student types, speaking in educated voices, the girls rather awkward. Next to them sat four noisy, extrovert lads of Len's acquaintance. Their voices had carefree Cockney inflections, but their appearance was all the more dressy. One wore a striped black Italian-style jacket, the next a fawn jacket over a blue pullover; all wore beautifully creased dark trousers and very white shirts. (Len told me some of the boys always washed and ironed their

own shirts.) Another quartet of his friends arrived in shiny black leather jackets, boisterous and eager, ordering steaks and exchanging comment with the music students. The proprietor, well-groomed, very Chelsea-ish in a canary-coloured pullover, switched on the radio-music from the Home Service. Len told me: "He's very strict, he won't have The Boys any more—he won't stand for any trouble in his place." As I had not been for years in a working-class restaurant like this, my impression was of the nonchalant breakdown of class barriers. Before the war, no restaurant mainly for wage-earners, which this still was, would have had such a Continental look.

It was interesting that Len, who worked as an unskilled building labourer, took this evening elegance for granted. It was a far cry from the street corner.

Cafés 2 and 3

Designated by Len as places where one might meet The Boys and learn of interesting bits of skulduggery, or plans for a fight, a punch-up, a lark. These were more like roadside cafés I might have walked into on my own. Dusty advertisements, boiling hot cups of tea or coffee, stale-looking cakes and sandwiches provided the dingy setting for groups of young men sitting pretty silently at tables with an air of time having to be killed. In the first café, all Len could point out to me was a trio who "dressed rough" because it was momentarily inadvisable for them to look affluent; their conversation, he told me, concerned a large crap-game to take place that night. In the second café, having joined and been introduced to a group of his former companions who looked like the most ordinary young workers, I found myself at first ignored and then made party to information about law-breaking which was either invented or, as appeared more likely, told to me as a deliberate dare to see how I would react; my reaction was fake nonchalance and fairly quick departure. Len told me that his ex-friends had assumed that he and I were living together until he told them I was a writer interested in "why boys went wrong". This explanation, he said, was accepted as quite normal and familiar. He also said that since the gang of The Boys, who had been a hundred strong a few years back, had broken up, some being sent off to Borstal and prison, some getting married, some having left the district, these cafés had become pretty quiet. And a good thing, too, I thought.

Café 4

This, on the other hand, was the popular teenager centre; Len felt already too mature to come here ordinarily. Open till 10.30 p.m.; a long, narrow room, with décor of four different, clashing wallpapers; boys and girls occupying every seat at the packed tables; the juke-box going incessantly behind a loud babble of talk. Some of the boys wore jeans; others were dolled up in coloured shirts, with careful fringe haircuts or sideboards like characters from a sinister French film. Collectively they looked taller, smoother-faced, more fluent in movement than pre-war youths in this area. The girls seemed above all extraordinarily young, some no more than 15; Len thought even younger. "You'd be surprised. Nowadays some of these young girls are terrible. They paint their faces when they're only thirteen." I found that my presence in this defiantly anti-adult company cast a blight; we left quickly.

Café 5

Last stage in the café-crawl, this was Len's idea of a "bloody awful" place. A café in a grimy side street near the crossroads, dilapidated-looking from the outside, but within surprisingly crowded. The two swarthy, broad-shouldered Cypriot brothers behind the counter looked determined fighters, and probably had to be. "Make trouble and they'll carve you up with a knife as soon as look at you", said Len. The crowded customers in the front room were youthful, noisy and boisterous. Steps led up to a second room where some girls sat at tables and were being eyed by other males. A narrow passage led to a back room from which juke-box sounds emerged. While I stood drinking another cup of tea, half a dozen girls dashed into the café and down the passage. Len invited me to note how dirty the place looked. The girls who came here were mostly on the game, he said, except a few very young ones, but they were "not much cop". We went down the passage to the larger room at the back. The juke-box drooled; two youths played expertly at a "football table"; boys who looked no more than 14 or 15 were putting coin after coin into gambling machines; in a small space two couples of vigorous and farouche girls rocked and rolled with each other. Standing about and looking on were local lads, young Cypriots in their own group, and one solitary, smiling young Negro who greeted Len with joy. "I don't hold with the Spades," Len said to me, "but this one, he's just an ordinary

young fellow. Everybody likes him." He himself did not often
come to this café. Fellows only came here when not choosy
about a girl to pick up because the place kept open till 1 a.m.
My impression was that it was probably allowed to keep open
into the night because useful to the police.

And this was all. After a certain hour of the evening, these five
cafés, with perhaps an odd milk-bar or two, served a London area
of about 200,000 people which probably contained twenty times
as many pubs. True, it was a pretty drab area, but the overall
impression was of an overwhelming urge among the young for a
new social life and inadequate means of meeting it.

A café-crawl like this could, I believe, be undertaken in any
similar urban area in England. Some indeed are served even worse.
I was told by a group of boys at the youth club at Friendship
House in Lambeth, that no other evening rendezvous place existed
within a radius of more than a mile, and this in an area of 100,000
population, where one tall block of flats after the other had sprung
up. (This was the group of boys who emphatically did not want to
have to go too often to pubs.) The need for meeting-places of the
café-type, where adolescents can gather after dark, has been
illustrated by the experimental attempts which have been made by
well-meaning organizations to open a few supervised teenage
coffee-bars. But these hesitant experiments only illustrate what
may be an acute social deficiency. A most useful piece of research
for a foundation could be an enquiry into the current rôle and
problems of the café as a meeting place for young people.

At the moment the lack of balance between the adolescent
demand for facilities for social life and the supply of such facilities
undoubtedly creates social strains. Because cafés kept open into
the evening for young people generally don't pay, there are too few
of them. Because they are so few, youngsters have no choice where
to go and as often as not end up in cafés taken over by the Teddy
boys, whose gangs in this way enjoy undue influence and draw in
recruits.

In other words, the rise of the new café life and of the Teddy
boy movement are not identical developments—they only overlap
somewhat. But against this, the availability of cafés where members
could meet night after night has given the young gangs a cohesion

they might otherwise not have possessed, especially in keeping up their sense of outlawry from society. Conversely, the knowledge that well-known gang members could be met at certain cafés has often given these places a romantic local attraction and thus made for a steady stream of new recruits. In this sense, the Teddy boy society has been very much a café society, a product of the curiously belated, in some ways beneficial, in others sordid, development of the café as an institution of English working-class life.

CHAPTER VIII

A Spot of Sub-culture

UNTENDER IS THE NIGHT

To return from the wider topic of café life to the narrower confines of Teddy boy society.

A time to kill: one does not require many encounters in this society to discover that its culture is one of incessant efforts to fill an empty expanse of time. So, perhaps, is that of many city dwellers of today. The distinction is that for the Teds this problem can become obsessive, and the means of killing time therefore take on the same importance.

One point which emerged in conversations is that for boys of their type the night life of London is dull and short. Pubs shut early, cinemas close, buses stop. Especially if a boy is making a respectable evening of it with a girl. "Suppose a fellow is out with his girl-friend: by the time they've been to the pictures, the evening is running out on them. He's got to take the girl home. Most girls have to be in by 11.30, that's the rule. If a boy wants to get on the last bus, it's usually before twelve o'clock. London isn't like places I've seen abroad."

When the boys are out with each other, the hours of being up and about may stretch ahead of them far into the night, and yet you can feel that time is short: you can stay up later—but doing what? In one group with which I had a brief encounter in North-East London, and whose meeting place was at a coffee-stall outside a Tube station, some of the boys would stand at this stall through half the night, like spectres. But what else, so their thoughts ran, was there to do after a certain hour when the cafés had closed? There was usually a game of dice going on at the nearby women's public convenience (it was locked, but the boys had a key), but for that you required cash. There might be a single late-night café open, but you'd know it was a dirty place and the girls who would still be up would be mostly scabs. The night seemed that much waste. That was why the boys were so often driven to "organize" something—a night train ride to the seaside, a raid into some other territory, a spot of breaking-in, just for a laugh. But in one way or another, organizing anything often meant organizing trouble. . . .

Side by side with rivalry over girls, it is, I think, this underlying sense of boredom in Ted society which is responsible for some of the continuance of gang warfare. In the original heydey of the Teddy boys in the early 'fifties, this was pretty elaborate. Some of the gang leaders-in-chief were called "governors". Their local subordinates were the "assistant-governors". It was a point of honour for a proper "governor" to be able to call out a ragged force of a hundred youths for a purpose which as often as not was a mock battle, but sometimes turned into a real one. By and large this phase is over. The smaller gangs of today are more knowing and purposeful, and probably some degrees more criminally inclined. But to judge from incidents reported, the spirit of this warfare still goes on. In the boredom of the night-time cafés, insults by one group against another are still brooded over. Evening after evening the rancour grows, until tempers are worked up, telephone calls are made, the boys tool up, and a punitive expedition is organized.

This warfare remains the Teddy boys' special little contribution to culture. But in the main, in their outlook on leisure they are affected just like others of their generation by the current mass media. The cinema remains a basic addiction. Television has entered into their lives, but less than one would have supposed; on the other hand, the cult of "pop" music has become an integral part of their day and night-time life. Apart from this, fashion consciousness has remained a passionate interest and mark of status.

THE ANODYNE OF THE PICTURES

Not long ago I sat in a vast suburban cinema alongside three dolled-up Teds and their girl-friends. During the preliminaries of the performance they had made a nuisance of themselves by exhibitionist laughter and catcalls. All this stopped, however, as the main feature came on. This was a gangster film, put over with that powerful realism which Hollywood direction sometimes achieves. The sordid side of American city life was forcefully conveyed—one felt that those making the film had raked this mud with a venom. Then came the dream-cliché of relentless and night-marish pursuit. With all hands against him, the hunted killer-victim stumbled round corners and over walls and down alleys. All in vain. As each new avenue of escape beckoned, it was barred by more men with guns. The trap was closed. This was it, the pay-off.

Happening to glance at the lads at my side, I thought that they were watching the climax of pursuit as if the dream were their own. Their silly dead-pan expressions were relaxed. They seemed to have forgotten the girls at their side. For them, too, this was it—the pay-off, their own fears and desires represented artistically, their amateurish ideas of ambushing and gangsterism writ large. When the lights came on, it took them quite a few moments to gather their wits and resume their swagger.

While cinema-going among the general population has under the impact of television dropped by over half during the last ten years, this seems markedly not the case in Teddy boy society. Here the Pictures still supply a basic emotional need—the lack of cinemas is a common adolescent grievance in New Towns and outer suburban estates. Small boys seem to play truant from school much as ever before to slip into the Pictures. Older youths may take their girls to the cinema twice a week and more. To break the deadly monotony of a Sunday afternoon, they will queue up early in daylight outside the local Odeon. I was often told by youths that when out of work they would spend one afternoon after the other at the cinemas. It is not hard to see why the cinema should remain this ideal time-killer. Its vast, comforting darkness offers not only relaxation but, to a Ted, temporary relief from the strain of being "somebody". The cinema is sex-dominated, the sanctioned place to take one's girl to, with sex on the screen and a good deal of it in the auditorium too. The values of the films often approxi-mate to those of the boys themselves. Emotions are there to be gratified. When obstructed by an opponent, the hero uses his fists. When rejected, he reaches for the bottle. The magnified hero and heroine seem to demonstrate how one can live fabulously on any social level. Or again, there is the gangster film, most popular of all with the Teds and as if tailored for them.

Not for them alone, of course. But it appears a fair assumption that the Teds, as a group of youngsters who have rejected their traditions, are therefore peculiarly open to suggestion from the mass media. The influence of the film on the Teds has the danger, first, that it presents a gaping negative. As my Irish informant put it, "It's not just the violence. A lot of people go to Westerns and gangster films and it makes not the slightest difference. But these young Teds, they've got no standards; in their dim way they're always groping, and the trouble with the films is that they show them a way of life, an American way, which they think they can copy, yet which in reality for them is non-existent." There is also the positive danger that the idea is implanted at least in a dream-like way among the susceptible that they, too, can live fabulously. Only one thing is needed, namely money; and if money is lacking, well, one way of getting it is through breaking and entering, or, if you're a girl, by just a little harmless prostitution. This effect of the films is not direct and measurable, but in talking to the dimmer sort of Teddy boys and listening to their ideas about the desirable life, one can usually note how strongly these have been coloured by film clichés.

An incidental fact I was surprised to learn was how many boys and youths get into cinemas without paying. I often heard from Teds how, as small boys, they used to dart in through back exits. What surprised me was to hear how they sometimes still got in free as young adults. One way of doing it was for a group to shoulder their way roughly through a crowd, each with a gesture that the one behind was paying. The attendants might, too late, be aware of this, but often would prefer to make no challenge. Where the youths concerned belonged to a tough gang, they might indeed be quite well advised not to.

THE TEDS AND THE TELLY

By contrast with the cinema, the impact of televison on Teddy boy life seems still to be surprisingly small.

Perhaps one should expect this. Viewing usually drops to a low point at the courting age when adolescents, stirred by their instincts, find it far more exciting to collect in the stairway of a block of flats rather than sit at home in front of a television set. Nor has television in England become acclimatized in public places, as in Mediterranean countries. In England there are no sets in cafés, and in any crowded public-bar, where people can talk, the occasional shimmering television screen is commonly disregarded. All the same, in view of the staggering statistical increase in British television viewing, I was a little surprised to find Teddy boy circles apparently little affected by the new medium, and indeed apt to talk of it with a certain scorn.

There appear to be some fairly obvious explanations. Television does not fit in with the sex *motif* that runs right through Teddy boy life. There is little point in sitting with your girl in front of some living-room television screen. Either adults are present, in which case you are not at ease, or else, if you are alone with a girl, there are better things to do than to watch telly. Another difference is that television lacks the streamlined sex-appeal of the films, perfected by Hollywood at the cost of so many millions of dollars. The performers in television drama are not "stars" in the Hollywood sense, but just ordinary English actors and actresses, and so in adolescent eyes conditioned to Hollywood glamour they are vaguely wrong. I also found the boys irritated by the interruptions of uplift or current affairs in television programmes—such interruptions showed that the whole television programme was not "theirs", that some hostile adults were trying to sell them something, that they were being got at—and similar reactions were even shown towards the advertisements.

This impression tallied with what I was told at youth clubs. The television rooms, which were installed at many clubs a few years back, were mostly neglected once the novelty had worn off. "The sort of youngsters we're concerned with have rather lost interest." In those clubs which catered for "difficult" boys, I even found leaders in considerable doubt about the benefits of the new medium. Some were distinctly worried about the constant scenes of violence shown on television, certainly in so far as these were directed at their particular charges. One comment was this: "The gang type we get in, if they watch at all, watch television with a moronic eye. They're only interested in the violence—for them unfortunately it's one way of learning how to torment people. They start out to do it themselves, to bust up the club—'just for a lark', that's the first thought, but before they know it's sadism."

Another, older club leader thought that the spread of television had to some degree coincided with that of youthful vandalism. While parents were more often in front of the television set in the evenings, their children were more often out roaming the streets. "Even small children, I think, are staying out much later round here because parents are busy viewing, and don't want to be disturbed. It's a sign of this growing callousness that they should be out at all."

In this general disregard of television, some programmes are, of course, exceptions. As I have mentioned before, programmes about themselves, that is about "youth" or "the Teddy boy problem", are often watched eagerly by the boys, who find them flattering, and find it natural that they should be discussed. Intermittently popular programmes are those presenting football, boxing and hot music, though here the basic appeal is that of sport and pop music themselves, rather than the medium of television. Altogether, I vividly recall the comment of one precocious young ruffian who seemed to sum up the whole impact of television on his young life in a few succinct sentences:

> It's getting so boys like us can't stay at home any more. It's telly every night: I say it get's boring. You take the·television room at the Club. One time it used to be crowded, now you never get more than a few fellows, and then mostly it's kids. It's all those advertisements. They're something horrible. You see a bloke with a gun just going to shoot somebody, and next thing you get "OMO adds Brightness", and when it starts again you see the police are already in the room.

What could be more concise?

As the reader may have gathered, the above criticisms apply almost exclusively to commercial television, for the good reason that, apart from a few sporting and musical shows, BBC television seemed almost unknown in these adolescent circles. The one reason above all which was given to me was that the BBC voice is still the ruling middle-class voice, that of teacher and of authority, which sends these boys and girls scurrying for cover—or to the familiarity of the brisk and half-American salesman's voice of "the Commercial".

MUSIC HAS CHARMS

While television has made only this little impact, exactly the opposite is true of commercial pop music. Its influence is hard to overestimate. The ordinary Ted's mind moves to the rhythm of rock and roll, and his body to that of jive. Here he is no rebel. The point where he feels most at one with the culture of contemporary society is within the commercial musical *ensemble*, in the world of pop records and record players, juke-boxes and radio disc-jockeys, the whole accompaniment of manufactured voices bawling, yearning or whispering at the boys and girls, trying either to incite them to movement or else (as I think Aldous Huxley once put it) asking them to swoon on waves of softest syrup.

In their enthusiasm for this brave new world, the Teds are of course only in line with most of their generation. And with its predecessor, too—after all it can be said that the British fought the last war to the sound of the Light Programme left continuously switched on in the Other Ranks' mess. Since then, the gigantic American and Anglo-American musical entertainment industry has made further spectacular progress in these islands, and above all among the young. It is hardly possible to count how many millions of pop music records are sold annually on the teenage market. Lately the possession of a modern long-playing record-player has also become the fashion among the very young. Of the half-million record-players annually sold in Britain, the majority are bought by very young boys and girls. At an average price of £15, which means paying a couple of pounds down and the rest by instalments, they are well within reach as new status symbols.

These facts about the youthful pop music boom are common-place. But what I felt was significant was that in participating in this enthusiasm, as he certainly does, the average Ted was for once not in opposition to society, but *sharing* in a positive reaction.

This is shown in a number of ways. Pop music is a pastime where he may often, just like other boys, spare no expense. I remember an occasion when I tried to talk to some young toughs about hobbies and their faces remained bored and blank, as if hobbies were a thing for their old man but no longer for their generation, until I mentioned records, and this changed everything. They all kept them. One 16-year-old announced: "*My* hobby is collecting LPs. You have to pay 35s., but its two guineas for the old stars.

I got dozens of those." Well, perhaps he had them. In darkest Notting Hill, not long after the riots, a youth leader told me:

> Record-players are the thing these days among the boys. You just don't find a house without one; they're just about taking the place of the telly, expensive ones, too. Television seems to mean little to the youngsters these days—the only thing they bother to watch is boxing and football—but it's remarkable how well they know the records. Even little girls at the club will ask if we've already got the latest hit, "Babyface" or something. Tunes are the one subject where you can be sure of getting them to talk.

One can go further. Ordinarily the Teds, as young rebels, are automatically against any ideas of working hard and "getting on". Sweat and toil to learn music is one of the few exceptions. A boy willing to devote every evening to practise in a band is not derided for his pains. Even in tougher Ted circles, musical ambition is generally regarded as legitimate. In fact, some of these dim circles show a pathetic longing to be "in" on jazz-as-art and to be knowing about traditional and modernist style and the rest.

In other words, his love for pop music appears to be the chink in the Teddy boy's armour of non-participation. This is already recognized in the well-meaning efforts "to talk to the boys in their own language". I remember visiting a café in the drabbest district in an industrial town which had been opened in an attempt to bring in some large groups of wild and footloose boys and girls. The café had remained almost empty until a manager was appointed who was himself knowledgeable about the Top Twenty of the Month, and what changes to ring on the record-player. As if he were the Piper of Hamelin, his café became a popular centre night after night. When I saw it, it represented the odd spectacle of a crowd of overdressed, bizarre and desperate-looking adolescents milling around in a confined space, yet under the spell of music all impeccably on their best behaviour, "living" themselves into the part of being good boys, like actors guided by The Method.

Many clubs in difficult areas have had a similar experience. By setting aside a room for records and jiving and leaving the youngsters in it fairly unsupervised, they have brought in drifting boys and girls who otherwise might have stayed resolutely outside.

It is true that in club circles there has already been some opposition to this move. The sight of an overcrowded, untidy room in which a few youngsters dance, a far greater number merely stand about, and the record-player is continuously turned up to top volume, is not edifying. It is said that if youngsters merely drift into a club for this one passive amusement and nothing else, very little is really gained, except that they are off the street.

Even so, I kept on feeling that this musical enthusiasm of the Teds was something positive which could be the starting-point for contact with them, if only one could understand just what it meant. It is perfectly true that this enthusiasm is constantly stimulated by the pop music industry through a skilful sales appeal, whose flattery begins with the faces on the glossy record sleeves, and ends with the yearning note in the lyrics directed explicitly at every boy or girl. But I also felt that the rhythmic music impinged directly on an aspect in the life of these youngsters to which they and society had done absurd violence—simply, their youthfulness.

Some time ago, Humphrey Lyttelton gave me what I thought a telling explanation why jazz should have become a modern urban folk-music which appealed so powerfully to the younger age-groups and only to them. If jazz was a music of revolt, he said, it was so in a general, youthful, undramatic sort of way. It appealed to young people coming up in the world because it demanded no great *expertise* either to perform or to listen to. It was democratic, in that on the stand even the band leader was only just another performer. It was international, in that the idiom was the same in every country. Lastly, it was an idiom which the young felt their elders did not understand, and they rather liked this.

The reasons for this difference in the reactions of the old and the young to jazz are also fairly simple. Jazz, even in its derived forms, is still a functional music, that of a vigorous and youthful dance, whose basic step is the athletic jive. Hence it remains a lively, almost nervous music, whose rhythm older people find unsettling, but to which the young instinctively respond with their bodies.

If all this applies to jazz proper, it remains true even of its debased forms. When a particularly catchy tune is put on in a juke-box dive, it is a common sight to see even the most passive dead-pan young Teds quicken to life, nod rhythmically to the beat, and look almost eager. The reason is that there is something youthful, appropriate to their age-group in this music to which they can respond, not as pseudo-adults, but as boys—as what they really are. And it always seemed to me that here one was on to something, that this response to pop music also indicated the long-term solution to the problem of the Teddy boys: that they must be enabled, guided or if necessary impelled to step out of the pose into which some quirk in society has forced them—and made to become boys again.

CLOTHES AND THE MAN

I accompanied a young friend, Len, (not my café-companion from the previous chapter) on a visit to his tailor, whose shop was in a busy South London street. I had met Len in a jazz club. Though he still lived in a South London slum, he was at twenty already earning good pay as a printer. He was assured, purposeful, devoted to hi-fi, to playing in a band, and elegant clothes, aiming for the suburbs when he got married, seeing few obstacles to rapid social advance.

Len was ordering a suit for a special occasion. Mr B, his tailor, was Jewish—efficient, very friendly and forthcoming. I had not thought it possible to discuss the question whether the vent at the rear of a jacket should be two, three or four inches long in terms of major fashion trends and of the historic derivation of vents from the original riding habits, but Len and Mr B did so with practised ease. A single vent of exactly two inches was finally agreed upon. "With your build I'd say that's just right," Mr B told Len. "You don't want to be an extremist. You've no need to deviate."

"Extremist" and "deviate" appeared to be the fashionable words.

The new ritual also seemed as elaborate as in Savile Row, if not more so. "You take the young fellows round here," Mr B told me. "Some of them may be earning as much as £12 or £14 a week. To you that still may not be so much relatively, but it does give them more scope. They are also better educated and so their brains are looking for a line in clothes, you might say. They have become fashion conscious." He occupied himself with Len's jacket.

"Fish-mouth lapels. I know the style you want—you want the coat to lie nicely in the hipline."

"I don't want a jacket that looks as wide in the seat as in the shoulders," said Len.

"Don't worry, I get you," said Mr B. He hitched up Len's lapels. "See—this gives you the manly appearance, yet not spivvy, if you get my meaning. What about the pockets?"

The discussion became precise on the subject of pocket flaps. "I'd never wear a jacket without flaps," Len said to me. "That's cowboy style. I don't go for that." There was the question of the width of the flaps. "Now some young fellows like them as narrow as one inch, but then again, they're the extremists," said Mr B. Len said he wanted no exaggeration. "Quite so, you don't want to deviate too much," said Mr B again. He turned to me. "I know exactly what's wanted. How? It's quite simple. I feel the pulse of the public; I make a model, I put it in the window and if it catches on it's soon copied. You take this young fellow, for instance. He's a good customer and I know he doesn't want to be extreme, I know what he's after. The sleeve cuffs tapered, I imagine?"

Len squinted along his horizontally raised arm. "I don't want the sleeves too long. I like to show plenty of shirt cuffs."

Mr B measured the sleeve carefully and the conversation proceeded to the details of the trouser line of the suit. "There, I think I'll give you a natural run down to a sixteen-inch bottom. Now how much turn-up? These days some fellows like cuffs on their trousers two inches high, but again I'd say that for you it's too extreme—a cuff that high must produce a strain on the trouser leg which you don't want."

After the turn-up, the trouser seam. "I want proper raised seams," said Len with some enthusiasm. "I had a suit made with raised seams and fellows used to say, 'That's a smashing suit you've got', and you won't believe it, I wore that suit for two years. I only wore it once a fortnight and I always let it hang in between, but the style was so good nobody knew it was two years old."

"One of ours, eh?" Mr B looked up at me. "You see? It's our style. There's another thing, talking of the way things have changed. Round here, we've got the most cosmopolitan crowd of customers, we've got Greeks, Irishmen, Coloured."

"Do your Coloured customers prefer any special style?"

"My experience is the Coloured round here are of two kinds," said Mr B. "The Ghana gentry, they're more genteel, they like to look cityfied. The Jamaicans—there are more of those—when they first come over their fashion is double-breasted coats and they like a trouser thirty inches at the knee with eighteen-inch bottoms and three-inch turn-ups. That way a suit takes a full yard more cloth, but they are quite ready to pay the extra, they tell us what they want and we do it." Mr B reflected. "Of course, that's changing, too. Lately I've seen quite a number of darkies wearing Italian cut."

"They're a bit flash," said Len, looking at his sleeve again. "Don't forget, I want to show plenty of shirt."

I asked about the local Teddy boys, if they could still be called by that name. Did they still dress in distinctive style?

"I know the customers you mean, Tony boys they call some of them now," said Mr B. "No, I wouldn't say a distinct style. Not like that old velvet collar business. That blew itself up and blew itself out. Today you might say that certain types like to be extremists. For instance, they ask for extra tight trousers, fourteen-inch bottoms, and exceptionally short jackets."

"You can tell those blokes by their behaviour," said Len. "They don't know how to behave. They come into a shop like this and they'll shout and be rowdy, throw things about."

Squaring his shoulders, Mr B laughed. "Don't you worry about fellows coming in here to try and bully. I don't go for that. The other day a fellow in the shop tried to call me a bloody Jew. Before he knew, I had him out on the pavement."

"They've got the money, though, they're the spenders," said Len.

"If you're interested, here's another question for you," said Mr B. "Where do some of them get the cash? We had one young fellow in here, in the last six months he's ordered nine suits and an overcoat. I have another customer, he's one of our regulars. He likes to order a suit a month, and when he's worn them he gives them away to his pals when they're out of work. In some cases, I myself would like to know where the money comes from. I had a kid in here the other day no more than so high who ordered a jacket. I tell you he wanted it as big as an overcoat, he wouldn't have it cut any other way. A kid of fourteen, still at school, and he orders an £18 suit."

"I'll have to go in a minute," said Len. I had noted that for the last few minutes, while the tailor had talked to me, he had been staring without interruption at his reflection in the full-length looking-glass.

I asked whether one might say that the young men of today had become almost as fashion-conscious as young women were.

Mr B almost jumped. "Hey, you've got to be careful, you mustn't ever say that, that they are like women," he advised, with a quick look at Len, who was, however, still looking absently into the mirror, quite unmoved. "It's just a general style—all younger people are wearing brighter clothes today. Like our latest styles— Costa Brava Grey or Cha-Cha Check . . ."

"Cha-Cha Check, what's that?" asked Len. "Another Prince of Wales Check?"

"Well, it is, basically. It's one of our names for this season," said Mr B. He turned to me. "You should see our selection."

We went out into the High Street which on this Saturday morning had a bustling market atmosphere. In Mr B's window the Italianate names proliferated: Napoli Grey, Fantoma Weave, Coracle Weave, Biscotti Brown, Ice Grey, Montefiore Grey, Cellini Blue.

"Cellini Blue, I haven't seen that before," said Len to Mr B. "Don't forget, I want the suit before the date I gave you. Before I wear a suit I want it to hang for two weeks so I can properly brush it down."

"You'll have it, Len, don't you worry," said Mr B. "Have I ever let you down?"

ORDINARY AND ABNORMAL

From an ordinary little encounter like that in Mr B's shop, one could see how far fashion had progressed in the 'fifties: what had begun with the outlaw bravura of the Teds had by the end of the decade become the elegance of the ordinary working-class boy who took pride and pleasure in his appearance.

If the successors to the Teds, to whom clothes meant rather more than this, could no longer be picked out by their appearance at a glance—the old velvet collar days were in the past—they could, however, still be distinguished, usually in two ways. First, by their "extremism", by their preference for dressing in a challenging and grotesque way even within the prevailing fashion. Secondly, many young gang members still have an obsessional attitude towards clothes—one still finds that their passionate identification of clothes with status and an outlaw way of life can border on the hysterical.

Especially in poorer districts, one meets cases where a boy may be up before the Court for theft and it is discovered that he may have half a dozen suits (or ten or more) hanging in his wardrobe. A social worker from Birmingham told me how in a young semi-criminal gang he knew, the boys consistently ordered suits far beyond their means, committing themselves to hire-purchase payments, whether they had prospects of meeting them or not. They were not interested in argument about this: a new suit was the badge of status, of manhood, not to be questioned. If they could not get the money for it from regular earnings, e.g. because they were in the meantime out of work, the first thought was to get it some other way. . . . The same informant also told me that he himself had become so conditioned to regard the suits as part of the boys' personality that on the rare occasions when they took them off, as when they went swimming, he found it hard to recognize them as the same boys. "With some I began to realize that the reason why they would not join in games was that they didn't want to remove their precious jackets."

A youth club leader from the East End told me a similar tale. "Last summer, when we took a fresh batch to our annual camp, we found that the older lads wouldn't stay a night in the tents on any account. Some even went into lodgings in the town and came back in the morning. Later we found out the reason—because there was no room in the tents to hang up their suits. This year we therefore provided a special store hut with proper hangers, and it worked like magic. Even small boys brought their best suits to camp."

To sum up, two trends should therefore be distinguished. The first is the advance in clothes-consciousness among British working-class boys in general. At the same time, in the peculiar little world of Ted society, clothes still play their exaggerated special rôle. Expensive clothes still seem to be regarded as going not only with status but also with defiance and lawlessness.

CHAPTER IX

Thrusters and Drifters

THE MEMBERSHIP

To turn from the cultural to the social viewpoint—how is the Teddy boy society constituted and recruited? In trying to answer this question one has admittedly to generalize, lumping together sophisticated London adolescents with a taste for the clubs of Soho with small-town boys and girls in provincial juke-box cafés. All the same, I found that teachers and social workers in different localities usually had a pretty clear idea about the character of their local Teddy boy society and that the impressions tallied fairly closely.

To those who had to deal directly with the problem of the Teddy boys, and who were often highly unsuccessful in trying to influence them, the cult of deliberate and anti-social irresponsibility among these youths and boys often seemed *sui generis*. In fact they were not so unique.

A friend from Oxford gave me a neat sidelight on this. He had been struck, he said, by the close parallels between the bloods, the top set among Oxford undergraduates and the South London Teddy boys among whom he did some social work. Both groups were alike in seeking provocative emphasis in dress: there were even traces of sartorial similarity. Both groups, each on its own social level, had similar tastes for women, fast cars, jazz and the West End life. Above all, both the young Oxford bloods and the London Teds were intent on living irresponsibly—the essence was that they both felt free from social pressures; each group, for instance, felt free to set off on a night's expedition at a moment's impulse.

Situated between these two groups, as my friend saw it, was the great majority of State-aided undergraduates at the university, who never felt free from social pressures. They sat in their rooms and worked, they worried about examinations, about making ends meet and what jobs they might get—in any case, they worried. And this hard-working majority had as little social contact with the carefree Oxford top set above them as with the irresponsible Teddy boy *jeunesse dorée* below. Each class went its own way.

While the other two groups are, however, well established, the emergence of a *jeunesse dorée* life among unskilled adolescents is still a very new phenomenon. For this reason, probably, one is struck in this milieu by its atmosphere of constant thrust—living for kicks—and of defensiveness towards outsiders.

I felt very conscious of this during a conversation arranged for me with a set of adolescents from one West London gang. The meeting took place in a youth club which they sometimes frequented. Warned of my presence, the first-comers entered without saying a word, sat down and nonchalantly picked up magazines, without taking the slightest notice of me; but I could see that they were nervously flipping the pages faster than they could observe what was on them, thereby betraying some tension.

When all the twelve boys sat round me in a circle, they willingly engaged in candid conversation, answering questions without ceremony, showing me something new; their sophistication. As a group they were pretty tough. Two of them had graduated through Approved Schools. On the other hand one good-looking youth among them talked of becoming a ballet dancer. Ballet or Borstal—it was all equally casually accepted. They were also worldly-wise. Their picture of themselves was of a generation struggling against frustration. They were misunderstood, they claimed, because they matured earlier. "You take a young fellow of 15 or 16 today, he's like what they used to be at 18, mentally." How did they know? They had read all about it in the *Daily Express*. They also knew all about discussions on "youth" on television—some of these programmes they thought childish. Not one of them, it appeared, had thought of staying on the voluntary extra year at school, nor was anyone attending courses at Technical College. It stood to reason: any boy who did so would then not have had money to go with the gang to dance-halls and places like the Lyceum in the Strand. One of them argued with conviction: "Extra school won't get a boy any place. There's automation coming anyway. That means more work for a few people with brains and for the rest of us doing the same thing all day." They talked readily of their grievances—minor grievances against youth club leaders who wanted them to engage in activities, and passionate grievances against their enemy, the police. Then, as the impulse seized them, they made abrupt, nervous departures, not merely without special notice of me, but even without politeness. One after the other, apparently on the spur of the moment, they abruptly got up to walk out into their private night-life. "You did well to keep them talking for over an hour," said my acquaintance who had arranged the meeting. In actual fact, I was acutely aware of having been made to talk across a gap of class and age—above all across a gap.

Two or three of these boys were only just 15. A second point to note about Teddy boy society is that it is strikingly youthful. In this respect it reflects the genuinely earlier physiological maturity of the present generation of teenagers. Although the boys them-selves are aware of it, this acceleration of adolescence seems a phenomenon about which surprisingly little has been written, perhaps because its implications are so startling. But there can be little doubt about this change. A number of studies in Britain, the U.S. and Germany indicate that, on the average, teenage girls today arrive at biological maturity a year earlier than their mother (and probably two years earlier than their grandmothers) while the boys have also kept pace.

The causes of this acceleration are still speculative—it is thought to be connected with changes in diet and infant care and the fact that modern teenagers are also taller and heavier than those of the past. Whatever the explanation, the change itself has already begun to create complications: for parents whose sons and daughters at 15 or 16 claim an independence which they them-selves only enjoyed at 17 or 18; for teachers in Secondary Modern Schools who find themselves—as some have complained—facing "sex-excited louts and hussies"; for the authorities at Approved Schools, and so forth.

As for the Teddy boy society, its age composition also quite clearly reflects this earlier maturity. A good many Teddy boys, as they leave school at 15, buy their uniform from their first earnings. If we take it that in so doing they are proclaiming their open rejection of school and parents and asserting their adult status, the point to note is how early in life this claim is made. As a rule, youths from 17 to 21 are still the actual leaders of gangs—it is they who usually appear in Court—but in many gangs boys of 15 are already members, adeptly working their passages upwards, and this precocity clearly poses new problems.

CLASS AND THE TEDDY BOYS

To return to the class aspect of Teddy boy society, while its life may illustrate the social advance of working-class adolescents in Britain, it is also clear that its members are drawn from a very narrow class of these young workers, one which under the current new stratification is also a class left over, left behind. Perhaps this is best shown by a process of exclusion. First, through the 11-plus examination, the 20 per cent. of grammar school boys are creamed off; they have no truck with Teddy boy life. The same is true for the minority of boys going into skilled apprenticeship. As young apprentices these don't earn enough money to keep up with the flash café life. On the other hand, once they become skilled workers, they feel it is beneath them: their earnings are then on a level where they are on the contrary pulled in the opposite direction, towards what is today called an "Americanized" style of working-class life, a life of suburban houses, cars, household gadgets, respectability—in any case, right away from Teddy boy café society. The latter is thus recruited mainly from those left over, from the young unskilled workers whose earnings are too low and irregular for them to take part in this *embourgeoisement*. But if they cannot take part in this, their earnings are at the same time much higher than in the past and enough for café life and fashions. Without the status of the white-collar worker and the prospects of the apprentice, and probably with resentment on both scores, a young unskilled worker can, at least at the age of 17, spend more money than either of the others. This is the economic basis of Teddy boy society.

Finally, within this changing life of a special class of unskilled young workers, the Teddy boy society is a still further minority phenomenon—a concentration of the insecure, of unstable adolescents, those with weak family ties and the fewest special interests, who are drawn to this nightly café life as to a drug, to hold back their anxieties.

This cannot be proved precisely by statistics, but all the evidence, especially the experience of social workers, points to the conclusion that the Teddy boys include a majority of insecure youngsters from bad or broken homes. One senior Borstal officer told me that in his experience of Teddy boy offenders, more than half came from family backgrounds which were "absolute hell"; another quarter from homes which looked superficially all right but probably were not; while less than a quarter came from genuinely adequate homes. From my own limited impression, too, it seems justified to regard the Teddy boy society as a new way of adolescent group life which like a magnet draws in the most psychologically insecure among working-class adolescents.

THE DRIFTERS

This need to find security in gang life is most pronounced in the case of certain younger members of the Teddy boy society to whom a social worker in Notting Hill always referred as The Drifters. It seemed an appropriate name. The Drifters, as the term is here used, could be described as a minority within a minority, the extreme wing of the Teddy boy society, or perhaps more accurately described as its lowest stratum. They are boys and girls who appear adrift, without apparent direction in life, or recognizable moral standards, rejecting all authority, living only for the immediate gratification of desire and the search for security in the mob.

When one goes into the individual background of such youngsters, one usually finds that they come from deprived homes. "Among these particular youngsters," one informant told me, "I have never heard one affectionate word spoken about parents, indeed always the opposite. They are laughed at and ridiculed, sworn at and deceived, and if they are not ready to pass over the easy five bob then it is taken from them." Usually the same youngsters are also the product of a bad area—Notting Hill is a good example, or the neighbourhood around Kings Cross, where 16-year-olds feel already completely worldly-wise, cynically weary of life, with no feeling that there is anything to learn or any attachment to district or country or anything but money. But other special circumstances, too, can produce groups of adolescent Drifters to whom vandalism, promiscuity and petty crime mean nothing, even on a new council estate, provided determined ringleaders appear and there is no counterpull.

As the lower stratum of the Teddy boy society, as a problem of today, the Drifters seem to be a recognizable entity. Indeed, the picture built up in my mind from conversations with people struggling thanklessly with this problem was like that of a single unintegrated, defiant and dangerous problem child—only this child was in actual fact a collective of adolescents. To me the most remarkable aspect about this collective of the Drifters is that they should exist in London at this present day. Yet the Drifters do exist. What follows is some documentation about it which I have gathered from various places. As elsewhere, I have thought it best not to give names and places too exactly, and the opinions of my informants are given more or less in their own words.

SHIFTLESSNESS

The first and foremost characteristic of the Drifters which makes them so untractable is their extreme shiftlessness. Perhaps this is due to the fact that most of them have cut themselves off from their homes and so are in a vacuum. At any rate, their state of mind is one where it simply does not occur to them that an impulse, a desire which seizes them, should not at once be gratified. This freedom to follow impulse is what the gang seems to sanction: hence its attraction. In this freedom to follow impulse they also find emotional security. Any attempt to guide them, to interfere, is therefore like an attack on their security and at once opposed or evaded as such. This is what makes the Drifters so difficult to deal with and has made pessimistic social workers coin words like "unreachable" or "unclubbable". Youth club leaders are well aware of this floating antagonism among some of the boys and girls they are trying to draw in. As one leader from a notorious London area told me:

Perhaps this latest generation is even more delinquent than the last in pinching motor-bikes and cars, but what strikes me is the way they do it—the growth of sheer irresponsibility. The other day some of our boys went to the market and simply began to throw goods from stalls all over the place and so they came up before the Court. But for them it was just having fun. They would pinch a car in the same way. You saw what an impressive new club building we have; for a good twenty-five per cent. of the 14-16 age-group it makes no difference. They will never be constructive. They just come in for a game of darts, a coffee, they flit in and out, nothing else. We thought: "We must give them easy things to do." Right: we organized badminton groups, judo groups, a snooker tournament, but they never stuck at anything more than half an hour. Then suddenly one of them would say: "Comin' out . . ." and they'd all flock after him like sheep. If you ask where to, they'd say, "To the chip shop" or "Sit in the café." It's just to be somewhere different, to move about, with no objective.

But then they've got no objective. They've got no faith, no religion, they don't see why they're in this world. Basically, it's a matter of seeing how selfish you can be. They're not interested in their jobs—money is the only thing that counts.

A depressing picture. What is worse, their amorphous restlessness can take them not merely to the chip shop but far afield and into trouble. The following story from a club in North London is typical of quite a few that I heard:

One Saturday evening a number of boys were idling in the place and there was a vague unrest. None of them had any money. Suddenly someone said, "Let's go to Brighton for the week-end." There was an instant's pause and with a sudden concerted movement about ten of them rushed out into the night. I was somewhat taken aback and I must have shown my surprise. "What's the matter with you then? Can't they have a week-end by the sea if they want or is that just for the rich like you?" said someone belligerently from the corner. He so enjoyed his own venom that he was soon earnestly and with great charm discussing with me the delights of a week-end in Brighton. "But they've no money," I said weakly. He smiled condescendingly and kindly told me how to travel on the railway without the embarrassment of a ticket. The only hazardous moment is getting off the train on the non-platform side.

What happened on this particular jaunt is that the boys were seen on the train by a guard and the Brighton police were notified. As a result, some were apprehended and only a number escaped in an uproarious chase across the tracks. But for some hours these managed to have quite a wild time. They tried to break open and rob cigarette machines, they damaged property in public conveniences, they staged a brawl on the sea front and eventually were rounded up and put under guard into a London train. There they started another minor riot in which two boys cut themselves so badly in breaking glass that they had to have hospital treatment. But as they told the story, all this did not matter. Being arrested, being wounded, it was all an ordinary occurrence of their life, soon no doubt to be repeated.

DESTRUCTIVENESS

Another characteristic of the Drifters is their destructiveness, their evidently compulsive desire to smash, to destroy, to harm. Perhaps our age has encouraged some such general tendency. Not long ago, when I watched a rock-and-roll session which had been arranged in a London Town Hall by local voluntary workers anxious to do something positive for the young, it occurred to me that there was more than a trace of this in the collective exuberance. Inside the hall, the scene had a touch of bedlam; what looked like a thousand boys and girls of ages ranging from 14 to 19 were sitting closely packed at the tables, or shoving to get on to the crowded floor, with a resentful and jostling queue outside. The crowd effect, the rock-and-roll rhythm and the continuous noise clearly provided a special excitement. The youngsters were enjoying themselves, shouting, laughing, smoking and pushing past each other to drink coffee and lemonade; the girls had an air of keeping themselves continuously on display; boys were dancing with their heads to one side, seeming not so much interested in their partners as intent on displaying their skill as dancers or their newest suits. But what was distinctly noticeable, in addition to the excitement, was a hint of mob callousness and destructiveness. Youngsters making for the dance-floor shoved their way ruthlessly through the crowd; I saw cigarettes thrown on the floor or stubbed out on the tables; chairs were kicked out of the way or pushed over; at one spot, where crockery was smashed and stewards hurried anxiously to the scene, there were shrieks of laughter.

Now, all this disorder was quite obviously under control. The dancers were plainly nice ordinary suburban boys and girls who would presently grow up into ordinary suburban adults. And yet

I thought that an undertone of mob excitement and destructiveness, which is a mark of the age, was distinctly to be felt. Take away the restraints holding it in check on such occasions, carry the urge to an extreme, I thought, and one arrived at that wanton attitude of destructiveness which is a mark of the Drifters, which is let loose above all against public property and from which youth clubs in exposed areas have also particularly suffered.

Since this destructiveness of the Drifters springs from unrestrained primitive emotions which are always there, even a small pretext is enough to set it off. A common cause is the feeling among the members of any such group that they are being deprived or excluded from anything they want. I was told a story of this kind from a new London housing estate where, in spite of the warnings by the local youth leader, the permanent premises for a youth club were given lowest priority and still not built two years after the estate had gone up. As a result, my informant told me, the estate quickly had its gangs of juveniles who tended to become unclubbable; the boys especially seemed absolutely frustrated because they had nowhere to go:

All we had for the Club was a converted air-raid shelter and we had such a long waiting list that there was no point in adding to it. Among those who weren't allowed in was particularly one wandering gang who came to the doors several times, ranging from a girl of 15, the youngest, to a youth of 21. One night after Whitsun week it was found that the Club had been broken into on Whit Monday and completely wrecked. The gang scattered tea and sugar, they smashed tables, tore out the electric wiring, they tore books into shreds ... they were found and caught. Four of the boys with previous convictions went to Borstal or on probation. Another eleven were between them fined £60. Yet my feeling was they were really victims. It all happened because they felt excluded, so their reaction was primitive. They actually agreed that they hadn't intended to do much damage at first—they just wanted to get in, but once inside they got excited and couldn't stop smashing.

It appears that an idea of having been excluded or unfairly treated, which can set off their floating resentment like a spark of fire, often underlies cases of vandalism. A café owner in a busy area who had set himself not to bar even the most unruly youngsters and felt confident of being able to handle any trouble told me:

> Of course it ultimately didn't work. There were some lads who were so psychopathic that they practically turned the place into a shambles. A few didn't even bother to order anything. I felt I had to put a stop to it, but as I had encouraged them to regard the cafe as a sort of meeting-place, any change in my attitude aroused fierce resentment. The place was burgled twice, in each case a retribution for "unfair treatment" on our part. In one case this was because we had fixed the juke-box so they could only get one record for 6d. instead of 3 for 1s. This so infuriated the gang that they broke in and removed the night's takings from the juke-box—and they were prepared to argue that we and not they were to blame.

From various parts of London one can hear a number of such stories.

WHAT ANSWER TO AGGRESSION?

How are these young Drifters to be caught and led back to a life of conforming with society? One answer is, through the Youth Services. But here lies the difficulty. The hostility of the Drifters is not only something which flares up when the gang feels thwarted or excluded. It is a basic emotional attitude—the Teddy boy antagonism towards society carried to a neurotic and dangerous extreme which makes these youths seem unclubbable.

Given the individual case histories of most Drifters, one can understand, in a way, why they should have an ambivalent attitude towards youth clubs. As they are only boys like others, they like what the clubs offer for almost nothing, namely the chance to drift idly into the premises for a spot of billiards or ping-pong, to listen to records, to enjoy the company of girls in the canteen. The chance to enjoy all this is obviously desirable, and to be excluded from it is to a Drifter not only an affront but a basic attack against his security. On the other hand, they must have these things only on their own terms of freedom to behave as they choose, and again one can see why. The characteristic Drifters of 15 and 16 have broken contact with largely loveless homes; they have consigned their years at Secondary Modern School to the dustbin and found a temporary security in the calculated egotism of the gang in which each of them can feel "somebody". Their attitude towards the authority of a youth club, even a minimum authority, is therefore often an irrational "So you want to drag us back to what we've escaped from? Don't think you can do it!" This is the point where violence often begins, where a gang of Drifters becomes like part of a "resistance movement".

I felt that this came out strongly during some talks with a dozen or so club leaders from council estates in difficult parts of London: their work seemed like a perpetual effort to snare shy game, only this game consisted of London boys and girls. In this social war there have been notable successes, but also enough disheartening failures to demonstrate the extent of the problem.

There was, for instance, Estate A, where the tenants' club for young people was never even opened through apprehension of the youthful gangs roaming the neighbourhood. "They've never been stopped, they are dangerous and they've bags of confidence: if anything, they're getting worse. They don't carry weapons as a rule, but in case of need are never at a loss where to find them. In one affray we had the lavatory chains torn off to be used as weapons for lashing." There was Club B, which according to its leader had had a wretched history: started, packed up, started again several times and then the police called in. "Not the local police—they generally arrived too late. If there's trouble the best thing to do is to dial 999. If you do, however, you can take it you've lost the confidence of the boys, even the good ones. You've shown that you can't cope and it means that you've also done something which in the eyes of the boys takes you right away from being on their side, so that their respect is gone. But what else can you do?"

There was Club C, whose manager confessed that perhaps he and his colleagues had made an error of judgment. A gang of dangerous-looking young thugs had come to the door and the youth leader on duty had not permitted them inside. "They went away with a chip on their shoulder and the damage was done because they turned up again as a gang of young rowdies out to torment us—'to torment people' is a phrase they often employ. Their invasion of us for several evenings running was quite systematic and followed the same lines. One of them might start the fun by treading on a ping-pong ball and looking at us challengingly; the second would take up a billiard cue and laugh and break it in two; another would take a gramophone record, smile and stamp on it. Do you know what they reminded me of? Gunmen in a Western film busting up the saloon. They had the same expression of craving violence, of spoiling for a fight, only we kept our heads and wouldn't oblige them. If you do that they usually pretend to lose interest and laugh and drift out again."

Club D, although situated in what was rather a criminal area, had coped surprisingly well with minor disorders, but there was now some anxiety over new developments. "The worse sort of trouble usually starts when you get a new leader in the neighbourhood, a real tough who is prepared to be ruthless. Often it's a type of that sort who's just out of prison, who can change the whole tone of an area—that's what happened to us, and our younger rowdies are round this new leader like flies. From one week to the next we could see their whole behaviour deteriorate."

The ways in which such aggression can flare up are also incalculable. There was the young club leader from Estate E in one of London's toughest areas who had made a point of going to neighbourhood cafés to try to get to know boys. "In the café, when talking to me, they would call themselves by different names. Some didn't give any names—never gave them away. If I did find out from someone else and called them by their name they would be startled, suspicious. 'How do you know my name?' They were like half-wild animals." Perhaps because most of the gangs he met included one or two psychopaths, the old tradition of "a fair fight" had hardly a flicker of life left. "Many of the regulars in the café thought it nothing to discuss complex methods of violence in front of me, about butting people, kicking them in vulnerable places and dealing with them." Fantasy also crept constantly into the idea of aggression. "I remember one boy in a beautiful Italian suit who carried not merely a knife but actually a gun. When I asked him why, he said: 'There's all sorts of Cypriots and Maltese walking about round here . . . you've got to put your hand on something.' "

The problem of making headway in this social war is not an easy one. Special clubs to attract boys of this type have been formed, but the difficulty is how to cope with their waywardness if ordinary club activities are at the same time not to be completely disrupted. Club leaders with exceptional understanding can do this. For instance, at Friendship House in Lambeth, the Rev. Douglas Griffiths has very successfully turned boys of this type into steady club members, but the following story he told me shows the patience required:

> On one occasion, for instance, four boys dashed into the club before it was open and in that very brief visit they cut the cloth on the billiard table and damaged the table-tennis table and a wall. And then they were out again through another door in no time. I followed them very slowly down the street, but just kept them in sight. After a while they stopped and let me catch up with them. I said to them: "Well now, why have you done this? I just want to understand you." And they said: "Well, last night, one of our chaps was hurt in the cinema. The attendant set on him and he's had to go to the doctor today. So of course we're feeling peeved. We've got to take it out of somebody. Wouldn't you?" And they simply thought that it was the most natural thing in the world that they should destroy somebody's property because somebody had hurt one of them. Well, when we knew what the trouble was, we were able to deal with it. . . ."

Another telling little story—this came from a West London area adjacent to Notting Hill—was told to me by a young professional youth worker who went out in New York style in an attempt to become a street-corner youth leader to a group of rather dangerous and delinquent young Drifters. Making contact was not so difficult, but as this young man saw it, being with these youths morning, afternoon and evening was rather like being in touch with mental illness.

He thought these youths were not unintelligent, though Secondary Modern School had made no impression on them, but in their defiant mood there was no such word in their vocabulary as "future". They took casual, unskilled jobs—when out of work they looked to other ways of keeping themselves. When some were convicted and sent to Borstal, the answer to the question: "Do you realize you may be away for two years?" was merely: "So what?" When they were destroying property, they were unconcerned about the feelings of other people, unless indeed they did it deliberately to make people angry, just for a laugh. . . . Within the group they egged each other on. The more violent a boy, the greater the respect given him by the others. They were often not aware of pain inflicted on other people because they simply did not see them as people.

I felt the decisive thing in my work with them was to convince them finally that they could not destroy me—that I was not afraid of their behaviour. Things did indeed become a bit different when they got to like me and were sorry if I got hurt. The extraordinary thing was that from one moment to the next they suddenly accepted me. Then they were most concerned about me and my welfare.

Such a picture of "mental illness" must, of course, be seen in proportion. Adolescent Drifters like this represent only a minority within the Teddy boy society and they are only a minute fraction of their age-group.

Even so, if it is thought that there are no more than a few thousand such adolescents growing up in London, they exist as a recognizable type, a strange product of the welfare state, and since many will inevitably graduate into adult crime, their existence poses disturbing problems. To give each group of Drifters the special psychological attention described above seems hardly feasible. Yet something needs to be done. A simple calculation shows that the share of young delinquents in the annual cost of the penal apparatus adds up to a sum larger than the whole contribution by the state and local authorities to the youth services. And if one wants to know what harm can be done by even a small number of such youths, neurotically equating aggression with "fun", one need only recall the Notting Hill riots.

CHAPTER X

Sex and Insecurity

SEX FOR THE ASKING

PERHAPS the simplest thing to say of the Teddy boy outlook on sex is that it is like that of the rest of present-day society—only more so.

This can be said not only of the psychopathic Drifters, but of nearly the whole of Teddy boy café society, including many very ordinary adolescents who by their mid-twenties will have forgotten all about dressing up and have become ordinary young married men. In its structure, Teddy boy society may be rudely governed by young adolescent males, but the sex drive remains the mainspring of nightly activity. The possession of the right girl to take to a cinema, dance or back alley is the symbol of status. As often as not, rivalry over girls is the starting-point or pretext for a gang fight—for going out "teamhanded" for a "giggle". Since Teddy boy society is also a concentration of the troubled, the intensified sexual chase also represents a search for reassurance. Its over-intensity somehow reflects a failure to mature, it is a substitute for lack of success on other levels, it is the topic endlessly chewed over in those night-time café conversations when dingy depression is only just kept at bay.

All this is a very ordinary story. As sociologists have found (and as one knew before), a nightly quest for sexual adventure is the common habit among young males at the bottom of the social ladder. Moreover, in a country like Britain, there is today noticeably far greater freedom in sex matters—this freedom has already spread far into the ranks of middle-class youth. Secondly, sex has never received such massive publicity as today, from the ubiquitous underclothes advertisements to the incessant erotic gossip in the popular press. This latter, it should be noted, goes much further than surrogate salacity like, say, the "Diana Dors" revelations which were run simultaneously in two popular Sunday newspapers in 1960, and condemned by the Press Council as "grossly lewd and salacious", while the standards of these papers were characterized as "debased to a level which is a disgrace to British journalism". In a way such dirt is already old-fashioned. More significant of the age, I think, are the streamlined pages of certain daily newspapers and of those glossy publications for teenagers which seem to carry the message that every adolescent girl ought to be in a perpetual flurry of erotic excitement.

It is not difficult to see the reason for this message. It's good for mass sales, and the advertisers like it.[1] Should one in this framework still speak of a special Teddy boy attitude to sex? A few points stand out. For instance, the precocity of Teddy boy sophistication. The typical Teddy boy takes his sexual pleasure where and when he wants it, and without further thought. Intercourse with a girl follows naturally after a rock session, a visit to the cinema or the chip shop, and in the circumstances much of it is back-alley sex. Common enough, but what is probably new is the youthful age of the boys. "By the time a boy today has reached 15," Mr Brian Carney has quoted a Birmingham club leader as saying, "he is ready for a full sex life—and the Teddy boy movement, by giving its group sanction to sexual freedom, helps him to get it. Even Teddy boys of 13 and 14 boast of their sexual adventures, and I don't doubt their word. Once they don Teddy boy clothing, the breakaway from conventional morality is complete."[2]

According to many observers, this early promiscuity induced by Teddy boy life goes with deliberate callousness, especially on the Drifter level. "I remember an odd boozy night. There was a girl well known for her antics. Ten of the fellows queued up for her. It was just an ordinary entertainment for them. Then they got into two cars and drove to a spot five miles out of town, but the girl wouldn't go through with it again, so they drove off and left her— left her in the middle of the night: they're callous, I tell you . . ." and so on: especially on the Drifter level, there is something of gang bravado in this promiscuity. The same callousness expressed in aggression might be displayed in café talk about a 14- or 15-year-old girl who has become pregnant. "Her own bloody fault . . . she asked for what she got."

However, such a precocious male sex life demands partners.

---

[1] See Chapter XXIII.
[2] *John Bull*, 10th March 1959.

What of the Teddy girls? In terms of being real gang members, a small number of these can be encountered. They are usually working-class teenage girls in complete revolt against their families and living dangerously and excitedly for the moment. But the more common type of camp followers are rather dumb, passive teenage girls. In my glimpses of them they seemed crudely painted up, pathetically young, appallingly uneducated, some of them probably in danger of drifting into prostitution—in any case, as I looked at their expressionless faces, I felt sorry for their future families.

Of course, not all girls in Teddy boy life are of low I.Q. As a sort of insurance, as if looking for the common exit from this racketing life, many a Teddy boy likes to have a respectable girl in tow, whom he sees separately from his friends in the gang— the pattern is frequent. In any case, in considering the rôle of girls in this life, one has to take account of what seems to be a fundamental difference in juvenile delinquency between the two sexes. If we accept the psychological explanation that a delinquent is frequently an emotionally deprived youngster who "steals love", then the equivalent to the boy who does so through stealing or breaking in is the girl who slides into prostitution. The revengeful delinquency is similar: boy and girl are both trying to get something of value while giving nothing in return (which is why the money obtained in this way is so often immediately squandered). The distinction is that a boy up before the Court for theft is always in danger of slipping through circumstance into a criminal career. The delinquent girl who is his psychological counterpart may end up on the streets, or else she may become a slut and an inadequate wife and mother, so perpetuating the evil. But as such she is unlikely to feature much in the criminal statistics, which explains, at least in part, why the proportion of boy to girl delinquents is six to one.

Another distinction is that girls have quite a different attitude to delinquent gang life. They enter it for different motives and so it is always easier for them to get out again. I was given an illustration of this by a young woman teacher in the North Country who had kept in touch with a group of girls who, on leaving school, knocked about with a lawless gang of youths in outlandish Teddy boy garb. The girls, when I saw them in a café, looked reckless yet also more wholesome than their London counterparts, better groomed, more self-confident. Yet they also seemed absurdly young to be leading this life. According to the woman teacher they were members of a large and loose gang, living away from their families; some had lived on their own from the age of 15, doing what they liked, accepting no authority. It was like a dream life: they were shop girls, and on the slightest pretext, if any wrong word were said to them, they were in the habit of asking for their cards and walking out. As it happened, the previous year had seen some unemployment in the town, and jobs for young people were no longer plentiful. But these girls still walked out of their jobs on the least impulse—they just could not grasp that they were no longer able to do this, and when they found that there was not a similar job to be got in the shop next door, they simply came to my informant in full expectation that she would conjure up such a job for them. On the occasions when these girls confided in her, she said, it was not hard to recognize the sense of insecurity which haunted these girls beneath their superficial air of independence and their determination to be adrift. She had little doubt that the basic feminine ideal of a normal home life with husband, home and children was the driving force even in their life in Teddy boy circles. The danger was that before they knew, they might come to be care and protection cases and normal life more difficult to attain.

Even so, even on the lowest Drifters' level, the chance for teenage girls to step out into a new existence of respectability is much easier, because it can be done through a mere choice of suitor. I found a young London Ted in a moment of self-criticism making this point to me quite explicitly, almost jealously. Women, he said, always have something extra in them a man hadn't got: "You take a girl that's got in with a gang of hoodlums. You think she's just a slut, but one day you will see her walking arm in arm in the High Street with a fellow and not even looking at the gang as she passes. Mind you, the boys would never tell. They might feel sorry for the fellow who didn't know what he'd got hold of, but they'd give the girl a chance to forget." There is an old masculine code—their own—even among Drifters.

Has the Teddy boy movement in fact had much impact on the life of adolescent girls in this country? It is hard to give an answer.

In 1958 there were by Home Office statistics about 11,000 un-married mothers of 16 and under in this country, a small number but double that of 1952. From another angle, about one unmarried woman in 80 in the under-20 group had an illegitimate child during 1938; in 1958 the figure was one in 50, in 1959 one in 40. This does show a trend, but the absolute figure remains small— the Teddy boy movement has been a mainly masculine affair.

To return to the boys themselves, the main harmful consequences of their sexual outlook is that in their violent conduct it is mixed up with deliberate callousness. Not, of course, for ever. In the end, even the wildest Teddy boy as a rule arrives at the point where traditional morality reasserts itself, usually at the point of the shotgun. "My girl's got a baby coming. Didn't want to get married, but what can you do?" Even so, the Teddy boy years may have their consequences: one observation to this effect was made by my Irish informant:

> The way they live, free sexual intercourse is almost universal. They get it where they want it. They don't care where. They'll go to a dance-hall, pick up a girl, have intercourse and finish with her, never see her again. The result is they've nothing to look forward to when they get married. These lads are worn out, they've got no excitement left in sex before marriage. So most of them can't make marriage a go and that's where the new trouble begins for them. Have you noticed one thing—these young fellows, at the start they don't drink. They'll stay all night in a café but you don't see them much in pubs. But when they're older, when they've settled down and got married, that's when they start drinking. They're restless, marriage means almost nothing, but if they start going back to the cafés the wife will get to know about it. But if they say they're going round to the pub it sounds harmless. They say they're just going round for a game of darts or bridge, but that's where they pick up women and go in for really heavy drinking when they're a few years older.

And it is then that they may also go in for the more dangerous types of crime such as pay-roll snatching.

ALIENS FROM OUTER SPACE

One can probably also see a revealing lack of self-confidence in the Teddy boy attitude towards the foreigners against whom they may run up—Americans, Poles, Cypriots, Irish, West Indians and Africans. London has been becoming steadily more cosmopolitan for years, but to the Teddy boys all except the Irish evidently still seem like aliens from outer space intruding into their manor, and fiercely resented as such.

Xenophobia is of course not confined to any country or class, but the Teddy boy attitude towards foreigners displays a particular nuance of anxiety. Sexual jealousy is naturally a prominent element—witness the hostile reaction of Teddy boys towards American servicemen all over the country which has led to a number of bars being declared out of bounds to American personnel and in general to a retreat from fraternization. The Teds are of course not alone in demonstrating such anti-American feelings. It has been the common experience in these islands that English working-class girls brought up on a staple diet of women's magazines have tended to find American servicemen glamorous while their boy-friends naturally reacted in the opposite way— there's a defensive ring in the word "Yanks". This has been surprisingly little affected by the mass media. If we take a typical young English worker who is in the habit of taking his girl twice a week or more to the pictures, to gaze at American films redolent with American values and speech, superficially such a young man might already look a little Americanized. That is, he might have picked up a few American slang phrases or an American style of haircut. But put this young man next to a real American G.I. and the result could be almost embarrassing. The two might well have almost nothing to say to each other. Real national character is not easily discarded in the dark of a cinema.

All this applies *a fortiori* to the Teddy boys and helps to explain their particularly strong anti-American feelings. On the one hand, their own social life is abnormally dominated by American films and pop music and imagined American behaviour—by what one might call their "Americanese" culture. On the other hand, this Teddy boy culture is also more than ordinarily superficial and unreal and here lies a reason for Teddy boy touchiness.

For example, let a group of real American servicemen come into a café crowded with Teddy boys who have been listening to the juke-box as it drooled in Americanese, and in a flash the atmosphere would be changed, the look on the faces watching the intruders would be guarded, hostile—I have myself seen this happen in the West End on several occasions. Nor was it hard to see the basic reason for the clash. As far as the boys in the Teddy boy suits were concerned, the presence of live Americans was enough to expose the non-existence of their own Americanese culture on which they laid so much value. The crime of the Americans was that they laid bare the vulnerability of Teddy boy society—something to which a Ted could only react by extra toughness. The ordinary Teddy boy might not be able to express his reaction in words, and probably would not want to; still, his hostile attitude to Americans as a whole reveals awareness of a real threat to his status and an instant reaction against this.

TEDS, CYPS AND SPADES

Another revealing relation in contemporary London is that between the Teddy boys and the Cypriot café owners in whose establishments the Teds spend so much of their time and their money. The post-war immigration of Greek and Turkish Cypriots to London has always struck me as a fascinating accidental consequence of Empire, if probably one of the last of its kind. Here they are, steeped in Mediterranean culture, these emigrants from Aphrodite's lovely island, with its classic shores and Crusaders' castles, its white-washed monasteries and minarets, its fierce sunshine and olives and vines. Now they are in their cafés among the brick and grime in Upper Street, around King's Cross, in the Tottenham Court Road and Hammersmith, swarthy men standing behind their tea and coffee machines, chattering to their families in demotic Greek, to the background noise of the juke-box, as they survey the London Teds and their girls who form the main part of their night-time clientele. What thoughts pass behind their dark brows? The picture to my mind was always one of mutual dislike; each side despising the other: the Teds looking down on the Cypriots as foreigners not regarded as quite "white", while it was not hard to guess how the Cypriots must despise these louts who provided them with custom and at the same time insulted them. As it happens, by coming to London and opening a number of late-night cafés, the Cypriots have largely aided the expansion of Teddy boy café society. But the operation has been attended by little goodwill. In Teddy boy talk of fighting in North London, that is, talk of battles far from those fought for Enosis, the "Cyps", that is Greek and Turkish Cypriots, their cafés and plate-glass windows, featured frequently as "the enemy". The hard-working Cypriots in their cafés were "raking in the money" which the Teddy boys spent. Although they were still new in London, they were rapidly getting on, while the Teds were not getting on. True it might be by their own choice, but then there was always an element of doubt about this choice itself—enough cause for anger.

General prejudice apart, I think the same anxiety lies also behind the fierce hostility of the London Teddy boys against the Coloured immigrants. Of course, other factors are involved. On the whole the Teddy boys have much the same amount of colour prejudice as the rest of the British population, sometimes more, sometimes less, but to understand the reasons why the Notting Hill riots attracted Teddy boys from all over London into the battle, one has to try to see what was involved for them. There was, for example, the question of status. To a Teddy boy who insists on a social status of which he is always unsure, it is vitally important that no Coloured immigrant should be better than he, or even an equal. The same applies to sexual jealousy: to boys to whom indiscriminate sex is a substitute for all their inadequacies, the sight of a Negro with a white girl may seem like a knife-thrust against their masculinity.

Then there is social and economic jealousy. When listening to the tale of Teddy boy grievances against the West Indians, I found that one of the first complaints was always that West Indians were making quick money and riding in flashy cars, and this money came from the immoral earnings of white and Coloured prostitutes. The complaint is revealing. After all, the typical Teddy boys are not against any man who makes money ruthlessly. They rather admire such a person. Nor are they against immoral earnings as such. In the ordinary Teddy boy café it does not take long to learn the identity of the local ponces, and the information is given without sign of disapproval. No, the rationalizations hide a more basic clash, namely that the Teddy boys and the West Indian immigrants who are working side by side are trying to travel in different directions. As new immigrants the West Indians are to begin with underdogs, but once they make good there are again no underdogs below the Teds. As new immigrants, again, the West Indians are very noticeably trying to get on, to make money and gain status. But the Teds don't want to get on; to join their movement is in fact to oppose getting on, to live in a dream of endless rebellion. In this dream picture, it is essential that the Coloured in their territory should feature as lesser beings. Any Coloured man who does not stay put but instead rises and buys up houses or a big car destroys this picture of security and so represents a profound threat. It is against this threat that the ranks in an area like Notting Hill have been tightly closed so that, for example, local youth clubs (even those visited by Prince Philip) have not been able to admit Coloured boys.

THE FEAR OF AUTHORITY

I think that much the same feelings have helped to produce the violent antagonism of the Teddy boys towards the police, about which something ought to be said.

It has been important for the development of the Teddy boy fashion that the gang should give its members a sense of reassurance. This feeling is, of course, quite irrational, at least as far as the authorities are concerned. Every new arrest exposes the futility of the whole rebellion, and this, in turn explains their violent antagonism towards the police. A hostile attitude towards the police is, of course, common to a good many working-class adolescents. For historic reasons, the police in England have been for long widely regarded as the defenders of upper-class property against the mobs from the slums, the revolutionary mob, i.e. a good part of the old working class. This hostile working-class view of the police is still strongly held, and much of it has survived slum clearance. "There's little sympathy among that class for the police," said an informant to me in talking about the families of Teddy boys. "In any tough criminal area there is never respect for the police: they are looked on purely as oppressors. When there was that stabbing in Holloway, when a policeman was killed, the one thing everybody said was: 'They'll make damn sure *somebody'll* hang for it.' Even the older working men in the pubs who usually dislike the Teds were talking in that strain."

It is this anti-police tradition, with its elements of old class struggle, which the Teddy boys have now turned into a social vogue. It goes naturally enough with the other aspects of their rebellion, but I think there is something more than just this tradition involved. Talking to boys of all ages in London, good and bad, Teds and ex-Teds, I found a single-minded acceptance of a state of Cold War between themselves and the police which was startlingly uniform. Indeed, in Teddy boy mythology it was the police who were the enemy aggressors. Like enemies, they were simultaneously despised and feared. They were despised, for instance, as cowards hiding behind their uniform. "You see a copper walk past a crowd of fellows when he's alone and if some-body calls out a remark it's ten to one he'll pretend not to hear—he'll walk on. They're only brave when there's two of them so they can give evidence." At the same time the police were feared because it was thought that their primary aim was "to get the Boys", to knock them about at the station, and to manufacture pretexts for charges. There was a prevalent idea that the police could always spoil a boy's career and frequently were out to do so. "I'm not afraid of the coppers, but I know, if they possibly can, they will put you on a charge. They will say anything, that you resisted arrest, that you were carrying horrible weapons. Result? You're put on probation. That means you've got a record—you can't get a good job." The police were also regarded as the enemy who stopped the Boys from leading their rightful and carefree social life. In one area they were held responsible for closing all the late-night cafés; in another, for the break-up of the large gangs. "It's all the coppers. These days, if they saw a dozen fellows standing together, they'll tell them they'll have them up for an affray. It's getting so they'll tell you to move on if they just see two blokes on the pavement."

And so on—listening to the plaintive talk, one got a sense that in these adolescent circles a constant state of war with the police was accepted as just one of the facts of life. Now, there may be some partial factual basis to this clash. After all, the juvenile crime wave *is* a reality. As the Commissioner of Police for the Metropolis reported in 1958, two-thirds of all arrests for shop-breaking, warehouse-breaking, etc., involved young persons under 21 (and two-fifths juveniles under 17). Faced with the rising wave of juvenile crime, and no doubt egged on by their superiors, the police in some areas have certainly taken to chivvying local Teddy boys suspected as being a cause of trouble. How much of this talk of the boys being beaten up at the station ought to be discounted is hard to say—it is by now almost a point of honour for an arrested boy to make this claim. But no doubt a certain amount of rough handling does go on and is a cause of genuine fear. I was for instance told on good authority about one gang of particularly reckless 16-year-olds: "No matter how tough these young fellows think they are, they remain dead scared of the police. They know once the police get them into the cells, they won't be handled with kid gloves—and that knowledge is always in their minds."

THE SHOCK OF RECOGNITION

Yet, at least for the older boys, the fear of being physically knocked about is not the most important thing. The real and overwhelming fear is that once a boy is arrested and sitting in a cell, his whole illusion, his whole fantasy of being safe as a member of a gang is suddenly taken from him, and it is this loss which is so terrifying. Each time another hero is arrested, a myth is destroyed. The power of the police represents in fact the flaw in the Teddy boy's dream of secure rebellion. The more intense the fantasy, i.e. the more neurotic a boy's belief that as a member of the gang he can live amorally, do what he likes and disregard the law, the more intense also becomes his hatred of the police, who threaten the fantasy.

It is of course not only the authority of the police which exposes the Teddy boy rebellion. Behind the police stand the Courts, the power of magistrates and judges. As the futile young rebels come up against the real strength of the society they had tried to oppose, the result is usually an overwhelming shock. There are of course a minority who remain hardened, but I have often heard the opposite stories of reckless young Teddy boy offenders who, when they find themselves in the dock, are at first as dazed as young prisoners of war whose entire familiar universe had collapsed. A social worker from West London who had attended the Court proceedings where some of his boys were up on fairly serious charges gave me this picture:

The thing which shocked me extremely was my own lack of preparation for seeing the boys in Court look so differently from what I had thought they were like in their normal social setting. They looked even physically smaller—they were really only infants, suddenly finding themselves completely helpless and without even being able to express it. When I asked them about this they didn't know how to put it into words, but what seemed to me the worst was the sudden awareness on their part that all their fantasy strengths were of no use to them. The boys were now surrounded by police, having to answer to a person who had very definite authority—it was not a matter of their giving this man authority—they weren't asked. I think their helplessness was linked with something else as well, that no matter how many do-gooders there were in their outside world, at this point they could not be helped. Where even that failed, everything had failed them.

Of course, this sense of shock—the shock of recognition—does not last. Youth is resilient and adaptable. Once sentenced, most boys adjust themselves. Even Borstal and Detention Centres become eventually slices of real life, with irksome restrictions but also the positive experience of companionship, and which in any case soon pass. Their reactions to it naturally vary almost infinitely, but two points seem to stand out. First, while the present crime wave indicates that the boys have outside become noticeably more troublesome, the authorities "inside" claim that they are no more difficult to manage than they or their predecessors were before, which seems to indicate that when the sense of insecurity is less, as it nearly always is in institutions, so is the need for defiance. The second point is the striking contrast between the intractability of some Teddy boy leaders when they are out in the street with the mob and their evident helplessness when they are on their own and have to face an unfamiliar situation. An older ex-prisoner, who had seen a good many characteristic Teddy boys pass through his establishment, put this to me with some contempt (his comments applied to the time a few years back when young offenders were still sent to prison in some numbers, which is now rarely the case):

When they're in a group together, they're ready to tear any place apart, but get one of them on his own—he wouldn't say boo to a goose. He might be definitely against the rules, but the warder would need only take him round the corner and clip his earholes for him and he'd cave in. I've seen them come and go. Once they're inside they're nothing. The first month they always write the same sort of letter: "Dear Mum, I'm very sorry for what I did and I won't repeat it. When I come out I want to go respectable. I'm going to go steady with Jeanie down the road, etc." They'd often cry, too, not in front of the others, but when they're on their own. I got friendly with one who'd been a sort of king of the Teddy boys down his way. I looked in one time through the spy hole—I was a "red-hand" then—and saw he was crying on and on, though of course he denied it when I mentioned it. The way they're helpless on their own is pathetic in the case of many of them. Immediately they're up against anything really important, any major decision, they're helpless.

That is, unless something—the right girl, the right friends, a job or merely the advance of time—helps them to pass from their adolescent insecurity.

However, the shock of arrest and the experience of detention can also have the opposite effect. One way of covering up fear and insecurity is by renewed defiance. And circumstances often encourage this. When boys get out, the same environment is often waiting to receive them again, the same street, the life of the Pictures, pubs and pool-parlour; the Boys still at the corner and in the cafés, the same old talk of clothes, sex, fights and nicking. How quickly before a boy is back in his old ways? With the difference only that what he has undergone has become a mark of higher status in the gang—now he can feel really tough. There is always this danger. As Lady Wootton has written, "It is easy to underestimate the effect of appearances in Court or of residence in approved schools, Borstal or prison, in creating a delinquent culture based on common experience."[1] How far this happens is hard to know. So are the ways of preventing it. But this is another story.

[1] Barbara Wootton, *Social Science and Social Pathology*. Allen & Unwin, 1959.

CHAPTER XI

Sports Day in the Meritocracy

A DIGRESSION

I WAS reminded of the opening of Orwell's *1984* where his hero Winston Smith slips through the doors of Victory Mansions on a bright, cold day in April "as the clocks were striking thirteen". In a sentence the reader is carried into a cold and eerie future.

As I reached Feltham in the Thames Valley on my way to attend a sports day at the local Borstal Institution, the same thing seemed to happen to me, only in reverse—I felt carried back into the past. In a weary other existence I had been writing of politics and the Cold War, but as soon as I drew up by car outside the little railway station at Feltham, I appeared to step into a smaller, more innocent and less-troubled world.

The heat wave sun was blazing down, the day was August Bank Holiday, and the little suburban station and the streets leading from it might have been a scene from a novel by H. G. Wells. The perspiring young policeman at the corner, who was talking to two girls as I approached, was friendly and forthcoming. "I know," he said, "everybody is asking me the directions to the Borstal. Those two girls are going there too." I whisked the two of them out of the bus queue and into my car. They were from the Midlands and dressed in Sunday best. They told me they had spent hours in getting to London and then this far, and were going back the same evening. No, they weren't visiting a brother. "We've come to visit her boy," said the taller girl on behalf of her friend. He had been at Feltham for six months. Yes, he now admitted he had been going with the wrong lot. Both girls spoke with a heavy Midlands accent. It did not go with the elegant lines of their gay nylon dresses, impeccably designed for them by Marks and Spencer. Nor did their make-up, their unsuitable high heels and coloured nails, I thought, but what did it matter? They were tremulously young and eager. This trip to London and a Borstal was an outing for them, and their excitement communicated itself to me. They had no idea what to expect—they would be pleasantly surprised when they saw the place, I reassured them.

Nobody bothered to check passes as I drove through the gates along an avenue of trees and drew up in what was already a crowded car-park. My companions looked in some awe at the complex of red brick buildings and all the cars and the groups of animated people all making for the sports ground. "I didn't think it'd look like this —I thought it'd be sort of cold and gloomy," said the one whose boy-friend was in forced residence here.

The path to the sports ground led us through the shade of a group of tall elms. Here the Governor, efficient, brisk, cheerful, looking younger than his years, stood receiving his guests. On his right was a roped-off staff and V.I.P. enclosure, with rows of chairs and groups of people talking outside a tea-tent. The setting might have been one for a local gymkhana or school sports day. There were the local dignitaries, the friends of the staff, the house-masters' wives, one or two distinguished figures of unmistakable military background, pretty young things, young men in flannels. . . . After a short time I slipped away to another enclosure, across the way, where parents, relatives and friends of the boys were waiting for them, and looked around me.

From here, too, I might have been looking at the setting of any English sports day. The field ordinarily was the cricket ground. On the far side stood a large, grey Victorian chapel, which on this day carried a big banner with the words "World Refugee Year"— as announced in the programme, the function and its sideshows were on behalf of that cause. On my left the field was enclosed by a high wall, above which I could see the tops of buses with their advertisements as they travelled along the road. Elsewhere the ground was bordered by tall elm-trees, throwing their shade on the refreshment tent and a number of stalls for hoopla and similar diversions. The centre of the field held the paraphernalia of sports day, such as hurdles, and a stand for officials and loudspeakers. The enclosure where I found myself held a fair-sized little crowd, mostly of relatives of the boys, but including a few girl-friends. The hot sunshine had already sent the first customers in search of tea and minerals; middle-aged men sat on the benches in shirt-sleeves. A handful of Teds in their full regalia stood in a group by themselves; children ran about on the verge of the field; I saw the two girls I had accompanied, still looking a little lost, and waved to them.

At a signal the loudspeakers launched into a military march, and now, led by the Cadet Corps, the Feltham Boys entered the grounds, each House marching in its own column with flag held high—under the public school system usual at Borstals, Feltham had five Houses: North, South, East, West and New House. As this year's function was under the auspices of World Refugee Year, the columns also carried the flags of all the United Nations. I noticed the Hammer and Sickle, the Red Star of Yugoslavia and the green flags of the Arab States before losing count. How many sovereign flags there were today, I thought; more than eighty of them, easily enough for five marching columns! The boys paraded smartly in formation. At the head of each column strode its physical training instructor, chest out, arms swinging, eyes front. Next came the athletes in their running gear, and then the rest of the House in the Feltham uniform of dark blue jacket of battle-dress type and grey flannel trousers, and finally the Housemaster bringing up the rear. The music rose in volume as the columns formed up in line opposite the guests and the flags—all the eighty-plus flags of the United Nations—were held in salute. There was really an odd touch of cultural dilution here, I thought. This ritual of marching and flags had in the past been part of the patriotic tradition of King and Country and Empire. Was there any real meaning in holding up as many as eighty sovereign flags of the United Nations, even in terms of present-day enlighten-ment?

But the ceremony was already over and the Feltham boys were swarming into our enclosure. I found myself in the middle of family reunions. Here a mother flung her arms unrestrainedly round her son; there a father looked rather more embarrassed as he shook hands; all round me boys were eagerly or awkwardly, as the case might be, greeting their visitors, that is, those who had visitors, for quite a few had none. Certain boys now took up their places at the stalls. I walked over to the one which said "United Nations Association". On a table lay literature explaining the plight of the refugees. The two boys who looked after the stall did not seem to me very much concerned with it. The large poster behind them referred to the Palestine refugees and stated: "End their enforced idleness—give them the means to work!" Was there a touch of irony in this poster in this place?

The first runners were now assembling and the races about to start. Music emerged from the loudspeakers, the opening strains of the familiar recorded selections from "My Fair Lady". Across the sunny field floated the precise voice of Rex Harrison as Professor Higgins: "Look at her, a prisoner of the gutters, condemned by every syllable she utters." Shaw brought in musical guise to Borstal—was this also a sign of enlightenment or of a cultural dilution hard to assess? The music was abruptly cut off. After a moment's silence, the starter set off the hundred yards runners. From the boys around me came loud, brief yells of encouragement. Like all hundred yards races, this one seemed over almost before it had started. An educated masculine voice announced the result. On a stand showing the relative points gathered by each House, a red, a green, and a yellow disc were raised to varying heights. Then the music was back, and again it was Harrison as Higgins, demanding across the chatter of honest Cockney, Midlands and North Country voices around me: "*Why* can't the English teach their children how to speak?" And another voice, this time a live voice, announced: "The next race in your programme will be the mile." And so it went on.

It was hard, as the afternoon wore on, not to let myself drowsily lose the awareness of my surroundings. The splendid August sunshine poured down on to the field. In the mind of someone of my years, nostalgic emotions and remembrance were inevitably stirred by the deep peace of the whole scene, the sight of white-clad runners against the green grass, the ripples of applause, the relaxed Bank Holiday mood. The races followed each other; results were announced and the Houses went up and down in the lead. Rex Harrison entoned very precisely "I shall never let a woman in my life", the selections from "My Fair Lady" were succeeded by those from "Oklahoma". On the spectators' benches around me, everybody was relaxed. Hot brows were mopped, shirt collars opened, tea and minerals carried constantly from the tent. The smaller children, by now bored with the sports, were running to and fro in games of their own. My young girl from the Midlands was now with her boy. They stood with arms enlaced but quite motionless, as if not one second in these precious hours could be lost. The puzzle of the presence of the small group of Teds was also solved. They were recent Old Boys, alumni of Feltham, eager to show off their freedom and new clothes, yet still drawn by the old associations.

Keeping to the shade of the trees, I wandered as on a slow pendulum between the staff and V.I.P. enclosure, and that where the boys with visitors, and also those without visitors, were gathered. And in my mind, too, I swung as on a pendulum between the illusion that this was just another ordinary sports day and the knowledge that we were all inside a closed and relatively strict Borstal; that the whole occasion had been staged with considerable trouble and much care and goodwill to provide the three hundred boys with just such an impression of Bank Holiday normality—yet before long the scene would be ended, the visitors would be gone, the posters for World Refugee Year taken away, the boys would be back in the buildings, and keys would be turned in locks as if the clocks were again striking thirteen. Talking to some of the boys who stood in the shade of the trees, watching their faces and bearing, I tried to get just a hint of what was in their minds. Desire under the elms?—they were sweating out their time, of course, but what else were they thinking as they watched us?

IN AND OUT

I had been here before.

Some months earlier I had visited Feltham on an ordinary working day. Within the graded Borstal system Feltham was designated, as I knew, for boys of average ability or below and presenting some difficulty on that account. Many of its young offenders came under the heading of "retarded", that is, prevented by circumstance or emotional disturbance from attaining even the educational standard they should have reached. Some were also retarded in attaining their physical maturity. While Feltham was not the place for extreme problem cases of maladjustment demanding specialist treatment, through this selection a particularly large proportion of boys who were here had backgrounds of unhappy homes and disturbed childhood. Included in their number were young homosexuals and habitual offenders. All in all, they were a selection of boys who at the age of 17 and upwards still needed care and protection as much as deterrents. At Feltham they were kept apart from the type of young tough who was over-adequate rather than inadequate. Rather more than the ordinary run of boys sentenced, those in residence at Feltham could be thus described as victims of circumstances.

They remain at Feltham for an average of twenty months, during which time it is endeavoured to provide entirely different circumstances for them—the basis of the Borstal system is, after all, total control. During my visit I had walked through the dormitories where, beside each bed, clothes and possessions were laid out neatly in boarding school or institutional manner. Above the beds I saw pin-ups of film stars and also—I don't quite know why I felt there was a slight pathos in this—photographs of admired young singers like Tommy Steele and Terry Dene. Passing out of doors, I saw parties of boys in overalls, all busy at work. Some were being trained in the machine-shop and carpenter's shop. In the latter, a woodwork instructor proudly showed me a kitchen dresser which a boy had just completed and demonstrated how precisely the shelves and drawers fitted. "Any cabinet maker would be pleased to have done this," he said and, as I complimented him, added without prompting: "This is one of the deep satisfactions we get from the job." In the building workers' section, other boys were learning to lay bricks and to paint and paper walls. There were some parties who went out on lorries to work on surrounding farms. Within the walls, other boys in overalls were at work in hothouses, in the kitchen and the laundry. If I made myself forget all kinds of things and concentrated only on the visual image, the scene was like a mixture of the atmosphere of army life and an agricultural school.

In the later part of my visit I looked over the facilities for leisure time; the football, cricket and netball fields; the swimming-pool; the library and television facilities. I was shown photographs of the Feltham Cadet Corps and of tousled boys at the annual summer camp. I visited the Compass Club, a pleasant little club premise with spick-and-span modern décor, a gramophone and a small canteen, where at certain times boys who had achieved the privilege of membership could meet and talk to visitors from outside. Outwardly, the whole effect of the institution was at times like that of an ordinary training school. The basic difference lay, of course, in the strict regulations and the visible and constant supervision. The boys were never alone. They walked in quick march to meals and to and from work. Their bearing betrayed an awareness that a constant eye was kept on them by the officers. I was told and could well believe that to certain boys this fact was not without a sense of comfort.

Feltham is not numbered among the experimental Borstals. On the contrary, from the nature of its human material it is run as a routine closed institution. Nevertheless, I thought one could see precisely in a place like this how in the Borstals of today the old spirit of the reformatory was fundamentally tempered by three influences. The first was humanitarianism. The average stay of boys was shorter. Even in closed Borstals like Feltham there was much less stress on lock and key. More boys spent their days in working parties outside the walls. More women were employed inside the institution and could be seen walking freely through the grounds. Much more emphasis than in the past was laid on after-care—the maintenance of contact with the families and with the boys after release had today become a specialist task. The second tempering influence, England being England, was still that of Dr Arnold, on whose public school lines the Borstal system had been originally modelled. Feltham's five Houses, with fifty to sixty boys each, had their own common rooms and were designed as units small enough for a boy to become attached to it. The Houses had their colours; at games the boys competed for their House. The carefully chosen Housemasters, always there for a boy to talk to, were key figures in the institution—authority embodied in firm but understanding father figures, or that was the basic theory.

The third tempering influence, which fitted in rather surprisingly with that of Dr Arnold, was that of Dr Freud. By now, even a superficial visitor to a Borstal institution is made to realize how far the doctrine of the decisive importance of early childhood experience and of the unconscious motivation of aggression is accepted at every stage of a boy's rehabilitation, at any rate in theory. This is illustrated by the reports of psychiatric social workers or of psychiatrists in the files of many boys, or in the investigation into a boy's family life, where the cause of his offences may lie, and the attempt to rebuild his family ties so as to restore his sense of security. What struck me most, because it was not so in the past, was the general present-day acceptance of the view that a member of the service should never react directly to a boy's aggressiveness, but should always appear unmoved and seek to lower the emotional tension. That is to say, the attitude of a boy arriving after a preliminary stay in prison at a Borstal was usually one of "all you screws are so-and-so's", but after a number of weeks he almost always came to realize that the screw was not necessarily a so-and-so, but also an ordinary person. I was told that today this point is undoubtedly reached much sooner, now that every "screw", too, was aware that the obstreperous boy in question might have had a raw deal, perhaps a drunken father or neglectful mother, and so was transferring his hostility against his parents to other authority figures such as the screw himself—one should therefore try to understand his aggression rather than react in kind.

In all these ways the Borstal system has certainly become more enlightened, and, if the word can be used, scientific—one could observe these trends clearly even at a strict unexperimental institution like Feltham. And yet progress is not easy. Indeed, quite the reverse. In conversations with officers one always came back to the basic difficulty of trying to effect a total social control within the gates which would be related to the society outside. And this difficulty was always renewed.

"To you these boys may look like a quiet, pleasant-looking bunch, but if you went into some of their records, you'd be horrified. It's lapses, again and again. I believe that these days we run the danger that the boys become too easily institutionalized. While they're inside with us they're fine—but they can't stand on their feet in the outside world."

There has been some disappointment that, as fairly rigid statistical research has shown, the Borstal system has a degree of success in the re-education of boys, but it is not as large as was hoped at one time.

"To my mind," said another officer, "these recurring lapses show the difficulties which boys of the lower I.Q. groups face as society grows more complex. They have not only got to know how to handle complicated machinery at work. To keep up with the talk of the other fellows, they are nowadays expected to be conversant with things like motor-bikes, portable radios and record-players. They have got to find their way through tabloid newspapers and know how to play the Pools. Just take this one example. I recently asked a whole class of boys whether any of them had filled in a Pools coupon. Not one of them had done so—because their minds weren't up to it. Just think what this means when they are with the others."

I let my own thoughts stray. "To an outsider like myself it would seem that what these boys need is a leisurely rural society, where they could walk slowly down the lane with the horses, or assist the cobbler or blacksmith. But that's the one thing you can't give them."

"We can't. All we can give is more specialist training in cabinet making and deeper psychiatric study and more extensive after-care. . . . In these directions we advance every year, but even so some of us are afraid that we can go too far in becoming specialized. In the old days, a Housemaster was in touch with all sides of a boy's life without the intervention of too many separate specialists. If he was an intelligent and devoted Housemaster, could he have done quite as much for a boy as is done more scientifically today? We can't say. We know that today we must try new methods to train these boys but we also know we are still in the dark."

THE LITTLE VICTIMS

My earlier visit to Feltham Borstal had been on a winter's day, and now it was bright mid-summer. The afternoon was waning and the end of the sports day was in sight. The flags of the United Nations stood on one side, unnoticed. As was traditional in the last stage of a sports day, the inter-House races were succeeded by a gym display (respectful applause), a tug-of-war (great yells of encouragement) and a father's race (loud laughter). Everybody on the field looked less tense and more relaxed than at the beginning of the afternoon, including the Feltham boys themselves in their blue battledress jackets. Watching their faces, I was still trying to decide whether I could gather any one general impression. There were rather too many unformed faces with a hesitant, defensive appeal. Collectively they looked like boys who'd had a difficult time and were not unaware of handicap. While no doubt mainly concerned with sweating out their time, they had already a touch of institutional adaptation. They were noticeably quieter than they would have been elsewhere. I had often had the experience that when I looked at such boys in the outside world even for a second too long, there was often a dark answering look or even a quick vocal challenge. Here (they knew better) there was none of this. When I spoke to any of them they answered respectfully and to the point. But they also showed a betraying touch of passivity towards their surroundings. When a member of their House looked like winning, they would cheer loudly, but as soon as he did not, their interest quickly waned. The influence of Dr Arnold on their lives could not but be thin. But so, when one came down to it, was that of Dr Freud, as represented by the reports and analyses on forms of different colours in their files. Even at best, how much could overworked officials, who must go quickly from case to case, discover about the causes of a boy's psychological disturbance in the course of a few interviews?

The important fact, I thought, was that after the total social control at Borstal, the uncontrolled street corner with its confused and accidental contacts was always waiting again for these boys. The tops of the red buses with their advertisements, which could be seen travelling along the road beyond the playing field walls, were a reminder of the world that began immediately at the gates of Feltham. Somehow this contrast gave me a disturbing feeling. I seemed to be acutely aware that the society into which these boys would go out was one where everything was growing bigger. It was a society where the concentration of business was continuing at a hectic pace, headlines were growing larger, and accepted moral standards more confused, automation made further inroads, competitiveness at every social level was growing fiercer and the intellectual caste system that had caused the name "meritocracy" to be coined for this form of society was growing more pronounced. How well would the Borstal boys who now stood under the elms fare twenty years hence in this society which by then would be that much more like itself?

The last competition was concluded. The sports day was over and concluding announcements were being made. Visitors were now invited on a tour of certain Feltham buildings. I stopped for a while at the swimming-pool, where some boys displayed the life-saving techniques they had been taught. After this, the whole surroundings began suddenly to look emptier. With the discipline of knowing exactly what they had to do, most of the boys were passing through doors which closed behind them. I went along with a little stream of visitors to the Compass Club. It looked crowded; dance music came from the record-player. The little group of Teds, the recent Old Boys, were still here, together with some present members. They looked eager and nodded and swayed to the music, safely back in the familiarity of the rhythm of rock and roll and of American voices. As I left the club, the locks were being turned elsewhere in Feltham. The car-park looked already empty and deserted and my mood turned to melancholy. I told myself that it was all not so harsh—later this evening, for instance, there was to be a film show for all the boys—but as I drove away and reached the main road, I was at once swallowed up in heavy queues of holiday traffic returning to London, and there was something almost sinister in this crowd effect. At any rate, there was one disturbing idea I could not get out of my mind. I thought of the three hundred boys I had been watching on this sports day. It seemed to me they had been hard dealt with by life. Some looked outwardly handicapped and others apparently normal—at any rate they were now all offenders, but more vividly than before I now also saw them as victims of a mechanized society where the slow went to the wall and, as the lines of intellectual caste sharpened, so the number of such young offenders who were left behind would shoot up. Perhaps this would not happen. It was always dangerous to extend present trends into the future. But the vision was disturbing.

Part Three
DISCUSSION

CHAPTER XII

The Penal Angle

LOOKING BACKWARDS

IN principle, what should one do to stop a juvenile crime wave—educate the young offenders out of the error of their ways, or use tougher methods to teach them a different lesson?

The discovery that the attraction of crime, and especially of juvenile crime, does not necessarily diminish with the spread of education, with slum clearance and enlightened prison reform, has in recent years caused confusion in a number of countries which are approaching that stage of material well-being described as "the affluent society".

In a country as conscious of its special history as Britain, this confusion in penal thinking has naturally had its insular bias. Visitors to these islands have often expressed astonishment at the inordinate interest of the press and the public in arguments about capital punishment and corporal punishment. In the 1950s they could also have noted a growing division of views in this penal debate. While Mr Butler, presiding over the Home Office, was expressing his pained feelings over the rise of crime in all age-groups and promising measures of penal reform and more research work into criminology, an extremely vocal body of British opinion was resolutely opposed to this soft approach towards offenders. At annual Tory Party conferences, Mr Butler was regularly commanded by the Conservative Women to bring back corporal punishment for crimes of violence and sexual assault—flog the hide off the young thugs! A sizeable group of Tory back-benchers at Westminster and of frequent correspondents to *The Times* also favoured reintroducing this time-honoured British deterrent, and the demand was voiced not only by lay opinion. It had the support of some magistrates and judges and in cautious form even of the Lord Chief Justice, Lord Parker, who declared in October 1959: "No one has ever suggested going back to the cat. That is brutal and makes martyrs. But what harm can there be in general in the cane or the birch? It has just that amount of indignity about it which is a deterrent."[1] Yet while this pressure was mounting, Mr Butler and his Home Office advisers showed no sign of yielding to it—on the contrary, they appeared completely preoccupied in collating the results of various research studies to discover to what degree various penal methods in use were in fact curative and/or deterrent at all.

To understand the current British penal confusion, it has to be seen in the context of some fairly obstinate historic British attitudes. Looking back to, say, 1800, one can see three distinct phases in British thinking about crime which could be called respectively the phase of brutality, that of humiliation, and that of enlightenment. All three have left their strong mark on the present phase in penal thinking, which to my mind began around 1950 and could be called an age of doubt.

To start with brutality. The early nineteenth century, the colourful age of coal and steam, the Corinthians and bare-knuckle fighters, was also an era of intensified penal savagery. The shock of the French Revolution had penetrated pretty deeply into the mind of the British ruling class; the vision of the tumbrils was never far away, nor was fear of the reputedly lawless and dangerous proletariat of the early Industrial Revolution. As a result, the list of offences which carried the penalty of death by hanging was steadily increased to over 200, including such pretty crimes as the proverbial stealing of a sheep or a shilling. If ever savage penalties should have proved a successful deterrent, it should have been under these shocking laws. Yet they proved a failure, for stealing and other crime went on and it was the Courts which had to impose such sentences which faltered. In spite of the conviction of eminent authorities that these penalties could not be relaxed without mortal danger to the State, public opinion forced a change: but this period of nineteenth-century brutality has clearly left a long-standing heritage behind in British penal thinking.

[1] From the Labour Party side, this support for corporal punishment was usually described as Tory class prejudice: but to the discomfiture of Labour spokesmen, a Gallup Poll investigation (*News Chronicle*, 21 March 1960) indicated that 74 per cent. of the British population wanted a return of corporal punishment—the emotional word was "flogging"—for crimes of violence, and 74 per cent. wanted judges to be given more power to hang.

The Victorian reformers tried new methods. They were bourgeois, self-confident, and in their fashion wanted to be humanitarian: for the ordinary run of offences they abolished the gallows and substituted long prison sentences. As rationalists they were convinced that if the result of an action was painful, the individual would refrain from it. To represent a painful deterrent against crime, Victorian prisons were therefore deliberately designed as repressive and humiliating institutions. But the Victorians also believed that solitary confinement, giving a prisoner the chance to meditate on his sins, had an outstanding moral value in leading him towards redemption. And they were most methodical about it all. It was Jeremy Bentham himself who designed the famous radial honeycomb of cells which became the accepted pattern of Victorian prisons. The result of all these combined views was a network of large, claustrophobic British prison buildings. The Victorians were great builders: starting with Pentonville in 1842, within a decade 55 prisons were built with a total of 11,000 cells where individuals unfortunate enough to offend against society could be kept suitably out of sight.

As deterrents against the prevalence of crime, however, these great prisons failed just as hanging had done—this was the lesson. The Gladstone Commission at the end of the century noted that because they demoralized and brutalized their inmates, the grim prisons acted in fact as breeding-grounds of new crime. So again there was a change of view in penal thinking, and the first half of the twentieth century could be called a period of steady if incomplete penal enlightenment. These were in any case years of persistent social reform. The Victorian belief in the rationality of all human behaviour crumbled; Freud had initiated his revolution in psychological outlook. The emphasis in penal thinking, too, shifted from retribution to rehabilitation, and offenders began to be seen as victims of circumstance. Prison sentences were accordingly reduced in length; the introduction of the probation service marked a significant advance in penal reform; so did that of aftercare for prisoners and of such amenities as prison libraries, lectures and entertainments. Step by step, corporal punishment was also consigned to the past. The progress of enlightenment was never uniform—for instance, the humiliating convict crop and the notorious striped-arrow uniform were not abolished till well into the 'thirties. In the life of the country, the prison system remained always a little outside the pale; no new buildings were constructed, and the régime of discipline imposed retained its repressive Victorian pattern. Still, the first half of this century was certainly an age of optimism in British penal thinking; on the assumption that crime sprang largely from poverty and ignorance and slums, it was expected confidently that with the spread of education and social reform most of it would eventually disappear.

Instead, and this brings one to the present day, the opposite has happened. After the Second World War, the crime figures began to go up again and in the 'fifties they did so at a rate which ushered in a depressing new age of penal doubt and uncertainty, for it seemed that if both hanging and heavy prison sentences had failed as deterrents against crime, so evidently had the new enlightenment. At any rate, the upsurge of crime in the 'fifties brought a twofold crisis. As the crime figures mounted, many glaring shortages and the neglect of decades in the penal system were harshly shown up. Largely because of inadequate pay, there was a national shortage of police officers—in 1959 the Metropolitan Police alone was 3,000 men below strength. There was a grotesque accommodation shortage in the prisons. Overcrowding reached the stage where on an average 6,000 prisoners were being kept 3 to a cell, that is, confined together for around 19 of the 24 hours of the day in a tiny space without sanitation. There was also a much publicized and criticized shortage of places for young offenders in closed Borstals and detention centres. The probation service was sadly under strength, and many of its harrassed officers had to carry twice the accepted optimum case load. There was also a shortage of Approved School personnel and prison and Borstal officers. In fact, wherever one looked, the penal apparatus looked overstrained.

The second aspect of the crisis was ideological: in the new climate of penal uncertainty, voices were suddenly heard again calling for harsh penal measures one had thought consigned to the past. This was like an echo of history. Just as in the British welfare state one can still see the outline and trappings of a feudal-aristocratic society, so the persistent call for more capital punishment and the preoccupation with flogging seemed to hearken back all the way to the memories of the early nineteenth century. If it could not be dismissed simply for this reason, it seems worth recognizing this.

The Victorian penal age had also left its heritage to the twentieth century, but a rather different one—namely its actual edifices. Public opinion in 1959 was startled to learn that not a single new English security prison had been built for over half a century (Everthorpe, the one exception, had been converted to a Borstal). Most prisons still in use were about a century old and with their bricks and stone seemed to have preserved the whole claustrophobic atmosphere of Victorian gloom and humiliation, and often of nineteenth-century sanitary arrangements. These period-piece prisons, the authors of the 1959 White Paper, *Penal Practice in a Changing Society*, were moved to say, "stand as a monumental denial of the principles to which we are committed. . . . It is no more possible to train prisoners in these obsolete conditions than it would be to carry out modern hospital treatment in the unimproved buildings of the pre-Victorian era."

The crisis in the crime wave year of 1959 was thus both administrative and ideological. The choice before the Government was either back to repression or forward to further reform, and as the title of the 1959 White Paper *Penal Practice in a Changing Society* indicates, the choice was reform. In answer to the crisis, Mr Butler and his advisers decided quite unequivocally to give the educational approach to crime a more extended trial. The White Paper declared that prison inmates were for instance to be given more satisfactory work and realistic pay incentives. The old, rather military, prison discipline was to be lightened. Prison officers were to be re-trained. From being mere guardians of security, the traditional "screws", they were now to take on an active rôle in the rehabilitation of prisoners. In return they were promised a review of their salary scales; so were probation officers and other personnel.

Finally, Mr Butler appeared as master-builder. To render his reforms more than academic, he proposed a ten-year programme of building modern prisons described as "unprecedented in scale for the century". Well, so it had to be, since there had been no large-scale building of prisons since Victorian days. Perhaps it was a pity that the programme was not still more generous, since at the end of the ten years there would still be 1,500 sitting 3 to a cell, and in keeping with obstinate tradition these cells would still be without modern sanitation. But these were details. Taking the building programme together with the proposals for improving the prisoners' lives, it was fair to say that in spite of alarming crime figures and against considerable pressure both from the public and the judiciary, Mr Butler and the Home Office had rejected repressiveness and decided rather boldly to experiment further with the educational answer to crime.

It therefore seemed that at long last the penal outlook of the nineteenth century was to be really left behind and that Britain was to have a modern prison and penal system appropriate to an age in which its citizens had never had it so good.

THE YOUNG NONCONFORMISTS

This general sketch of the British penal system for all age-groups may have been a digression, but it is relevant for a discussion of juvenile offenders just because the problems of effective treatment for the latter are today rather different.

In the treatment of juvenile offenders, the break with the nineteenth century had been achieved at a much earlier date. The juvenile penal system had its problems, but these did not include overcrowded Victorian buildings nor underpaid "screws" trained under a repressive régime. In spite of archaic survivals (e.g. that children were deemed criminally responsible before juvenile courts from the tender age of 8 upwards, instead of from 12 to 15, as in most other European countries), it could be said that since the end of the First World War the British treatment of young offenders was by international standards reasonably humane, sensible and progressive. The years between the two wars saw an increasing acceptance both of humanitarian principles and, rather more vaguely, of Freudian psycho-analytic theory. In 1927 the White Paper on the *Treatment of Young Offenders* laid down the principle of guardianship as basis for all juvenile court procedure. The Children and Young Persons Act of 1933 stated that in the case of any child or young person "every court shall have regard to the welfare of the child or young person brought before it and shall in a proper case take steps for removing him from undesirable surroundings and for securing that proper provision is made for his education and training".

As a broad principle this was unexceptionable, and the increasingly close association of probation officers and other social workers with the juvenile courts worked strongly to make such guardianship more of a reality. Though the duty of probation officers towards their charges was primarily "to provide a steady and correcting influence until they have grown out of their delinquency", the economic distress of the 'thirties turned them inevitably into something like additional welfare officers.

In fact, on a long-term view the trend in the juvenile penal system was one of steady enlightenment. For example, the Approved Schools, catering for youngsters up to 17, remained at the end of the 'fifties still something of a characteristic case of British compromise, being run on the model of boarding schools by boards of managers appointed by religious, charitable and other voluntary bodies, while at the same time financed by the State, and since 1933 under the direct authority of the Home Office. The defect of this mixed system lay in the sharp difference of standards between one school and the next, but it had its advantages too. It drew public-spirited men and women into doing voluntary work on behalf of young delinquents. It allowed for differences of religious atmosphere and individualism in education. The introduction of Classification Schools made it possible to organize quite a variety of specialized training for backward children, for the deprived, the maladjusted and the psychopathic. Under Home Office guidance the overall trend was slowly but fairly consistently away from repression and towards giving every child individual attention and re-education. Broadly speaking, therefore, it could be said that up to about 1950 the British penal system for the under-17s was working quite well in its basic methods and aims. Its faults, though highlighted by the occasional Approved School scandal, were mainly those of bureaucracy, inadequate budgets, underpayment of staff and the common human shortcomings.

One might say the same about the treatment of the next age-group, the young adult offenders between the ages of 17 to 21 who, if convicted of a crime which in an older person would have meant prison, were instead committed for Borstal training.

Here I must confess to a personal view. After knowing little about it, the more I have learned about the history of the Borstal system, the more I have found it fascinating. In its original, undiluted public school form, the Borstal system was so paradoxically English that it is not hard to see why it became famous as a national institution, indeed, a part of music-hall folklore. The whole notion of curing Hoxton or Liverpool toughs from their predisposition towards lawbreaking by submitting them to a shadowy public school régime with prefects, house ties and team spirit had a touch of eccentricity almost from the start. Today, when public school boys on their way to the laboratory or machine shop would themselves blanch at hearing slang about "playing the game", it must seem so all the more. Yet I think the real paradox lay in the unexpected virtues of Borstal as a penal system.

First of all the Borstals were from the start penal institutions of a modern pattern. They were designed according to the nineteenth-century precepts of Dr Arnold, it is true, but because the first such boys' prisons at the village of Borstal, near Rochester, was set up only in 1902, they received this public school spirit only in its enlightened, twentieth century, essentially bourgeois form.

It is also admittedly true that the Borstals were very much institutions reflecting English class-consciousness. They expressed the deep confidence of the English upper class that even for the poor blighters in the Borstals, nothing was as beneficial as a touch of that decent education which they had missed by being born into the wrong class, naturally added to such measures as "teaching them a trade". But it was because the Borstals were so intimately bound up with the English class sense that they also attracted outstanding men with a sense of religious and public service into the ranks of their governors and house-masters, especially following on the reforms of Sir Alexander Paterson. In this respect, the Borstals had a distinct advantage over the more mechanically designed reformatories found in some other countries.

In the third place, the Borstal system was almost by accident simultaneously old fashioned and modern. It was old fashioned in all its obvious class snobberies. It was modern in that, taken out of this framework, the public school system has many valuable psychological features. The Borstals were designed to place their young charges under a system of authority, working from governor through house-master down to dormitory captain, intended to be firm but also friendly, personal and intelligible. They were also designed to give uprooted young offenders a sense of belonging— to a group, a team, a house, an entire little society. In theory both aims were like a copy-book example of what modern psycho-therapy says that young people need.

Of course, time marched on and the public school prefect system, which the Borstals had copied, soon began to be dated even in the outside world. It became apparent that young offenders could not really be "trained for freedom" under such conditions of authoritarian security. But again, it speaks in favour of the Borstal system that the transition from closed to open institutions was so easily achieved. It was in the unpropitious economic crisis year of 1930 (when the total of unemployed was approaching the 3 million mark) that a group of boys from the strict Borstal at Feltham hiked all the way to Lowdham, near Nottingham. They walked on their long march without uniforms or guards. At Lowdham they lived under canvas while they themselves built the huts of what was to be the first open Borstal. This was the start: set against the reactionary social climate of the time, this gesture by the Prison Commissioners seems almost like an experiment from an *avant-garde* socialist society.

It also speaks in favour of the system that since the last war the majority of training Borstals have been open institutions: that is, leaving aside the minority sent to prisons, the *majority* of British young adult offenders between the ages of 17 to 21 were being re-trained without bolts or bars. One side of life in an open Borstal which has been much remarked on by penologists from abroad is that the officers and their families, from the governor and his family downwards, all live on the actual premises. Historically, this of course simply followed the public school pattern. In actual penal practice, however, it makes it easier to run an open Borstal as a self-contained community where, in theory, officers and boys are all living and striving together for one dominant purpose, the training of the boys for return to society and for their earliest suitable discharge. At any rate, this community life in open Borstals has been particularly praised by experts from the United States, where even advanced juvenile penal institutions have seldom reached this stage.

PORTRAIT OF THE ARTIST AS A BORSTAL BOY

The conclusion from the above remarks is that, contrary to popular ideas, the Borstals represented a relatively progressive system of penal training for young adults. A witness I should like to quote here is Brendan Behan, the young Irish dramatist, and also the author of an entertaining slice of autobiography called *Borstal Boy*.[1] Drawn into I.R.A. underground work in England at the tender age of 16, Behan was arrested in the middle of the last war and, as he relates in his book, packed off for two years' training at Hollesley Bay Colony, a well-known open Borstal.

Behan's picture of the war-time English local prison, where he was initially kept detained and kicking his heels for some weeks, is not unexpectedly that of a grim, grey, depressing world of low-I.Q. human contact, of slopping out, degradation and hate between screws and prisoners. Very probably the picture is sharpened by Behan's recollections of his hate for the Protestant English enemy, but it is fascinating to see how the whole tone of his story changes as soon as he recalls his arrival at the open Borstal on the coast. The atmosphere and the talk—Behan must have a wonderfully retentive ear—conjure up images of the vanishing confident tradition of English upper middle-class life. This is conveyed already in Behan's account of the Governor's informal opening speech to the new arrivals, in which he put them on their trust not to abscond: since there were no bars or bolts, there would be no glory in the feat nor much point, as the absconder would only have to break in again somewhere for clothes and money and so would be involved in further lawbreaking to his own loss. The Governor then added:

"If, as we all do, no matter where we are, or under what circumstances, you find life unbearable, I ask you to come and see an officer or your Housemaster or the padre or myself about it. . . . More than likely, you will find that your differences with the staff or other men will straighten themselves out after a time, but it's always worth having a chat with someone if you feel your troubles are getting beyond you. . . . It may happen that the working parties to which you have been sent don't suit you. I can't always guarantee that I can transfer you to work

[1] Brendan Behan, *Borstal Boy*. Hutchinson, 1959.

to which you are better suited. Obviously, though some of you may be good sailors, I can't put you on a ship."

The blokes laughed at this.

By and large Behan's early relations with Housemaster, Librarian, Dormitory Captain and the boys around him were also friendly enough. He recollects candidly that when a little later he was asked to abscond the excuse he gave for refusing, that as an I.R.A. detainee he would be hunted down at once, was not the full reason:

> The place seemed all right. The Governor seemed a decent sort with a bit of humour to him. The screws were all right, and I liked the other blokes and lastly, although I didn't like saying it to Ken, I didn't like double-crossing the Governor.

If he lost his anger, Behan kept his sharp observer's eye and most of his memories of his two years at North Sea Camp seem agreeable enough in the circumstances. There were outdoor working parties and getting to know his companions; minor punishments that were easily endured; secret swimming expeditions in the summer. Behan recalls a speech day that might have come out of an Evelyn Waugh novel, at which an eccentric old colonel delivered his unchanging set Public School speech to the Borstal boys; occasions where he himself could sing Irish songs from the concert platform. He was intrigued by the eccentric figure of Matron, who talked to him about Yeats and Stephens, who impressed the toughest boys by her fairness, but always kept herself to herself, a solitary, puzzling figure as she strolled about the grounds with her dog. Behan also found himself slaving to win an essay competition; he even played in the Rugger Fifteen. Almost suddenly his time was up. The sergeant witnessing his release was the same officer who had arrested him in Liverpool.

> "They've made a fine man of you, Brendan," he said. Well, I had to admit I'd been well looked after.

Of course, one should not generalize from this. As a member or ex-member of the I.R.A., Behan was at North Sea Camp more in the position of a prisoner-of-war than of a sentenced offender and so would not have shared the special feelings of guilt, defiance and boredom of the ordinary sentenced Borstal boys, who were simply sweating out their time alongside him. All the same, they must have been exposed to the same influences, and since so authentic a writer can rarely have looked at a Borstal from inside, it is noteworthy how many of Behan's memories are pleasant ones and how many acts of kindness he could report.

ATTENDANCE AND DETENTION

Borstals and Approved Schools are both institutions for the long-term training of offenders away from their homes. Under the Criminal Justices Act of 1948 (which also ended corporal punishment), two new institutions for shorter treatment for young offenders were experimentally added. These were the Attendance Centres and Detention Centres and it is symptomatic of present penal thinking that some imposing research studies into their results were immediately set on foot at respectively Cambridge and Oxford.

The first innovation, the Attendance Centre, was a mild type of institution, designed to give a minor salutory shock to boys and girls of school age who are merely considered wild and out of hand—or who may have broken a probation order—by depriving them of their peak-hour leisure time. They are sentenced to spend a succession of their Saturday afternoons at drill or handicraft at an Attendance Centre, under supervision of members of the local police force. The hope is that, in addition to this mild shock, the experience may also guide them towards more constructive use of their leisure, e.g. joining a youth club. The police in some areas favour the experiment as a means of contact with youngsters in ordinary human guise. My recollection of a London Attendance Centre, which I visited on a heat-wave afternoon, is of perspiring constables in shirt-sleeves taking small boys in courses of gym and basketwork. The atmosphere could not have seemed more good-natured. What I found unsettling was merely that this institution seemed to reflect the lessened authority of parents and school. Why was it necessary?

The Detention Centres were designed as a much more serious deterrent. Their avowed purpose was to administer a "short, sharp shock" of 3 to 6 months' duration to older offenders where this was thought more appropriate than either a short sentence of prison or else a long spell of training at an Approved School or Borstal. Life in a Detention Centre appears to be rather like that in a closed Borstal, only much more so and much more disagreeably so: the régime of hard work and drill is conducted at a brisk, strenuous tempo; discipline is strict, and privileges few. But the Detention Centre régime is not brutal or humiliating—only severe; it does not, like prison, throw boys into the demoralizing company of adult criminals; it is designed to be carried out under modern sanitary conditions and with educational supervision. It seems, in short, a penal treatment appropriate to our age: for young offenders who have failed to conform to society, here is a short, sharp shock to teach them better—but with everything done to make it an antiseptic shock.

All in all, it could therefore fairly be said—and this is the decisive point—that the penal crisis of 1959-60 had its different aspects for adult and for juvenile offenders. While the penal and prison system for adults required historic overhaul, the methods applied to juvenile offenders were modern and reasonably designed. However, before all the new methods could be given an extended trial, the entire system was jolted by the crime wave of the 'fifties which produced some fresh problems.

Within the under-17 group, admissions to Approved Schools rose in 1959 to the record figure of 4,000. The Approved School authorities complained that with earlier maturing, many of the new crop of boys and girls were more difficult to control—the Teddy boy outlook also added its share to these difficulties. It was also noted that a higher proportion of this new generation, the boys especially, appeared to require special treatment for the mal-adjusted and neurotic. Among the young adult offenders of 17 years or more, at the Borstal age, the sheer growth of criminality threatened to swamp the whole classification machine. Angry magistrates complained that it was as hard to find a place for a boy at a Detention Centre or closed Borstal as at an exclusive public school. At the same time the Prison Commissioners gave it as their conclusion that short prison sentences were ceasing to have any effect on a certain category of cynical youthful criminals. Often they only invested them with glamour.

LOOKING AHEAD

This was the penal crisis which faced Mr Butler and his advisers on the juvenile front. Here it was not so much an administrative crisis, to be met by a building programme alone, as very clearly the result of far-reaching changes in society. From this viewpoint, the 1959 White Paper was in its immediate proposals for juveniles also a boldly liberal document.

First, the separation of the young from adult criminals was to be carried further, which made good sense. So that boys due to go to Borstal or Detention Centre should not have to spend a demoralizing waiting period in prison, special Remand Centres were to be built for this purpose.

Secondly, short prison sentences for young offenders were to be reduced to absolute minimum, which also made sense.

Thirdly, the White Paper proposed bringing together prison and Borstal treatment under "a single indeterminate sentence of custodial training" of up to two years. This was an interesting innovation. It meant that *after* the conviction of a young adult offender, it would be decided by careful and expert study at a classification centre whether he was best suited by prison or one of the forms of Borstal. The fact that the sentence was indeterminate, i.e. could be periodically reviewed according to the offender's progress, was yet another move away from the concept of retribution and towards re-education.

From the point of view of the penal reformers, all these were proposals in the right direction: the question was only how soon they would actually be carried out. But from the view of the wider public, the trouble was that even so the White Paper held out few hopes that the number of delinquents would go down. This was shown by the unprecedented building programme for young offenders which was also planned; and the added fact that the White Paper listed as many as 32 official research projects into juvenile crime and penal methods showed effectively that the 'sixties had become an age of penal doubt—what, indeed, was to be the rôle of the penal system in a changing society?

CHAPTER XIII

Some Penal Reflections

CHANGING VALUES

WELL, what is to be done? If there is one sure generalization that can be made about crime, it is that it is associated with male adolescence. Current figures show that law-breaking is still a preoccupation of boys and youths in the 14-17 and 17-21 age-groups. After the age of 21 the incidence of criminality declines significantly, to dwindle rapidly after the age of 30. We can therefore take it that a good many boys are driven to commit offences only during the erratic years of adolescence, but will get over this as they reach maturity.

The figures relating to boys and girls admitted to Approved Schools in the 'fifties show that after discharge about nine girls out of ten and four boys out of five could be counted on to disappear sooner or later into law-abiding anonymity (on the figures of 1955, the actual "success rate" for boys discharged from Approved School was 58 per cent., a success being counted as a boy who was not re-convicted for three years after discharge. However, of the remaining 42 per cent. about half only reappeared before the Courts merely for some trivial offence that was no more than an episode on their way towards adult respectability. This left roughly 20 per cent., or one boy in five, as likely to continue with criminality even as an adult.) To keep such youngsters under safe supervision for what is presumed to be their difficult phase is therefore only common sense. Whether our society is moving in such a direction that the number of young rebels and victims to be kept under supervision will increase is another matter. But there is one accompanying difficulty which has arisen. In recent years the British juvenile penal system has progressed notably in the classification of offenders and in providing psychiatric treatment for the maladjusted. However, the basic method of re-education is still that each penal institution should be fashioned into a little society to which the young offender can feel that he or she belongs and so learn to live in the greater society outside. Now the question is—what should such a little society be like? How far should it reflect not only the theoretical but the actual values of the outside world, where these are changing rapidly? This is not a new problem, but one has only to talk to the staff members of penal institutions to see that it is one which has fast become more complicated.

There is, for instance, the basic general change in the moral climate. The early Borstals of a generation or two ago still functioned within the framework of a generally accepted morality. To the middle-class mind, at least, this still seemed a fixed morality, based on religious observance, patriotism, respect for the law, respect of the person and property, the ideal of honest work, and so on. Today this morality has become less assured. Not only because of wars, the Bomb, and the arrival of psycho-analysis. Disintegration of values has come nearer home. Suppose an Approved School boy showed his Housemaster the issue of the *Evening Standard* of Christmas Eve, 1959, whose editor had chosen to proclaim in the largest front-page headline type available the two words: MANIAC MURDER. Should the housemaster criticize this editor and express disapproval of the commercial principles on which the popular press is run? And if not, what should he tell his charge?

There are also changes in the whole class structure to be taken into account. As was said earlier, the whole Borstal system was designed very much on the lines of English upper middle-class ideas. It is true that of its message of public school virtues a good deal probably passed over the heads of most working-class Borstal boys, who took it simply as part of the peculiar moral lecture they had to endure from "them", their social betters, because they themselves had broken the law and been silly enough to get caught. But at least such boys accepted the unchanging existence of this morality imposed on them from above. "They", their social betters, were always there; and so was their authority.

Today this is already much less the case. An Approved School housemaster who tries to set the right tone, to talk about a steady job and the virtues of saving, has today to compete with the appeal of the young pop singer whom an incessant publicity portrays as leading a glittering life of fabulous wealth, with no mention of thrift whatever. A boy who is obliged to attend religious service knows that after his discharge it will not be chapel that is waiting for him but the cinema, the dance-hall and the record shop.

It is also no accident but a reflection of social priorities that the representatives of penal authority have suddenly been allowed to become relatively poor. An illustration of this problem can be drawn from the situation of housemasters and housemistresses in Approved Schools. In this category of responsible key workers, roughly one post in five was in November 1959 being advertised as vacant. In view of the salaries offered this was not surprising. Mr Hugo Charteris, in an article on this subject,[1] quoted the following advertisement from the *Approved School Gazette*:

> Wanted: Housemaster . . . salary £575 rising to £845 if qualified, otherwise maximum £725 . . . possibility of some night work. Female Supervisor, £460 rising to maximum of £540 less £166 for board and lodging.

Such pay scales, which have a look of 1929 rather than 1959, had two consequences. The direct effect was that posts remained vacant and others were only inadequately filled. The indirect effect at a time of full employment was like counter-propaganda. In the eyes of boys who were fully aware how much money their friends outside were spending, the cramped style of life imposed on a housemaster and his family inevitably diminished his personal authority and what he might have to say about saving and a steady job. Boys who after discharge had got a good job in a factory, said Mr Charteris, were "often in a position to come back and flaunt their relative riches and liberty at housemasters who only a few weeks ago were their foster-fathers and arbiters".

No doubt this disproportion between the salaries of Approved School staff and what their charges can earn will presently be corrected, especially as the public enquiry into the breakdown at Carlton House School focused attention on this point. As *The Times* pointed out editorially, "less derisory salary scales" would be at least one way of attracting professionally qualified social workers into the service. There seems to be no question about this. At the same time I feel that the task of adapting life in penal

[1] *Daily Telegraph*, 17th November 1959.

institutions effectively to a changing society goes much further than this.

A mile or so west of the sleaziness of Shepherd's Bush, hidden away among quiet Victorian stucco terraces, lies Stamford House, the London County Council Remand Home for boys. Here the telephone rings day and night as the police are at the other end of the line and boys are brought in. Boys arrested for an offence; boys who had run away from home or an institution; boys whose parents could not be found to bail them out—the parents often seem to be in Ireland. From their particular viewpoint, the officers at Stamford House were given constant insight into the ragged edges of London life. In the opinion of one experienced officer, the instability had lately been increasing—it was the usual tale:

> The raising of material standards has meant an increase in selfishness. Mother is financially independent of father—the mother is working in ninety per cent. of the cases we get here. You get a boy of 15 brought in here with £5 in his pocket. The parents are often not in need: the kids are left with a high proportion of what they earn, and no sense of responsibility in spending it. . . . The parents don't supervise leisure time. You ask what was Tony doing last week, and they haven't the vaguest idea. He was knocking about in some other part of London, in dives or caffs—they didn't even know.

Apart from being a Remand Home, Stamford House serves a second function, namely as Classification Centre for boys from 8 to 17 whom a juvenile court had thought fit for Approved School. Such boys are observed for four weeks. They are submitted to the battery of standardized modern educational and psychological tests; their behaviour is observed by housemasters and supervisors and, if need be, by consultant psychiatrists; while this goes on, social workers investigate the family background. Finally, working from elaborate dossiers, a classification conference of experts tries to allot each boy to the type of Approved School most suited to his need (provided that there is a vacancy). This is by now already recognized routine. What I found particularly instructive was the special life, the special little society created at Stamford House.

The picture I had carried away from a visit to a Remand Home just after the war had been of silence, of boys slumped apathetically at tables, supervisors looking on sternly. In 1959, by contrast, the first glimpse of the main hall at Stamford House was a bewildering one of boys of all sizes in khaki shirts and either flannel trousers or shorts, milling about in what seemed like market-place activity. The central hall looked bright, colourful, airy. The walls were decorated with colour prints—Cezanne, van Gogh, Breughel. Some boys were playing ping-pong; others crouched over draughts-boards; some, beyond an open door, were watching television, others were just standing about; most of them appeared noisy and unrestrained; the supervisory adults present looked informally at ease. The hall also contained four aquariums, a cage of budgerigars, and a parrot; a dog was dashing about and barking.

Intent on their games, the boys took little note of the entry of a stranger like myself. On closer sight, I thought that they had perhaps a trace of the Approved School look, shown in a certain slouch, a crudeness in expression. Yet there was no doubt that they looked both eager and at ease. My attention was caught by a boy who was six foot tall, incongruously still wearing a guards-man's uniform. I was told he had been brought in only a couple of hours before, picked up at a railway station. A few weeks earlier he had given a false age when enlisting. Overgrown and clumsy, he was now eagerly retrieving ping-pong balls for boys half his size, trying to please. He noticed me and for a moment I saw him staring at me with bewildered blue eyes.

Upstairs in the dormitories, where sleeping-clothes lay in neat baskets at the end of each bed, one of the younger officers gave me a summary of the method employed. The informality I had witnessed was no accident. A boy arrived with a record; he had broken the law, charges had been laid against him, but this was only one side of the case. At Stamford House the job was "to eliminate biased reports by biased observers and get down to scientific objectivity". This could not be done under a repressive régime. Boys anyhow became test-conscious too quickly. "A proper classification job, as we see it, requires not only the usual tests but getting beyond a boy's glibness, always seeing how he moves with other boys and with adults." For this reason the discipline was deliberately kept light, with little standing to attention. While this light touch was a means to an end, to put the boys at ease while they took the tests, my informant said, it was remarkable how quickly almost all the boys responded to it. "A new boy of today is already the old boy of tomorrow, telling the others the ropes." For many a boy, indeed, this easy informality was his first sensible contact with adults for years. In the second place, however, the boys also had to follow a strict timetable of work, tests and play, of cooked meals whether they liked it or not, and regular showers (the physical side was important). And to this sense of order they also responded. "Basically, all boys want to know what the rules are. If they approve of them and find you're not talking down, they are usually law-abiding. Very often the time that a boy is with us is the first time he has known real security, in the sense of knowing what the next day will bring. There's a remarkable change to be observed in such boys—as a rule it happens already in the first days."

I felt that what I saw confirmed this. When I returned to the hall downstairs, a bell had just rung. The boys came crowding from every direction in the untidy manner of schoolboys. They were called up to take their evening snack under supervisory eye, yet informally. The boys looked well fed, good physical specimens. Above all, there was an eagerness about them which I remembered from my own school days: those extra quick movements, the raised voices, the look of keen group interest, in fact that air of market-place activity I had noticed at my first entrance. It was hard to think that these were a scattered collection of problem boys who not long before had been brought in by the police or removed from home for their own protection.

Later I was shown the room where the outfits were kept which the boys had been wearing when picked up by the police. It was as if the suits had their own life. Row by row, there they hung, grotesque and expensive, the tenth-rate imitations of advertised ideals, the suit in Ted style, in pop singer style, in the imitation of the Californian thug. It seemed hard to believe that they had been worn by the same boys I had just seen in open shirts, shorts and flannels. The young supervisor at my side laughed—he said the room always made him laugh, like some of the boys when they first arrived:

You would hardly believe it—they turn up in tight jeans, with fancy haircuts, suede sandboots, iridescent shirts and linings. . . . They are given the khaki and flannel clothes and told to change into them. With this change it's hard for them to keep up the pretence. As they get into normal clothing, they drop the façade.

Some of them at first are rather shocked—they feel they are committed to school again—but in a couple of hours they usually come round and join the other boys. Some resist—they say "no bloody shorts"—but we don't have to use coercion. We just say they can't join in, and leave them sitting in another room. Pretty soon they are laughing at themselves and let us pull their legs.

Or more or less like this. The contrast seemed to illustrate at least one-half of the delinquency problem.

On the one hand, Stamford House indicated the sort of life these boys ought to be living, namely quite simply as *boys*: to dress like boys, to play and to learn like boys, to be guided by adults as boys should be. (It was true that to maintain the society in a Remand Home was a subtle and expensive business which for a population of 100 boys demanded the service of 50 trained adults. But this did not alter the case.) On the other hand, the suits in the cloakroom stood for those influences of an acquisitive society, a society dominated by grasping mass entertainment, which had forced these boys into a false maturity, a moneyed life long before they were ready for it, a pseudo-adult life which for many of them had proved far too great a strain.

Of course, this was not all. As I saw at a final classification conference, each of these boys was a "problem youngster". It might be because of a broken or hostile home, a history of truancy, failure at school, repeated convictions for dishonesty—the cumulative picture was depressing. At this round-table conference, which was also attended by an eminent psychiatrist, one could not but be impressed by the care taken to agree on the special handicap of each boy, whether it was lack of affection at home, emotional immaturity, neurosis or a learning disturbance, and to compensate for this by sending him to the most suitable Approved School, strict or permissive, for the well or the maladjusted, emphasizing ordinary teaching or manual crafts. (Once again, if there was an available place at such a school.) All this was efficiently done. But the impression in my mind, as I left, was still of what seemed to me the primary contrast between the boys, dressed and behaving as I had seen them, and the pseudo-adult suits in which they had arrived, standing for the pressures of society which had helped to make them delinquents. Here was a destructive element that lay outside psychiatric control.

GREEN MANSION

I felt conscious of the same contradiction during a visit to one particular senior Approved School for backward boys—let me for anonymity call it Green Mansion.

Already the approach to Green Mansion made it hard for me to feel that I was going to a penal institution. For the last few miles I was driving along winding lanes through a stretch of secluded, peaceful countryside. The school was housed in a Victorian stately home, standing in green and spacious parkland. The curriculum included both building work and horticulture. Every day squads of backward boys worked on the mansion and in the grounds so that at the first approach, and in the sunshine, they looked almost improbably spick-and-span.

Indoors, the high-ceilinged Victorian reception rooms with parquet flooring, through which I walked with the headmaster, were now the common rooms for the "Houses" into which the boys were divided. I caught a glimpse of bright, modern wallpaper; the usual colour prints were well framed; the television sets and record players in the corners looked new. A few boys were indoors—they were really youths of 15 to 19, wearing open-necked shirts and blue overalls. They greeted us with institutional politeness. Out of doors we met more youths who were marching heavily-booted to working sites, carrying their tools. They had an emphatically proletarian and awkward look. To see them against the setting of this house and park was somewhat like a scene from a Russian film, in which the workers had taken over the former aristocratic mansion—only these young proletarians were here by compulsion.

After lunch I walked through the grounds with the headmaster, who talked to me about plans for the future. He conformed to a type I had been meeting in the penal service, one of the enthusiasts, who, once caught by the spell, would not think of other work. Tall, strongly built, with a firm handgrip and quickly mustering eyes, he looked eminently like a man who from experience knew exactly how to handle boys, how to set the right tone, to deal with awkward sex problems, to take both cricket-net practice and prayers. Only now he was talking to me in the technical terms of modern psychotherapy.

He had just returned from a week's conference with colleagues in the service. As we walked in the grounds past landscaped trees and an ornamental lake (I had guessed from hints that the school was a show place and the headmaster an exemplary guide), he talked about new ideas. It seemed to me that his plans for progress all concerned improved psychotherapy, while his problems derived from greater *social* disorder.

Plans for progress. Green Mansion took in some 80 boys of three related categories. The first was boys classified as immature, which meant a negative selection: one could not mix lost little boys with sophisticated back-street toughs. Secondly there were boys without a normal home, through circumstance, who had become over-institutionalized. Thirdly, boys from particularly bad homes who had suffered from cruel or neglectful parents or an emotional problem like illegitimacy or a hostile step-parent. In other words, all were boys who lacked some element of a normal background. True, they had also all done some wrong, committed some offence which could not always be traced directly to their circumstances. Still, a defective family life was the most recognizable common factor in their delinquency. This meant that the education at Green Mansion must have a social slant. As he himself saw it, said the headmaster in a telling phrase, "here are eighty-odd personal lives which have become unravelled, and have to be knitted up again into a sensible pattern".

Green Mansion had already a successful tradition of teaching boys good manners, self-respect and how to work. Now, said the headmaster, this was to be backed up by more specialized forms of treatment. Green Mansion was already being visited regularly by a consultant psychiatrist. He had also asked for the addition to his staff of a full-time psychologist to deal with the harder cases, and of a full-time social worker who would concentrate on those instances where there had been a complete breakdown in a boy's family relationship. He had also reorganized the functions of his teaching staff. In the old days the teachers simply gave their scheduled hours of instruction and then knocked off. Under his re-arrangement, each teacher also saw some individual boys in the evenings and at week-ends; he might take them swimming or canoeing; he would encourage them to talk about their worries—in fact, participate actively in casework.

The purpose of all these changes, said the headmaster, was to help his housemasters, the key figures at Green Mansion, whose task it was to know about the problems of every boy in their charge, to build up his confidence, to keep in touch with his family and his after-care representative. Relieved of other duties, each house-master would now be able to concentrate on this rôle of being a real substitute father or mother figure to every boy in his charge, which was what these particular boys needed most.

As we retraced our steps from the furthest extent of the park, I asked the headmaster about his own worries. Here we were immediately back in the world of current and increasing social problems.

There was the question of inadequate pay and consequent staff shortage, about which I had already heard enough. There was the ignorance of certain parents. If some appreciated what educational advantages Green Mansion offered their sons, at a weekly cost of £10 per boy, others remained dull-wittedly antagonistic and indifferent. No wonder that, whatever one did, many boys still thought of their time at Approved School as "doing a stretch". The Approved Schools were still in need of more psychiatric facilities—this might surprise me but he would give me a typical case: "He's one of our lads—I'll call him John Smith. His mother was a prostitute who abandoned him in a gents' lavatory in the West End of London. He was taken over by the L.C.C. and has never known what it means to have a proper home. He has known plenty of care, but it's always been a life of dormitories, a row of beds, bells ringing. Sometimes this doesn't work. In this particular lad's case it's no wonder that his attitude became completely anti-social. When he got here at the age of 16 there were fifteen different addresses in his file."

By this time we had completed the tour of the grounds and were back on the terrace of Green Mansion. On the way I had seen boys working as carpenters, in the tailoring shop, the greenhouses and on the building site. A group of the latter, led by a fair-haired Cockney youth, trudged past us. "Hello, Norman, I'm glad to see that you've finished that wall," called the headmaster, and then to me: "That particular lot are working without supervision. That's another line we are pursuing."

He seemed able and confident. Everything in *his* school was under control. Yet as I stood looking out across the parkland— there were boys at cricket practice and I could see a shimmer of water—I felt that I could see the flaw in this whole penal work. To catch John Smith and to prevent his start in life in the gents' lavatory from leading him into an anti-social career of crime, Green Mansion was being turned into a more and more efficient instrument for psychotherapy. But if society produced more John Smiths, and if this evil was not attacked at the source, would there be need for more and more rural retreats like Green Mansion to cure them?

POLLINGTON

Another interesting experiment in teaching young offenders how to adjust, by creating a special society for this purpose, was something I saw during a visit to Pollington Camp. This is an experimental open Borstal, housing selected boys, who according to the Mannheim-Wilkins prediction test are by and large not expected to commit any further offence. At Pollington they are given a short, intensive education in self-discipline.

Pollington stands without fence or gate right beside a busy highway in Yorkshire. In appearance, it is like an encampment of army huts round a parade ground which had just been spruced up and polished for a general's inspection. The impression on the morning of my visit was of bustling work on every side. Cheerful-looking youths in overalls were getting down to their tasks. I met them in the carpenter's shop, in the kitchens; some were scrubbing floors or polishing windows in the dormitory huts; another lot were piling into a lorry to be taken into the fields. In the background, among the prefab houses with small gardens where the staff live, I could see children playing and could faintly hear their voices. Something in the look of the place reminded me distantly of an Israeli communal settlement. I could tell from the firm posture and relaxed expressions of the boys that they were not the usual Borstal boys but the pick of them.

This was confirmed by Johnnie, a tall boy picked out at random to show my companion and myself over the institution with explicit freedom to comment. He took us through the dormitories, explaining relative points of spit and polish and neatness that gained or lost marks—Johnnie laughed at this. Six foot two, tousle-haired, he was engagingly frank. In his present institutional situation he had no inhibitions. He had the look, I kept thinking, of a confident young man who back in his home town would go far, who would presently be a solid citizen, perhaps a works fore-man, driving his new Austin, with his children perhaps going to Grammar School.

As we stood at the edge of the road I suggested that it would not be difficult to get away from Pollington. Johnnie agreed; all one had to do was to thumb a ride on a lorry. But where would that get him? Only back to the punishment Borstal at Reading.

"So you wouldn't do it?"

"I'd be silly, wouldn't I?" said Johnnie. "Today I *think*. I'm supposed to be learning self-discipline. That's why I'm here—because I didn't know how to think."

He came from a small town in East Anglia. There was an American air base in the neighbourhood and an R.A.F. depôt not far off. The town had coffee-bars and pubs with bands; it was a place of many fights; there were rough places, a lot of Teddy boys about. His father kept a small shop there. He himself was the only son.

I asked how he had managed to get himself sent to Borstal. "Just for a laugh. It's a fact." There had been trouble in the family, father and mother at it every evening, then finally mother walked out. For a while his father made him help in the house. "It was enough to get you down." Going out nights to get away from home, he had got in with a rough mob. His mate at the café said to him: "Do you want a laugh tonight?" He found it meant breaking and entering—well, it meant breaking into a television shop, but the way he was feeling about things, it would have been chicken to refuse. And in any case, "I just didn't *think*. It's a fact. I'd know different today."

Johnnie had two more months to go before his discharge. On the face of it, if he had learned nothing else, he gave every sign of having learned to think cautiously about looking after number one.

At Pollington the training spell in self-discipline, in learning how to think, is short, on the average only ten months, but intensive. The boys rise through four grades of increasing privileges, provided they obtain a minimum of points which are allotted each day for conscientious work. Loss of points can mean additional days' stay. The self-education extends further than this. The camp has a number of elected committees; a kitchen committee with some scope for varying menus; committees for running entertainments and sports; most important, a disciplinary committee, with one member drawn from each dormitory with responsibility for seeing that minor rules, like quiet after lights out, whose breach could mean trouble, are properly kept and with the power to impose small fines and penalties.

The basic idea is that for the committee members this means learning self-restraint in not abusing powers; for those who offend against the common well-being, it means learning how to accept discipline from their fellows without rebelling, because if they do so the staff need not be involved and so no precious points for behaviour need be lost. All these committees are elected by a fortnightly camp meeting of all the boys, to which they are responsible. From the staff side this meeting is attended only by the Governor himself, who acts as chairman.

The second experiment at Pollington is group counselling, which as a penal method was first started in California and in 1959 was being tried out in half a dozen British penal institutions (including Dartmoor!). The assumption is that these boys who arrive at Pollington are usually suffering from particularly strong adolescent emotional disturbances, from sub-conscious grievances against parents, sensations of failure and the like, which could do with an airing. And so about eight to ten boys meet regularly once a week for a session with a particular officer, to talk on a footing of absolute equality about anything, but preferably about themselves and their problems. In fact, the more a group starts off as a grievance committee in which the boys shoot their mouths off, the better. In this way, deep down grievances over which a boy may have been brooding to the point of obsession will at least be brought into the open and talked about to others. If a boy can see his troubles through the eyes of others, he may learn that they are not unique and perhaps not even as bad as he thinks. In any case, the hope is that they will seem to him diminished.

The whole of Pollington Camp is divided into such groups. (At the time of my visit it was still too soon for proper evaluation of the experiment.) The boys, including Johnnie, with whom I talked about group counselling, were evidently able to laugh about their plight—shut up in a camp and with no girls!—and the silliness that had led up to it. They appeared already conditioned: the eager cross-talk about themselves which made up our conversation sounded almost like another counselling session. Some of the chief topics which came up at the sessions, so the boys told me, were their grievances against "them", the camp authorities, who opened parcels and did other unpleasant things. But I also caught deeper echoes. "You see, this bloke, he says everyone's against him, so in the end all the fellows told him it's his own blank fault, it's him that's selfish, it's up to him to change." The arguments seem to be drawn with fascination to the subject of fathers and their unjust attitude—almost as if the boys had read Freud. Johnnie put the opposite view. He remembered, he had once told another fellow it was no good going on and on about his own father, the blokes were sick of hearing about it, and besides, supposing his father had a good reason for doing what he did?

How important all this was I could not tell. In contrast to the Californian system, where the group counselling was to be conducted by trained psychologists, the men in charge at Pollington, after some preliminary coaching, were the ordinary officers, including the security officers. How highly the officers I talked to regarded its results I could not tell either—they probably had their own reservations. But the very fact that the counselling was done not by psychologists from outside but by officers who were actually living with the boys seemed to me to have its advantage too. As I drove away from Pollington in the twilight across the flat Yorkshire plain, I felt as if the whole camp was like an organization geared single-mindedly to the task of teaching these youngsters who had got into trouble the simple social lesson of today: learn to think and to conform.

MORE CONFORMITY

The methods used at Pollington are for the Borstal élite. Is it possible to apply them more widely? It seems quite likely. Penal reforms which seemed *avant-garde* ideas thirty years ago are today accepted without much trouble, and no doubt more far-reaching changes may be expected.

In the case of the Approved Schools, for those under 17 years old, there has been a growing demand for their rationalization, for taking them over into a single State system which would fall into the administrative sphere of a single juvenile penal authority. This would be of help in raising conditions of work and salaries to a reasonable modern level. Under a single authority there would also be more flexibility in applying the various penal methods available to an offender under the age of 17 and reviewing his case when necessary.

From the Approved School representatives themselves, a strong demand has come that boys and girls should be sent to them at an earlier date. As things were, the Courts generally sent an offender to an Approved School only as a last resort, after all other means had failed. This meant that in the eyes of parents and boys even the most permissive Approved School, with small classes, excellent teaching, psychiatric facilities, had a penal look. It stood for the stiffest punishment in the juvenile code, a young offender being sent away "for a stretch". It also meant that when a boy went to Approved School he might already have defied several other penal methods and be a tough little criminal.

In the view of Approved School authorities, the modern classification technique made it quite possible to pick out likely candidates for re-education before they had been convicted several times over. If they were packed off earlier this would have several clear advantages. It would remove the historic stigma from Approved School of being a last resort. Boys would be removed before they had been infected by the modern gang life. In addition it would give the Approved Schools a better chance to give a youngster from a bad background continued and intensive re-education to put him right.

As for the Borstals, I was given some current advanced ideas about their further reform from a critical young intellectual who had joined the penal service (one of the few who had done so recently).

He thought the basic Pollington ideas about self-education could be applied not only to a chosen minority but to the ordinary majority of Borstal boys though perhaps in not quite the same way. What he thought wrong in the system as a whole was the gap between the society "inside" and the changing conditions in the outside world. The authority of the housemaster as father-figure was still of therapeutic value. But beyond this, the public school prefect system had seen its day. So had the historic emphasis on setting the boys to "learn a trade"—in modern industry the widest range by now was of semi-skilled jobs which could be learned in a few weeks by any one with some *general* technical training. Instead of all this stress on "vocation", my young critic wanted to see the Borstal system as re-training in *choice*, not merely between behaviour and misbehaviour (as was the case even in Pollington) but of choice between positive alternatives with a chance for the offender of learning from mistakes.

In practice this would mean considerable changes. A boy might, for instance, start in a closed Borstal and on attaining a suitable standard of progress go on to an open one. As for training in work, instead of a boy being simply ordered on to this job or that, there should ideally be a series of jobs open to him, so that he could work his way up the ladder. Pay for these jobs should be on a scale which would enable a boy to learn with some purpose. For instance, a boy might have to make at least some payment for skilled vocational training. Instead of skilled training being something which was simply handed to the boy through his saying "I want to be a mechanic" and being told "Right, we'll put you in the machine shop", it should be something which, with proper advice, he could see as an aim—one for which he himself could decide to make some sacrifice. Similarly, a boy should be able to acquire some extras for his cell, like a picture, a rug or a bookshelf—these would depend on his work and saving. An approximation like this of Borstal life to life outside, so my young informant thought, would in itself call for the general establishment of the sort of self-government by committees in practice at Pollington.

THE NEW RE-EDUCATION

Advanced reforms of this kind may or may not be realized in the near future. But even visits to a few institutions are enough to show how the winds of change are blowing through the whole juvenile penal system. The White Paper only confirmed what was often already being done, or planned, in the actual field. Stern legal morality is going out and the educator and psychiatrist are moving in. The shift is away from the historic concept of the young offender as a law-breaker who has to be punished for a moral wrong. It is towards seeing him or her as a young person who for various reasons has failed to conform to the demands of society and must therefore be re-educated to find new adjustment. Moreover, the reasons for the original failure are often regarded as having their roots in the offender's childhood, in a defective early family background, so that they need to be tackled by psychiatric methods. With the emphasis all on education and psychiatry, penal officers, including security officers, thus find themselves increasingly drawn into an "active rehabilitation rôle".

These changes in penal outlook, which are by no means confined to Britain, have called forth a good deal of criticism. Some of this, like the persistent clamour for severe measures and corporal punishment, come from quarters which are simply out of step with the whole new trend. But there has also been more serious and penetrating criticism of what is going on. In a special section of her *Social Science and Social Pathology*, Lady Wootton has expressed misgivings against the progressive advance of the psychiatrists into the penal realm, which to her mind involves a dangerous departure from some of "the basic assumptions of ancient and honoured legal systems" on the concept of the individual responsibility of the offender.

Already in many countries, among which England must now be included, the first steps down this slope have been taken; and the possibility cannot be dismissed that the relaxation of definitions of responsibility, which is already in progress, is the beginning of a process which, in the remoter future, is destined to result in the total destruction of the concept itself.[1]

[1] Barbara Wootton, *Social Science and Social Pathology*. Allen & Unwin, 1959.

While one can sympathize readily with Lady Wootton's misgivings, it is obvious that this change in penal philosophy did not come by itself. It did not come even through Freud and the psychiatrists. The classic concepts of right and wrong, lawful and unlawful, did after all not exist in a vacuum. They reflected the morality of an established ruling class, certain of its authority in its attitude not only to questions of law but also to the rôle of the individual and the State, to all issues of religion and property, sex and family life.

It is this traditional moral authority, I should like to call it bourgeois authority, which is receding in our changing society. The young offender of today does not only hear the call urging him to be an obedient citizen. The loudest voices calling to him are anonymous. They are asking him to spend and to consume, to be a mass reader, a mass viewer and listener, a mass motorist and purchaser of gadgets, and always to fall into line with whoever and whatever is most up to date. This is the basic change. I have a feeling that in a society dominated by mass advertising, the penal system simply cannot be out of line. (After all, what is the authority of a magistrate or judge compared with the influence of the films, of television and of magazines?) And so, in practice, the penal system has already inevitably shifted its stress—away from the ideal of obedience to authority and towards the ideal of conformity with present-day society as it really is, and of re-educating young offenders to adjust so that they, too, can enjoy the gifts of so beneficent a society.

This is my first general conclusion. The second is the point, obvious indeed, that in spite of periodic public clamour that the penal system should cure the social disorder of crime, any possible penal system has in this respect its narrow limits. The measures it can take follow only after the event, after an offence has been committed. It represents at best only a piece of apparatus for social patching up. To attack the causes of crime, and even really to search for them, one has to look at society itself. To quote Lady Wootton again: "Instead of measuring a man's mental health by his ability to get along with his environment, we should find out what environment is itself conducive to mental health."[1] This is surely true above all for the young.

[1] *Ibid.*

CHAPTER XIV

Myth and Sociology

WHO ARE THE DELINQUENTS?

IN my view it is not difficult to show how the current environment in Britain is affecting delinquency.

British society in the 'fifties produced an increased number of young delinquents of a distinct social and psychological type. They were boys and girls (many more of them boys) from the more disorganized sections of working-class life. They tended to come from broken homes or to have inadequate parents, towards whom they often felt violently antagonistic; many of them could be described as neurotic or maladjusted; they tended to have indifferent school and bad employment records. They were concentrated in so-called bad areas, but there were in general enough of them about to create a new style of gang life which provided a collective sanction for their defiant outlook. The delinquency of the boys was usually expressed by larceny and breaking and entering—here the figures went up sharply. The trend of the girls was towards some shoplifting, but more often towards early sexual promiscuity and prostitution—this is not so easy to measure, but the number of illegitimate births among teenage girls did go up quite noticeably. Lastly, this rise of delinquency during the period was so marked that it must have had its special causes.

I realize that as soon as the word "cause" is used, one has to qualify carefully. Delinquency is a loose term, to be identified with the statistics of actual court convictions only on an overall view, and it is in this general sense that I use it here. All the most painstaking research has not yet really shown us why any one individual boy or girl will become a delinquent. From the same catastrophic family one youngster will turn into a delinquent and his brothers and sisters not. Some maladjusted or low-intelligence youngsters will seem drawn into crime with inevitability, while others with no greater expectations go through life unscathed. Certain boys from a "bad area" where the population is perpetually at war with the police will in the natural way of things grow up into thieves. Others from the same streets may ten years later be found as respectable householders in the suburbs. We can in fact only talk in delinquent *trends*.

On the other hand some of these trends do not appear difficult to define—this proposition is worth restating, because it has been the subject of some recent debate. For example, in her Nuffield Report, Lady Wootton has sharply questioned the statistical validity of a number of recent sociological and psychological analyses of the causes of crime, and the relevant sections of her work represent something of a hurdle which has to be taken by anyone venturing into discussing these causes—fortunately it does not appear as formidable as made out.

In the first place Lady Wootton charges certain researchers with middle-class bias. By trying to study young working-class delinquents in purely psychiatric terms, they are ignoring the temptations which rain down on such boys and girls in a stridently acquisitive society. The point is a fair one (and one would have liked Lady Wootton to carry her study of this acquisitive society further), but it is not really an argument against talking about the general causes of crime.

In the longest section of *Social Science and Social Pathology*,[1] Lady Wootton presents a subject-by-subject analysis of twelve expert British and other studies of the association of juvenile crime with such factors as poverty, low intelligence, broken homes, mothers going out to work and maternal deprivation, the decline of religion, non-membership of youth organizations and other factors. Her considered conclusion is that such association remains largely unproven—statistical information is still too scanty and too contradictory to enable us to speak in precise terms about causes of crime. This may be true in the sense that the results of these studies do not tally with the same mathematical precision as studies in the physical sciences. But that does not make them valueless. I have a feeling that, after exposing various contradictions in these results, Lady Wootton rather too severely leaves it at that. Take for example her final summary of what she feels can be concluded from all the twelve studies, which I think worth quoting in full:

On the whole, it seems that offenders come from relatively

[1] *Ibid.*

large families. Not infrequently (according to some investigators very frequently) other members of the delinquents' (variously defined) families have also been in trouble with the law. Offenders are unlikely to be regular churchgoers, but the evidence as to whether club membership discourages delinquency remains "wildly contradictory". If they are of age to be employed, they are likely to be classified as "poor" rather than as "good" workers. Most of them come from the lower social classes, but again the evidence as to the extent to which they can be described as exceptionally poor is conflicting; nor is there any clear indication that their delinquency is associated with the employment of their mothers outside the home. Their health is probably no worse than that of other people, but many of them have earned poor reputations at school, though these may well be prejudiced by their teachers' knowledge of their delinquencies. In their school days they are quite likely to have truanted from school, and perhaps an unusually large proportion of them come from homes in which at some (frequently unspecified) time both parents were not, for whatever reason, living together; yet even on these points, the findings of some enquiries are negative. And beyond this we cannot go.[1]

This passage has a curiously negative air, yet the more one looks at it, the more it appears as a considerable summary of statistical knowledge which by and large supports the ideas of penal officers and experienced social workers about the delinquents of today. I feel tempted to put the same facts into the following *positive* paraphrase which, though crudely put, would not be unfair: "On the whole it seems the delinquents come from 'the lower social classes'; not necessarily from the poorest families, but from those involved in social or moral disorder—in an unusually large number of cases from families where the father and mother were at one time not living together and/or some other member of the family had already been in trouble with the law. Such defects of family background frequently seem to handicap the delinquents in their social lives outside the family. At school they are likely to be among the truants and to earn poor reputations. In employment they are likely to be classified as 'poor' rather than 'good' workers. They are certainly very unlikely to be regular churchgoers. On the other hand, no overall statistical conclusion can be drawn about the

[1] *Ibid.*

membership of delinquents in youth clubs, since intensive efforts have been made to open clubs precisely for the benefit of young people who have already been in trouble with the courts. Many have been drawn into membership of such clubs, and though they have in this way at certain times been 'kept off the streets' it is hard to say how far this has diminished actual delinquency."

EFFECTS OR CAUSE?

Such current information about the young delinquents seems quite enough to go on to the question of explaining the increase in their numbers.

For example, one could argue convincingly, if a little fancifully, that the sharp rise in juvenile delinquency in Britain from 1955 onwards was linked with the arrival in that year of British commercial television, and this would not be entirely absurd. Not just because from that year onwards, the television screens were filled with a much greater variety of gunplay, murder and other violence, though I think at certain low I.Q. levels this also had its corroding effect. No, the main argument would be a different one, namely that with the advent of commercial television the insidious voices of the advertisers invaded yet another sphere of British life. Since the popular press had to fall into line and become more popular still, the domination of British society by the advertising of consumption goods advanced further, and with it the outlook that material possessions equalled happiness and glamour.

With this, a great many more mothers went out to work, and family cohesion was weakened. More boys and girls in their last year at school were induced to think only of leaving in order to earn and spend, and the authority of teachers was diminished. To obtain the money for what television proclaimed as essential to a life of glamour, an increased minority of boys and girls yielded to the temptation of dishonesty, and up shot the delinquency figures.

In short, one could argue convincingly that the advent of commercial television had increased the trend towards "materialism" in British life, which in turn is often blamed for the increase of delinquency. This last view seems also that of a leader of the legal profession and a former socialist, Lord Shawcross:

When a young man looks around and sees how lax our standards are nowadays in regard both to sexual matters and to matters of honesty and loyalty, it is not altogether surprising that his own behaviour is not of the best. This is our responsibility, ours as a nation, I mean. There is the appalling petty pilfering, the tax evasion, even the avoidance of doing a good and honest day's work in one's employment. In all these matters our increasingly materialist attitude has led to perceptible demoralisation. Mothers and fathers must realise they can never abdicate their responsibility for bringing up their children well to the State . . .[1]

This sort of moral lecturing is, of course, pretty pointless, a mere delving around among symptoms, without trying to see the underlying social and economic changes of which they are the result. For if we look more closely at most of the trends which are frequently blamed for rising delinquency, it is not hard to recognize them as themselves not really causes but effects—the results of a far greater social and economic revolution which is taking place today.

For example, take one of the favourite "causes" blamed for the unruliness of the young, "the decline of religion". Since a good part of the English working class has long been estranged from formal church attendance, what is really meant by this charge is the declining influence of the Christian Churches as a source of conventional morality. But quite apart from spiritual changes, one can see evident social or even physical causes for this decline. How can a church or chapel remain the old sort of focus in an industrial society where people are always on the move, living in one locality, working in a second, and taking their pleasures in a third? Or if one thinks of the volume of high-powered advertising and entertainment directed at the citizens of today, what actual room is left for the propagation of religious faith?

In the same way, other favourite developments blamed for delinquency are strictly speaking not causes but effects of deeper social change. What is the use of talking of "too much easy money for the young" or blaming "inflated wages" if these are simply an outcome of supply and demand in industries dependent on youthful labour, while entire other industries are dependent on the

[1] From a speech by Lord Shawcross in Eastbourne, quoted in the *Daily Telegraph*, 27th March 1958.

spending of these wages? When it is said that "parents should not abdicate their responsibility", does anyone really expect—for this is the usual reference—British working-class parents to retain their old authority over their sons and daughters when the latter are exposed to the call of so many other authoritative voices out to teach them how to enjoy an affluent life? "Mothers going out to work?" But what else should one expect in a society dominated by the advertising of consumer goods? "The chronic shortage of policemen?" This too is not surprising when a constable's weekly pay is two-thirds the wage of a car-factory worker. (The policeman's wife also reads those women's magazines in whose stories the heroine never marries an ordinary constable!) Finally, as ingenuous speakers like Lord Shawcross complain, there is the alleged decline in national moral standards. Yes, but it's not morality that is being advertised from the hoardings, nor does morality determine the choice of sensational headlines in the popular newspapers. And what are the economic realities which make such newspapers what they are?

It is surely not so much social symptoms which matter in the search for the causes of delinquency as the evident transformation of an entire society which is in progress. To understand how this bears on the young delinquents it is, I think, necessary to leave their pathetic little world for a while—perhaps to regard the increase in their numbers as a danger signal—and to look at the shape of the new society which is producing them.

CHAPTER XV

The Passing of the Bourgeois Age

THE FUNDAMENTAL CHANGE

THE belief that we are rushing into a new society is today found all around us, but the definition of the basic nature of the change is less easy. Some would see it in the incessant march of scientific technology; in the age of jets, rockets, artificial materials, electronics and of automation advancing already from the factory to the office. In an industrial country like Britain, this revolution is particularly evident. One can see how on top of the historic divisions between the two nations of England in terms of social class a new division is being superimposed—a rift between two cultures, between those who are familiar with the new scientific age and those who are not.

Some again would put the main emphasis on social levelling and the spread of new habits of mass consumption and entertainment. These have indeed spread fast. In 1960, the great majority of British households owned a television set. It was expected that well before the end of the 1960s the majority of households would own a car. Among the countries of Europe, Britain has probably already travelled furthest into Subtopia. Since the war three million council houses have been built on what at times looks like a single pattern. At a certain hour of the week in 1959 one-third of the population was (said to be) watching the American television serial "Wagon Train". One of every three younger citizens read the *Daily Mirror* and one in three at a higher age group the *Daily Express*. From an office in London, E.C.4, the directors of the *Daily Mirror* group could, in 1961, take decisions on the editorial policy of women's magazines read by eight out of every ten British women and girls.

In connection with this mass culture, some saw the signs of change in the arrival of new figures of authority, the take-over bidders, the advertisers, the gossip columnists, the publicity men. Yet not only these were making headway. A telling sign of social change, to my mind, was the growth of the teenage market and of a mass youth culture. I recall a remark which made a particular impression on me, made to me by the head of a youth club founded half a century ago in what was then still the darkest East End of London. "Today our motoring club has sixty motor-cycles and thirty motor-scooters. The girl friends act as secretaries. They'll arrange the logistics of a tour to the Pyrenees without any ado."

On whatever outward signs of a new age one likes to put the emphasis, to my mind the essence of the contemporary change is that the great bourgeois age, which went with exclusive middle-class privilege and middle-class culture, is passing. As it recedes, it is being gradually replaced by a new affluent society (after thinking of alternatives I come back to Professor J. K. Galbraith's term as the most apt)[1] which is based on mass consumption, and the increasing participation of practically everyone in a new good life and many other things alongside.

Of the fundamental character of this change there can already be little question. It was the age of bourgeois exclusiveness which launched what we know as Western industrial civilization. This bourgeois age has had a long innings, but almost any middle-class European whose memories go back some thirty or forty years knows that a dramatic change has occurred in his lifetime which it is not easy to communicate to the young, and that the world of his own childhood with its large solid houses and its domestic servants lies already in another era. Writing in 1955 about the new look of post-war Britain and Europe, I tried to define what it had replaced:

> The causes of Subtopia lie in the social change more far reaching than the establishment of the Welfare State—in something like a change of ruling class.
> It is ruling classes which set cultural patterns and for more than a century the dominant culture of Western Europe has clearly been that of the well-to-do middle class, the *haute bourgeoisie*. It was a culture which went with those great English social inventions, the gentlemen's club (and the soft club chair), amateur sport, and the long week-end; with French *cuisine* and Finishing Schools, German scientific *Tuechtigkeit* and

[1] While using the term with acknowledgements, I am aware that here and on other occasions I am not using it in the same precise way as Mr Galbraith.

German music, Italian and Viennese opera; it went with family holidays in Scotland and Switzerland and on the Riviera; with large *appartements*, parlourmaids, and the solid house façades of Europe's middle-class cities. It went also with the distinguished European repertory theatre, the great tradition of the European novel (whose last representative was probably Thomas Mann), with liberal individualism, introspection in art, psychoanalysis—anyone thinking aloud could enumerate a similar list for himself. In all its aspects—and this was important—this bourgeois way of life was also a minority culture from which the lower-class majority of the population was by and large excluded.

It is this bourgeois minority culture with its exclusive appeal that has been crumbling. The process has gone further in the United States than in Britain, and further in Britain than in tenaciously bourgeois countries like France or Germany. What we are now entering instead is a social era based on mass participation. The keynote is that culture is no longer for a minority. Everyone must now participate.[1]

Writing the present chapter in 1960, I feel that the revolution has already gone further, and with it new problems are upon us. To understand these better, it is as well to see the sort of social structure which has been left behind us. In terms of what one might call "ruling-class participation", the bourgeois society which arose in Europe out of the French and the Industrial Revolutions represented a considerable advance on earlier aristocratic eras in which power and fashionable culture had been vested in only a small fraction of the population. The solid upper middle-class culture, the one which really mattered in the European bourgeois society, was shared in by perhaps ten to fifteen per cent. of the nation. This made it a comparatively broad culture, and yet it was still a minority culture in which the majority, and especially the working classes, had little or no share. And it is this exclusive bourgeois class system and culture which is today cracking up.

In retrospect some points about it are worth noting to illuminate the change. First, the system of bourgeois exclusiveness quite easily survived the political revolution of one man, one vote. It

[1] *Encounter*, June 1955.

has taken a second upheaval, the present one, to shake it. Secondly, even in a country of widespread wealth like England, the bourgeois culture was still that of a class small enough to base its social life on direct personal contact and relations. The contacts of the head of an upper middle-class family which mattered were nearly all direct and personal: with the fellow-members of his class, his profession and his club; with his family solicitor, doctor and public school-master; with his tailor, his personal shopkeeper, domestic servants and the like.

In the third place, bourgeois culture was also authoritative. It rested on a network of institutions which, particularly in England, derived authority from history and tradition: Crown and Parliament, the Law, the Church, the Armed Services, Oxford and Cambridge, *The Times* and *Guardian*, the Medical Colleges, the Learned Societies. But authority in the bourgeois society lay not only with institutions. It was also personally vested in individuals. The bearer of a title had traditional social and moral authority. So had a bishop, a judge, a senior Cabinet Minister and a Colonial Governor. The writers of editorials in *The Times* had *their* special individual authority; so did eminent lawyers and Harley Street specialists (who may have preserved it best of all); so did all kinds of figures like public school headmasters, and England and County cricket captains; and so on and so on. Of course, the whole system was buttressed by money, but not only by that: money still has its power. It was buttressed by the tradition of a whole close-knit class culture. If British policemen carried an aura of unusual authority and respect, it was because they were seen as represent-atives of a society sure of all fundamental belief.

THE CHANGE IN BRITAIN

It is this authoritative bourgeois order which has today become suddenly tenuous and is crumbling. Such traditions as public school exclusiveness, the ponderousness of Parliamentary debate at Westminster, even the right accent—they are still all there, but have become suddenly less significant. This observation is not new, but an additional point I would make is that the dis-integration of bourgeois values has gone further in England than some other countries—further than in France or than in Western

Germany where the restoration of old social forms has been remarkable—and this in spite of the English retention of titles and tradition and the importance of the so-called Establishment. Or perhaps just because the traditional surface of English life is still so sedulously maintained, the real social changes beneath it appear more dramatic. On the Continent of Europe, palaces turned into museums or municipal offices have usually been devoted to this purpose for some generations, but as for the English stately home now converted into a convalescent home or Approved School, people no more than middle aged can still remember how not long ago it was filled with guests, grooms and gardeners.

One can think of various reasons for the more rapid crack-up of English bourgeois society. There were the shocks of the First World War and its casualties, the drift of the inter-war years, the dreary years of dole queues and Stanley Baldwin, and the progressive loss of empire. Other European countries underwent similar experiences, but I think the sharper social cleavages of English society intensified the crumbling. The genius of Lord Northcliffe also had something to do with speeding the change. The fact that the British were conditioned to read far greater numbers of popular newspapers than anybody else did mean that they were exposed at an earlier stage to an influence destructive of the old order. The similarity of language also laid England more open to transatlantic influences. It allowed such American publicity figures as film stars and pop singers to be substituted for the traditional figures of British authority—this has also happened elsewhere in Europe, but nowhere to quite the same degree as in this country.

At any rate, historians will probably conclude that some decisive social change was set on foot in England in the bad inter-war years, some more pronounced drift, some greater loss of upper middle-class assurance than elsewhere, which had the effect that if the post-war British affluent society is not more affluent than others, it seems to be more stridently commercial than others and more destructive of social roots.

At this point it may be worth giving a rough definition of what I have been describing as "the affluent society". I would say that the affluent society begins to take shape when techniques of capitalist mass production have reached such a pitch that the wheels of the economy can only be kept turning over if in theory all citizens of the society are turned into consumers on a full scale. I would put its starting point in Britain at around 1950—really the decisive take-off date when all Western Europe began to advance towards an "Americanized" social life of cars, gadgets and mass media.

Among the many new features of the affluent society, certain trends seem to stand out. Mr J. K. Galbraith, in writing about America, has laid stress on the priority given to personal consumption, the growth of the idea that material possessions equal status, and the relative decline of the public sector. I would add that they also include three changes affecting family relationships, which I would put under the headings of "Women go out to work", "Loss of status of the father" and "All youth is golden".

All these trends have, I think, some influence on the relatively marginal problem of youthful delinquency which in turn throws some light on their effects.

CHAPTER XVI

The British Affluent Society

CONSUMPTION AS MAINSPRING

ANOTHER name one could give the affluent society would be the age of participation. Because of the shape which the economy has assumed, it depends for its stability not only on uninterrupted mass consumption but on consumption on a steadily expanding scale. Every citizen must consequently be drawn into the circle of producing and consuming at the maximum level. If the affluent society is to prosper, not merely a privileged minority as heretofore, but every man, woman and child must participate in the good life of modern living.[1]

Everyone must participate. In a country like Britain, one can see this trend quite visually illustrated in the contemporary movement of the British working classes away from their drab nineteenth-century streets, the darkened brick, the draughty passages, the worn sink, and towards the ideal of a new suburban life of small house, small garden, small car and large television set. In the new society it is public authorities which mainly provide the new houses, but private enterprise which provides all the rest, which gives the working-class housewife her modern kitchen and appliances and the whole family its mobility and entertainment. In face of this supreme drive to create customers in the mass, the old bourgeois privilege based on exclusiveness, large houses, domestic servants, has simply crumbled. It is crumbling the faster because other influences are also pushing in the same direction.

MATERIAL POSSESSIONS EQUAL STATUS

In the affluent society it is not enough that the wants of every citizen should be met. To satisfy the capacity of the largest production interests, new wants have constantly to be created. Mr

[1] I believe this to be the basic social trend even though I am aware of the fact that in Britain a substantial minority, estimated at several million people, were still living on the fringe of acute poverty, especially old-age pensioners, invalids, etc.

Galbraith has drawn attention to the distortions caused in American society as new wants are created and intensified by an advertising industry running at a rate of eleven billion dollars a year. The notorious example of an industry dependent upon the constant creation of new wants is the giant American motor industry, whose models have been deliberately built and stylized to become obsolescent in a few years and so to make replacement necessary. For many models no spare parts are even issued after five years: the motor industry could not stand the repairing of older cars. The British economy is not yet so far advanced, but on the same road. (One can, for instance, detect a trend towards built-in obsolescence in British cars, too. A significant feature in television advertising is the stress on "newness" in household appliances—some new gimmick, some new improvement, usually a minor change but presented as making the new model infinitely preferable to its predecessor.)

This creation of wants requires constant advertising. This in turn means that big financial interests must take over and enlarge the media of mass communication. The mass media must in fact become both a part of big business and themselves big business. In the British affluent society, the newspapers and magazines that carry the bulk of advertising are in actual fact already controlled by a handful of large financial interests, and television has followed suit. In some ways the close tie-up between the big newspapers, advertising and betting interests has already gone further in Britain than in the United States.

This take-over, in turn, has a result on the contents of the mass media. It involves them in the drive to create a new image of what is desirable—that of a world where through material consumption everybody is happy, wealthy, successful and enjoying the right status. An example of this image-creation is offered (not absolutely every time but often enough) by the *TV Times*, among all British periodicals perhaps the cleverest expression of the ideals of British advertising. In its pages, all articles seem written skilfully but indistinguishably in one single style adjusted to celebrity worship. All personalities, whether statesmen and scientists or pop singers and comedians, are brought down (or up) to the same denominator. All are presented as happy, successful, well-to-do, but at the same time as people who can smile at past failure and are essentially simple people like you or me—more than that, dear viewers, these wonderful people are only too happy to create further happiness by entertaining you: and so, week by week, world without end.[1]

This gigantic take-over by the advertisers has, of course, not been the only cultural trend in the affluent society. (There has been a noticeable hiving off of new middle-class culture, seen, for example, in the rise in circulations of the *Observer* and *Sunday Times*; while many television programmes on any channel have also been informative, vital and stimulating—television is, after all, only a medium.) By and large, however, it is already clear that before the triumphant onrush of the new affluent mass culture, geared with the aid of highly-paid talent to the advertising of consumer goods, the significance of the historic institutions seems suddenly to have dwindled, to be no longer in the foreground of British life. It was as if a glossy wand had been waved. The affairs of the Church, the tribulations of the Royal Navy (or for that matter of the T.U.C.), the uninspired Parliamentary debates at Westminster, the editorials in *The Times* (trying to renew and re-advertise itself) and the Left-wing views in the *New Statesman*, the attention paid to occasions like the Oxford and Cambridge Boat Race or the efforts of the Amateur Athletic Association to find a few thousand pounds—all these seemed to pale before the new foreground of the affluent society: the parade of television personalities, the arranged publicity for girl models and boy singers, the advertisements for electric mixers and Ford Consuls, the unending colour-print pages on fashions, foods and cosmetics in the women's magazines. Through the irresistible mass attack of this new artificial culture, everything else appeared suddenly pushed into the background, reduced in size, dated.[2]

[1] Writing about television advertisements in *Encounter* (November 1959), Mr Richard Hoggart pointed out that it was not "in the interest of the advertisers to be radical or searching, to break the audience into minority groups; they have to have mass audiences, audiences of masses". Mr Hoggart's *The Uses of Literacy* (1957) remains the most vivid study of this aspect of the British affluent society.

[2] A Labour Member of Parliament told me how sometime in 1959 he made the same point during a debate in the House and a day or so later in a popular television programme. The indications were that on the latter occasion he was actually heard by more M.P.s than at Westminster.

The consequences of this shift in popular values were not ignored. They have been noticeably criticized, for example, by Richard Hoggart and the younger writers of the Left who followed him, but I think it was not always seen clearly what this shift actually involved. Discussing the violent, inchoate protest by young writers against British life of the 'fifties, Mr Anthony Crosland has remarked that he could sympathize with their frustration, for one of the things which marked out British life from that of other countries was the blanket of smug, lethargic conservatism which descended on Britain in the 'fifties. Mr Crosland went on:

> This can be seen almost everywhere one looks: in our lagging rate of economic growth, the sluggish pace of technical innovation, the absence of civic initiative, the lack of revolt against the public schools, the number of taboo subjects from the monarchy to the trade unions, our laws on homosexuality and hanging, the level of public patronage to the arts, our insular nationalism, our attitude to Europe, and so on indefinitely. It is not only that these things persist longer than in other countries; but they persist with the full support of most of the population. No wonder that young, radical intellectuals feel discouraged and frustrated.[1]

But this political lethargy was only one side of British life in the 'fifties, as Mr Crosland ought to know (and has indeed remarked elsewhere). Side by side with it, the decade in Britain saw the sweeping march of the working class into suburban life, the dynamic advance of youth into highly-paid semi-skilled work, the spread of technical education, the revolution in mass motoring and other mass consumption, and the hectic expansion of the glossy advertisers' culture promoting it. This dynamic in everything which is linked with the progress of the affluent society has to be set against the lethargy in other spheres of British life; indeed, it was surely in part the cause of this lethargy. And if this social and cultural revolution has been more pronounced in Britain than other European countries, it was because Britain, among other things, started off with a far larger and more businesslike popular newspaper industry and a larger and more Americanized advertising industry. In these respects, other European countries are only just catching up.

[1] *The Spectator*, 12th February 1960.

The shift in social and cultural priorities also proceeded faster because the affluent society contains a built-in economic unbalance.

THE LAG OF THE PUBLIC SECTOR

The relative decline of the public sector in the affluent society seems the simple consequence of the identification by the advertisers of personal and private consumption with personal happiness.

The equation any government in a capitalist society must solve is simple. Every citizen likes to spend his income on consumption of his personal choice. All citizens equally dislike having a part of this income taken in taxation for public ends, even if as essential as schools and hospitals. The success of a government in balancing these demands against each other is a measure of its popularity. In the affluent society, however, mass advertising comes in to disturb the balance. Or to be more precise, since advertising is only an instrument, it is the fact that the giant producers have developed advertising as a scientific technique for creating and increasing the demand for their goods, which has introduced a new situation, since this technique is employed only on behalf of goods produced by private enterprise, and almost never on behalf of public services rendered by the state. Mr Galbraith has shown how in the United States this one-sided concentration of "the massed drums of modern publicity" has created a visible unbalance in the American affluent society which, if not wildly dangerous, has led already to a deplorable distortion of social priorities. The distortion is seen in the contrast between, on the one side, the fabulous American living standard in consumption goods, and alongside it the ugly problems of slums and delinquency in American cities:

To create the demand for new cars we must contrive elaborate and functionless changes each year and then subject the consumer to ruthless psychological pressures to persuade him of their importance. Were this process to falter or break down, the consequences would be disturbing. In the meantime there are large ready-made needs for schools, hospitals, slum clearance and urban redevelopment, sanitation, parks, playgrounds, police and a thousand other things. Of these needs almost no one must be persuaded. They are unavailable only because, as public officials of all kinds and ranks explain each day with practiced skill, the money to provide them is unavailable. So it has come about that we get growth and increased employment along the dimension of private goods only at the price of increasingly frantic persuasion. We exploit but poorly the opportunity along the dimension of public services. The economy is geared to the least urgent set of human wants.[1]

In Britain, a similar trend was during the first post-war years actively countered by the political decision of the Labour Government to give subsidized public housing and public health unquestioned priority over private consumption. But the Labour Government ran into some problems over this, and under Conservative *laisser-faire* in the 'fifties, the British affluent society has also begun to show distinct signs of social unbalance. On one side there was the steady rise in standards of personal consumption. Alongside this was the evident belief of the Government that the country could not *afford* to build a single new hospital—or prison: none were built during the decade. There was the lag in subsidised public housing; the inadequate provision for old-age pensioners; the relative slowness in replacing antiquated school buildings,[2] in providing youth clubs and playing fields. Above all, the lack of social balance was illustrated by the inadequate salaries and consequent staff shortages in public services vital to the welfare of society, but not falling into the sphere of private advertising. There was the persistent shortage of nurses (what would have happened but for girls from overseas?), of teachers in state schools, of policemen, penal officers, midwives, youth workers.[3] Setting these shortages against the boom in all kinds of personal consumption, and in the advertising industry itself, the picture of Britain in 1960 already shows the characteristic social distortions of the affluent society.

About this two comments could be made. Britain is still ruled by Parliament, not the mass media, and in 1960 some of the

[1] J. K. Galbraith, *The Affluent Society*. Hamish Hamilton, 1958.

[2] It is true that on an average eight new schools were built each week, but compare this with the twenty thousand new cars turned out weekly.

[3] And also of clergymen. The average income of a Church of England parish clergyman in 1959 was about £675 to £750 with a house provided —no longer an adequate middle-class family income.

problems arising from the decline of the public sector had already impressed themselves pretty firmly on public attention. The proposals of the Crowther Report for raising the school age to 16—even though postponed by the Government—and of the Albemarle Report for providing public finance for the youth services, could be seen as attempts to redress some of this un-balance within special fields. So could the setting up of an enquiry into the pay problems of the British police: clearly a point must come when an affluent society has to wake up and offer adequate pay to those who protect it. It was, however, also apparent—the General Election of 1959 showed this pretty clearly—that redress-ing the balance would be no easy task. For instance, there was always the one-way pressure of the daily press with its values geared to those of advertising. As a result of this tie-up, any tax reduction in the Budget—cheaper beer, cheaper baccy, sixpence off income tax—was automatic front-page headline news: it was good for the ads., good for business, good for circulation. On the other hand, talk about the need for more teachers' training colleges, for newer hospitals, for more probation officers—this was mere stuff for well-intentioned editorials, not read by nine popular-press readers out of ten. In this way, a persistent shortage of school-teachers was something simply taken for granted—consumption had to come first.

The second observation—and this, after what may seem a considerable diversion brings us back to our young delinquents— is that if we take the points where the public sector has most sharply declined, it is where working-class families and especially working-class boys and girls dependent on public services are particularly involved. It is they who have suffered from delays in rehousing; from the shortage of trained probation officers; from lack of playing-fields and sports facilities in poorer areas and from niggardly public grants to youth clubs; probably most of all from the shortage of school-teachers, from overcrowded classes and the consequent lack of individual attention. Mr John Townsend in his interesting account of teaching in difficult secondary modern schools[1] has, for example, shown how the constant staff changes in such schools and the need to make do with inexperienced "directed" student teachers and untrained Dominion graduates,

[1] John Townsend, *The Young Devils*. Chatto and Windus, 1958.

has not only debased standards but added to the sense of insecurity of problem children:

> Schools should be the one place where children from unhappy or unstable homes should find security and feel wanted . . . but in face of this restlessness within the profession, and the patch-it-up policies of government and educational authorities alike, it is almost impossible to provide this; or to build and develop character in their pupils, obtain good educational standards, respect for authority, or achieve any worthwhile corporate life.

In fact, if one takes just this particular social distortion, on the one side the intensified stress on money values in the message proclaimed by the affluent society to such youngsters, and on the other the visible lag in the social services designed to help them, one can see this distortion, perhaps, not as a direct and measurable cause, but certainly as part of the background of rising delinquency in the 'fifties. How much weight to give to it is hard to say, for the affluent society is also responsible for other great changes, namely in family relations.

CHAPTER XVII

The Family and the Affluent Society

THE RESILIENT MIDDLE CLASS

BEFORE leaving the subject of these basic changes in outlook in the affluent society, it ought to be said that they affect different classes in different ways. They have noticeably had a much stronger impact on the working classes than on the middle class.

What has happened to the middle class in the British affluent society is that it has changed from a bourgeoisie largely represented by independent professional men and entrepreneurs to a new and more dependent middle class of administrators and technicians, largely employed by big private and public institutions. Culturally, the change has meant a lessened sense of middle-class independence and self-assurance, perhaps also of morale, but in spite of much lament, the transformation has not been altogether to the bad.

It is already quite clear that in a highly conservative country like Britain the upper and middle classes can coast along success-fully with the new affluent society. Especially for middle-class youth, its initial impact has been distinctly positive.

It has in the first place brought a stimulating vista of expansion. The pages of advertisements of positions vacant in every daily newspaper show that the new administrative middle class of the affluent society will be considerably larger in numbers than was the old bourgeoisie. Secondly, the change has brought a very marked new spirit of competitiveness and discipline to British middle-class youth. Greater demands at schools and universities have introduced a whole new hierarchy of grades of merit. If the public schools have lost in social exclusiveness, this has been more than offset by reinforcement in middle-class numbers from the grammar schools. There are also more ladders to climb; science and technology have opened vast new avenues of employment—and how the young flock into them! Culturally, middle-class young people have been far less affected by the intensified power of the mass media than their working-class contemporaries. By contrast with pre-war philistinism,.the cultural horizons of British middle-class youth have, indeed, broadened noticeably. There is far more active participation in music (including esoteric jazz), more interest in modern furniture, the modern theatre, in motoring and in international travel. In fact, as the old economic class distinctions, like having servants and being the only people to have cars, have broken down, so new class differences have been reconstructed along intellectual lines; and these have, if anything, become more marked again as the controllers of the mass media directed at working-class readers have lowered their sights.[1]

In the first phase of the affluent society, in short, British middle-class youth has benefited in many ways, but especially, I think, through the increased working discipline which has been imposed. Of course there are the problems which arise from the bigness and impersonality of the new society, and which overshadow the lives of all young people. But against these, English class snobbery is still a powerful defence—witness the way suburban young people have flocked into the Young Conservative associations. Or again, middle-class youth can find an answer to the times in earlier marriage and more pronounced retreat into purely personal relations. (Across the Channel, too: discussing the new defensive outlook of French middle-class youth, Mme Françoise Giroud summed it up as: "*Comme ils ont le cœur frileux. Vite, se marier. Vite, avoir des enfants. Vite, edifier sa niche.*")[2]

The lives of working-class young people have been rather

---

[1] Since the war Britain has fallen into line swiftly with the United States and European countries in making a university degree an essential qualification for responsible administrative and technical posts. In an illuminating survey (*The Observer*, 4th September 1960), Dr Mark Abrams has shown how British graduates in annually increasing numbers are taking over such posts not only, as hitherto, in the professions but also—and this is the striking change—in business and industry. As Dr Abrams points out, this means that already by 1970 there will be far less of a cultural gap between "the businessmen" and "the intellectuals". The danger of this stratification is that, if left to itself, it may create a wider gap between the lower ranks of administrators and the majority below them; i.e. that the cultural gap between the readers of a successful "class" newspaper like *The Observer* and a successful "mass" newspaper like *The People* is not narrowing but growing wider.

[2] Françoise Giroud, *La Nouvelle Vague*. Gallimard, 1958.

differently affected in the affluent society. Not, of course, merely negatively. If we want to see how successfully one section of working-class youth is acquiring middle-class status, we need only look at the class background of boys and girls in grammar schools, at who works in the laboratories and who are the members of new provincial rowing and sailing clubs and at the classless world of jazz. As for the general benefits of the affluent society, it has, of course, brought most working-class families an incomparably more varied life. It has brought them modern housing through the estates, and mobility through motoring; it has brought music through radio and pop records; drama through the medium of films; comment on current affairs through television; domestic science through the women's magazines, and so forth.

The negative effects of the affluent society on working-class life are certainly less obvious and less important, yet they can also be discerned. The working classes are more immediately affected by the relative lag in public services. They are vulnerably exposed to the cultural assault of the mass media, for instance in putting across half-assimilated American values. Working-class families are also more vulnerable to the socially and psychologically harmful effects of rehousing, as expressed in a breakup of local community life. Researchers like Michael Young and Peter Willmott[1] have shown how even well-intentioned large-scale rehousing can diminish the tradition of warm family ties and the defensive community sense of the old slum street, for which fresh air and new suburban surroundings are no substitute, at least not at first. It is hardly an accident that the largest of all London housing estates, at Dagenham, has a particularly high delinquency rate.[2] If we turn to what is called "alienation" from work, it is the working classes who are most affected by mechanization of all production, which is turning many jobs into a meaningless ritual. (The complaint of "boredom" at work and out of work, so widely prevalent

[1] Michael Young and Peter Willmott, *Family and Kinship in East London*, Routledge and Kegan Paul, 1957.
[2] A local teacher put it to me like this: "The estate was a flipping ghetto from the start. Working-class families and practically nobody else were just pushed into the place as a class and today there are a lot of angry young men on the estate. The insecurity of the parents on the estate is also passed on to the children."

among working-class youth, is seldom heard on a middle-class level.) Lastly, it is working-class youth which has been most intimately affected by what is perhaps the most important change in social life in the affluent society, the change in family relationships.

MARRIED WOMEN GO OUT TO WORK

Yes, but should they?

This is no longer a question worth asking. The only valid question is how this revolutionary change in family life should so quickly have come about. The simplest answer is that married women are today going out to work in millions because for the first time they are able to do so. This is the initial revolution. Professor Titmuss[1] has calculated that from the mid-Victorian family of six or more the average working-class family had already fallen to an average of less than two and a half children from marriages contracted in the 1920s. In 1890 about a third of the life expectancy of a working-class woman was devoted to pregnancy and the care of small infants. Today it is only one-fourteenth of her life. By the time she has completed her cycle of birth and infant care, the present-day working-class woman has still more than half her life to live. At the same time, modern appliances have freed her progressively from household drudgery while the trend continues towards more and more State supervision of her children. Even so cautious an observer as Professor Titmuss has said that to speak of a "revolutionary change in working-class attitudes to child-bearing" would hardly be an exaggeration.

Secondly, most married women in the affluent society go out to work because their labour is urgently required. In the current British economy this demand has already attained such proportions that by now innumerable unskilled and semi-skilled jobs in light industry and the distributive trades could not be filled at all without the employment of married as well as unmarried women.

Thirdly, married women are going out into employment because every contemporary social force is pushing them in this direction.

[1] Richard M. Titmuss, *Essays on the Welfare State*, Allen & Unwin, 1958.

Advertising creates the desire for consumption goods, hire purchase the means. It is already a fairly regular pattern that the wage of the husband "keeps" the family while that of his wife provides for the purchase of possessions like a washing-machine, television set, refrigerator or car. Just as the advertising of consumer goods increased throughout the 'fifties, so did the outside employment of married women. In 1948, the estimated number of married women at work was two million, and in 1958 about four million, and there is no sign that the maximum has yet been reached.

Is this trend to the good or bad? Does outside work create a genuine conflict for the average working-class woman between her rôles as wife and mother and as wage-earner? The fog of prejudice and platitude around the subject is not easy to pierce, but a few points seem to stand out. First of all, the affluent society has arrived; its dynamic requires married women to be both earners and spenders; and in view of the change in the size of the average family, any idea of halting the exodus of wives into employment is futile. Secondly, the material benefits flowing from the added pay packet of the average working-class wife are so tangible that they hardly need mentioning. It is largely these combined family wages which have speeded the advance towards the current *embourgeoisement* in working-class life. Thirdly, outside work is by nów part of the whole process of emancipation of the working-class woman from the old drudgery at the kitchen sink. Dr Viola Klein in her survey[1] found that a large minority of wives welcomed outside work primarily because it enlarged their horizons; so did a minority of their husbands. Moreover, one can see quite a convenient pattern: a young married woman of today will go on working for the first years after marriage; she will then stop while she has children and they are small, and only as they reach school age and the State takes over will she go back to outside work.

However, not all women follow this pattern, and everything has its price. In the unplanned way in which it took place, the mass exodus of British working-class women into outside employment has also led to a weakening of family life—at least in certain cases

[1] Viola Klein, *Working Wives*. Institute of Personnel Management, 1959.

and on certain levels. This danger is not easily measured nor even easy to generalize about, but, I think, also not to be ignored. Certainly not in those cases where parents are already indifferent and negligent towards their children. The absence of a mother from home is, of course, likely to do most harm to the morale of her children where the family life is already inadequate. There are at least some signs of this danger. There are the familiar complaints from teachers about "latchkey children" who go back from school to an empty flat, bolt their tea and out again into the streets. There is the automatic way in which a penal officer, in looking at a young offender's record, will comment: "Mother out at work, of course!"—with the idea that in his experience this is a frequent contributory cause of the trouble.

The idea of such a direct cause-and-effect relationship should perhaps not be carried too far. As is often pointed out, working wives are numbered in millions and juvenile delinquents only in tens of thousands. Yet I think this counter-argument misses the point. The *general* exodus of married women, many of them mothers, into outside work, in itself helped to create a new social atmosphere, a new *general* way of family life, whereby "home" for many boys and girls becomes less important in their lives, and the companionship and rules of the irresponsible gang therefore become more important. It was a picture of such general change which emerged most clearly from my conversations with penal officers, social workers and youth leaders. In the outcome it may not be the boy or girl in the gang whose mother works the longest hours who will actually stray over the uncertain borderline into delinquency, but this is surely a detail.

There is also the argument that the mass movement of married women into outside work has led to an increase in the number of children suffering from "maternal deprivation"; that is, of children who through lack of that security which depends on maternal love suffer from a sense of rejection; who grow up emotionally adrift, finding it hard to feel any firm ties either to their family or to society, and whose delinquency can be described as a reaction against lack of affection—the stereotype of such problem boys and girls is well known.

Has there been a great increase in the number of such emotionally deprived delinquents? Well, according to the impression of penal classification officers, there has been some increase. Any causal link between this and the doubling in the number of married women at work during the last ten years is not easy to prove. Yet it stands to reason that, once one deals with millions of families in this situation, the actual physical absence of the mother from home must in marginal cases—and these may well number thousands—be the deciding fact which pushes an already disturbed child just that much further into psychological insecurity, and so towards delinquency. After all, and today this really needs no further argument, the relation of mother and child remains the basic human relation and an early failure here may handicap a child morally for life.

Of course, one cannot calculate how many marginal cases of children suffering from maternal deprivation may result from the outside employment of millions of married women, but one parallel has always been in my mind. When I have talked to middle-class married women with professional careers about their dual rôle, not one in my experience (and I think this is common experience) was prepared to say with certainty that her professional absence from home might not have entailed *some* psychological loss to the children and to family life. It is hard to believe that the wholesale movement of working-class wives and mothers into outside work has not resulted in a similar psychological loss in at least a minority of families—it may be quite a fair-sized minority.

DECLINE IN THE STATUS OF THE FATHER

Another change in working-class family life in the affluent society, which some would say was even more important, is the diminution in the status of the working-class father as head of the family. Here, too, we may only be at the beginning of a historic social change. It was the Industrial Revolution, breaking up the extended families of rural life, which forcibly put the industrial worker into the position of sole and vital breadwinner for his wife and children. Through this process, Professor Titmuss writes,[1] "Women became dependent on men, not only in economic terms, but in the pattern of psychological subtleties in their relationship.

[1] *Ibid.*

Authoritarian patterns of behaviour, sanctioned in the factory, were carried into the home. The survival of the family became more dependent upon the labour power, the health and strength of the husband and father—the one who now 'earned life' for the whole unit." Well, farewell to this authoritarianism.

It was this position of being the sole economic provider which made the feared working-class father such a common figure in English life and literature, and today it is equally clearly being broken down. Even in the household of a relatively well-paid skilled worker, the collective pay packets of his wife and, say, a teenage son and daughter may outweigh his own. In a society where respect is increasingly based on the yardstick of money, this must have a considerable effect on relationships within the family.

In addition, technical changes are today working swiftly to lower the prestige of industrial skill from which the older working man derived his status and self-respect. The men who today at the end of the shift pour in great crowds from the assembly lines of some huge works can make no special claim for the mystery of their crafts, certainly not to their adolescent sons and daughters. In the affluent society, as Professor Titmuss has also stated, the average working-class father is subjected to sharply conflicting demands. The effect of increasing mechanization in factory work is to reduce him to a passive human unit in a vast process of production in which he is required to display little initiative, if any. Yet at the same time he is asked to show greater care and forethought in planning the future of his children: because society regards each of the fewer children of today as more valuable; because educational opportunities are more varied and promising; or simply because there are more persons about, such as youth employment officers and careers masters in comprehensive schools who come to him with such demands. There is a conflict between these two claims, and what is generally apparent today is that the authority of the average working-class father over his family has diminished and is exercised over his teenage children for a shorter period than formerly.

The loosening of family bonds was further accentuated in the 'fifties by marked changes in the relative earning power of the different generations.

ALL YOUTH IS GOLDEN

As the first half of this century has seen the economic emancipation of women, so its second half may see a parallel emancipation of adolescents.

That young people of today have far more money to spend than their parents ever had, that a new teenage market and youth culture have sprung up and an astonishing amount of advertising is directed especially at the young—these are today commonplace observations. But they illustrate another change in family relationships.

The starting-point has to be seen in the changing techniques of production. In the British census of 1931, boys still featured largely as messengers, tea-makers, errand boys and in other dead-end jobs, while one employed young woman in three was a domestic servant. All this has been transformed. *Adolescent work is no longer menial.* Youthful workers are today drawn chiefly into new light industries (electrical engineering, home equipment, food processing) and the expanding distributive trades, that is, into the most modern sectors of the economy where many of them work as full equals with their elders. This new situation is naturally reflected in the earnings of adolescents. As between an ordinary manual worker or even, say, a ticket collector on British Railways, and his teenage daughter working in a factory or shop, the balance in earnings is shifting all the time in the latter's favour.

This is again chiefly a working-class phenomenon. Of Britain's 5 million young people between 15 and 21, some 20 per cent. were in 1959 still receiving full-time education at school and college (or else were in the armed forces), and so played only a minor financial rôle as teenage purchasers. It was the remaining 80 per cent., the mostly working-class majority of 3 million boys and girls in this age-group, for the most part in well-paid employment, who have created the phenomenally affluent teenage market. According to the calculations of Dr Mark Abrams,[1] the average weekly wage of a young unmarried male worker in the 15-21 age-group had in 1959 risen to £8 and of a girl to £5, 10s., real wages 50 per cent. higher than before the war. But this is only part of the story. Because their

[1] Mark Abrams, *The Teenage Consumer*. London Press Exchange, 1960.

parents were by and large also more prosperous, the new custom was for boys and girls to keep a much higher proportion of their earnings to spend upon themselves. Dr Abrams calculated that as a result the total personal expenditure of unmarried young people was in 1959 running at about £900 million pounds a year.

This assurance of easy employment and of the money which goes with it has helped to create something of a gap between the generations. Probably the greatest difference between young people in the 'thirties and those of the 'fifties is that the former grew up under the constant threat of unemployment, something which the youth of today just cannot understand, just as some harrassed working-class parents cannot reconcile themselves to the present carefree attitude of their offspring towards jobs.

Given this new spending power, it is also natural that new industries have sprung up on every side to cater for the youth market. It is in supplying such things as records and record players, motor-cycles and scooters, soft drinks, distinctive clothes for boys (especially Italian style), Junior Miss clothes and cosmetics for girls (especially French style), that big business in the 'fifties has made roaring profits. It has also been remarked that as a result, working-class teenagers are persuaded to spend their money on a comparatively narrow range of goods, mostly mass-produced. In 1959, many a youth spent more than £1 a week on pop records, and many a girl more than £1 a week on cosmetics and hair-dressing. Expenditure on this scale has naturally also led to a barrage-like concentration of advertisers on the youth market. Films, television programmes and magazines were created or angled to attract youth. An interesting step in this direction was taken when the proprietors of Britain's largest newspaper, the *Daily Mirror*, drew a lesson from the 1959 General Election, cut down heavily on politics and proclaimed that the new message of the *Mirror* would now be directed openly at optimistic youth living in a world of expanding pleasure. (The real change was not so drastic, but the reaction was significant.)

It is also on the basis of this spending power that the commercial "youth culture" has sprung up, which seems an integral part of life in the affluent society. There are several interesting points to be made about it.

In the lives of the individual youngsters caught up in this

commercial youth culture, it represents a fairly brief interim phase, confined to their years between leaving school and marriage. From the moment they marry, set up a home and have children, most young working-class couples have to become accustomed to entirely new spending habits, a transition for which they have not been well prepared.

Secondly, for all that the youth culture reflects a new affluence, it has in itself become a cause of new class distinctions. To quote Dr Abrams:[1]

> The teenage market is almost entirely working-class; its middle-class members are either still at school or college or else just beginning on their careers; in either case they dispose of much smaller incomes than their working-class contemporaries and it is highly probable, therefore, that not far short of 90 per cent. of all teenage spending is conditioned by working-class taste and values. The aesthetic of the teenage market is essentially a working-class aesthetic.

In other words, just as working-class boys and girls were in the past cut off from the social life of middle-class youth by their poverty, so today it is by their relative affluence and different spending habits.

Another point is that the youth culture flourishes mainly where it is based on commercial products which can be quickly mass-produced, such as pop records, soft drinks, glossy magazines, or films and television programmes going out to audiences of millions. In contrast, even though young people have a need to congregate, in such necessarily local and small-scale efforts as the provision of coffee-bars through private enterprise and of youth clubs through public effort, there has been nothing like the same progress.

The atmosphere of male dominance in the youth culture can probably also be explained in market terms. Boys in Britain today outnumber girls and also earn considerably more so that they dispose of about two-thirds of teenage spending money. This increased concentration of spending power in the hands of what are mostly unskilled or semi-skilled workers is a phenomenon

[1] *Ibid.*

which was noted in the 'fifties in a number of industrial countries; it helps to explain why these young men have lately been so much more in the news, whether in setting fashions or causing trouble. This masculine slant in the youth culture is also reflected in the astonishing popularity of young male singers. Apart from their talents, these can be seen as shrewdly manufactured idols of the youth culture—young men fabulously successful yet explicitly publicized as being of working-class origin, and in fact, except for their money and success, like any ordinary youngster who spends his money on pop music.

A final aspect of the teenage culture, which is especially noticeable in Britain, is its air of instability, of constant fashion changes accompanied by hectic advertising. Again this seems fairly easy to explain. Not only do growing youngsters quickly change their tastes. Over and above this, because the upper and lower age limits of the teenage market are so narrow, the interests supplying it annually lose part of their customers as they get married, and must think of fresh ways of attracting a new generation of school-leavers. The obvious recourse is therefore to fresh advertising, new fashions and sensations. In Britain this has also another consequence. Because the American teenage market is much larger, the interests supplying British teenagers are continuously drawing upon it and so promoting American values. At any rate, the net result is a commercialized youth culture, which has admittedly led to some broadening of interests because it could not help but do so. But its worst side is that it is outwardly Americanized but inwardly not, always intent upon the ephemeral and somewhat on the nihilist side.

There is little doubt that this youth culture also draws young people still further away from their families. Its whole drive is towards entertainment and expenditure away from home. And why not, one might say; young people naturally want to be by themselves. For instance, the more that they visit well-run places like the Mecca dance-halls, where they find pleasant entertainment and are taught new standards of modern comfort, the better. The answer is that many boys and girls don't go to Mecca dance-halls precisely because they are so orderly and well run. And on a broader view, the chief fault of the youth culture remains its commercially inflated size.

CONCLUSION

To sum up, therefore, after what may seem a long excursion away from the problem of delinquency, the arrival of the affluent society has brought noticeable changes to British life. The authority of bourgeois traditions has diminished while mass advertising and popular entertainment have become progressively more powerful influences. As a result, social status has become more closely identified with personal spending, while public services have lagged behind this spending boom.

The new influences have also affected family life, especially working-class family life. Considerably greater numbers of married women have gone into outside work. The authority of the working-class father has suffered a certain decline, and the new affluence of boys and girls has led to the growth of a large and well-exploited youth culture.

None of these trends is quite new, but in Britain in the 'fifties they were all speeded up—the dividing-line from bourgeois to affluent society was definitely crossed—and from this analysis one can also deduce why increased delinquency was a likely symptom of the change.

CHAPTER XVIII

Worse for the Also-rans

THE DOWNWARD PULL

IT is never possible to isolate the consequences, good or bad, of a major social upheaval; they are always mingled. A shrewd observer of working-class life in a northern industrial city said to me, speaking of the local increase in violent juvenile crime: "The parents concerned have lost economic control based on income, they have lost intellectual control, quite a lot of them had little control based on affection, and so breakdown comes where there is no affection at all." But my acquaintance was also concerned with the selection of local industrial apprentices for advanced technical education and he thought he had never met anything as promising as the generation of the late 1950s. "These lads possess a serene self confidence. At 17 or 18, they've already advanced right out of their parents' world." Enough has been written about the pattern of British working-class life of the past for us to know that it was often oppressively narrow. It involved much parental tyranny because even highly intelligent children were at the first possible moment snatched from school to work and earn. It certainly involved a national waste of ability. The present quicker emancipation of adolescents from home has without doubt helped many bright boys and girls to break away and mount the social ladder.

At the other end of the social spectrum, however, lie the harmful effects of this break-up. To look into the background of boys and girls who pass through the penal institutions of today is chastening. The collective picture is not only of a fringe of social chaos, broken homes and neglect, but also, it seemed to me, of continuing passive helplessness—what is a woman to do when her husband suddenly walks out and her son from that day becomes unmanageable? Have such problems become worse in recent years? The signs are that at least in a section of the population, the affluent society has increased the trends making for irresponsibility among adults and delinquency among the young. These forces are obviously not simple but many and complex: what follows is an attempt not so much to enumerate as to suggest some of them.

(1) *Weakened family ties*. The impression one could get in talking to social workers in difficult areas, such as the inner suburbs of London like Notting Hill, Hammersmith, King's Cross, Hackney, was that the new affluence had in some ways passed across the scene like a breath of harsh materialism, affecting personal and family relationships. The new generation of parents who were indifferent towards their children and the children who knocked about in the streets seemed alike to have become more openly cynical. More parents than before seemed content not to know where their teenage children roamed at night, just as the children now had the money to go further afield. The whole message of the mass culture seemed to sanction personal irresponsibility. Where a man had few feelings about his family, the "I'm all right, Jack," outlook made him more likely to walk out; where a mother put her own pleasure before care of her children, more money meant that she was more often away from home.

(2) *More young victims*. One evident result has been an increase of unstable young delinquents conforming to a common psychological type: the youngster who starts with defiance against one or both parents (especially a boy against his father) and carries on this defiance against other authority figures—teachers, the boss, the police, the probation officer, society as a whole. As was mentioned earlier, a very definite increase in the number of maladjusted youngsters has been noted among the admissions to Approved Schools. One could see a collective expression of such youthful feelings of hostility in the aggressive behaviour of the gangs of young Drifters. One could deduce an increase in the number of insecure children from the fact that the figures of truancy from school were back where they had been much earlier, in spite of better schools, child guidance clinics, and greater literacy all round.

(3) *Earlier gang life*. Another consequence of weakened family ties is that many teenage boys and girls are pushed into independence before they are ready for it and when they still feel uncertain about life and about themselves. As a result, they go out at a very early age to seek reassurance and social status in gang life. But for many of them, the life of the irresponsible gang also turns out

to be monotonous and frustrating and so more of them drift across the frontier into delinquency. The earlier recourse of adolescents to gang life has also sharpened the conflict between adults and themselves, a new phenomenon on housing estates.

(4) *The greater strain.* The indications are that the new life of the affluent society brings simultaneously greater wealth and greater mental strain to many teenage boys and girls. Society treats them as pseudo-adults, both at their work and even more so in the expensive amusements offered to them in their leisure time. For boys and girls of weaker fibre, this strain of having to live as pseudo-adults is often too much. "Some of them step out of one job into another," a probation officer in the Midlands told me. "They come into a firm and at once feel themselves the equal of old Charlie who's been there thirty years. There's a shocking failure of society to prepare them for the first phase when they have money."

(5) *Not keeping up.* The affluent society also imposes greater strains by making "keeping up" a more complicated process. Professor Galbraith has shown how in the United States poverty is already coming to be looked on as not just a misfortune but a kind of cultural disgrace, a blow to self-respect. One reason is that American magazines and television are constantly projecting fairly expensive standards of life as an absolute norm, with the implication that there must be something wrong in not attaining them. In Britain, too, one can see how the greater stress placed on money and on success at any social level has made life harder for the less intelligent, the less well-adjusted, the also-rans. Hence the violent defensive reaction by some of these: in their aggression, many of the early Teddy boys were in fact protesting against the idea of being also-rans. Both the outlook of gang life and of the commercialized youth culture also make it a greater social stigma for any youngster "not to keep up", which is why more boys and girls will steal (and girls try out prostitution) to get such extras as clothes, cosmetics, and pop records.

(6) *Social restratification.* The new educational distinctions have added to this problem. The Act of 1944, which set up three types of secondary schools, with children separated at the early age of 11, may have been passed with good educational intention. In the special circumstances of the British clan structure, its *social* results

have been disruptive, in some ways deplorably so. A new criterion for class separation has been set up. The 11-plus examination has come to be regarded as a visible test for creaming off the abler boys and girls and leaving the majority not chosen with a sense of rejection as second-class citizens which the best efforts of educators have not eradicated.

(7) *Increased moral confusion.* There are also many indications that through the greater impact of the mass media and the youth culture, the distinctions between what society *really* considers right or wrong are made more difficult for young people. It may or may not be the case, that as Lord Shawcross has declared, British moral standards have declined on every social level. But there is no doubt that it is moral laxness which makes headlines in the popular press. The impact of ambiguous advertising must add to the confusion. Television commercials tell a girl that by using one shampoo rather than another she is more likely to meet romance: true or false? The point is that this impact is today incessant. This over-exposure of young people has to produce some moral confusion. The effect is not necessarily that they more often do wrong but that it is harder for them to know what is right and wrong.

(8) *Rejection in fantasy life.* A view which was expressed to me several times was that the new impact of the youth culture and of advertising directed specifically at adolescents had added a new dimension to the conflicts of the young. Every adolescent had usually to fight a battle to achieve his rightful place in the family and another battle to establish himself among his equals. Today, however, he also has the problem of seeing himself realistically in relation to the glamorous fantasies with which the youth culture surrounds him. Children in every age read fairy-tales and adventure stories, but these were never quite real to them. A boy did not think he would become Prince Charming, but today it is incessantly and realistically suggested that he could become a Tommy Steele, just as any girl could become a Mayfair model. Interrogations of disturbed youngsters indicate that many never get over failure in this third conflict between the reality of their lives and the publicly accepted glamorous image of the teenager.

(9) *The lag of the public sector.* Young people are quick to know whether they are being valued or fobbed off with the second or

third best. "Niggardliness by the authorities who try to appeal is particularly harmful because the young have an acute sense whether anything is in their favour." In this way, the shabby premises of the youth employment office must affect the prestige of "a steady job". A youth club housed in dingy, antiquated buildings and lacking in equipment is poor propaganda for constructive leisure. If the police are under strength because, as every boy in the street has read, police pay is inadequate, this must diminish their status. If there is a shortage of teachers in State schools, it is the boys and girls in the most difficult schools who will suffer most from constant changes.

(10) *Uprooting*. There is much evidence that the process of large-scale rehousing in which many working-class communities have been involved has had an unsettling effect on boys and girls, especially if they have moved to new, still unfinished outer suburban estates, where they feel that no one bothers with them, and where in fact no provision has been made for any organization for them. The houses may be more attractive, but too many are inhabited by strangers; there may be more green around, but in the evening the street corners are quiet, unfamiliar and uninviting. The first generation of teenagers living in such estates not designed for them often feels cut off from life. They only want to get out of these places where boredom reigns as fast and often as they can, to make for the nearest real town with its cinemas and pubs, or simply for the nearest main highway with its roadhouses.

THE POCKETS OF LAWLESSNESS

These are some of the problems which their life in the affluent society had brought to certain classes of boys and girls. One could list others, but in 1960 one development was no longer in doubt. In many parts of urban England, what might be called real pockets of juvenile lawlessness had developed against which the social agencies found it hard to make headway. As for the consequences of such an atmosphere of spreading lawlessness, I would quote the summary of the Albemarle Report:

This acts disastrously in several ways. First, it digs a gulf between the young generally and the law-abiding older sections of the community, which it becomes almost impossible to bridge. Misunderstandings grow. Secondly, it deeply affects the young who would themselves never become violent. They are unsettled by the success of the lawless in society. This becomes the more true the more society fails to bring offenders to trial. Every teenager in a congested area knows of offences committed in the neighbourhood and not discovered. He hears them boasted about in public places. He knows that a life of crime, rarely discovered, is possible, and this shakes his faith in the order and dignity of the society in which he lives. The whole society comes to look hypocritical. Thirdly, crimes of violence (particularly if undiscovered) terrorize the other young. In one sense they are meant to. Bragging lawless teenagers hope indeed that their contemporaries will accept them as stronger than society and above its laws. This must seem to be true when a convicted youth appears in his old haunts and ready for his old pursuits, apparently unintimidated by his experiences in court, and on occasions even enjoying enhanced status within his group. Fourthly, crimes of violence create an atmosphere in which older people are unwilling to intervene to stop other crimes because they fear acts of violence against themselves. Everyone who has moved among teenagers in certain inner suburbs of big cities has had to face this moral dilemma at some time or another. The retreat from responsibility on the part of the general population for fear of reprisals leaves the police isolated in their tasks and hurt by lack of public support. It has a deadly effect on the young who wish to be law-abiding, and who read from this the growth of social pressure to tolerate or at least not to oppose the tough in any risky way. What has to be asked for in face of this moral withdrawal is a clear and strong indication from society of its social condemnation of rising violence and destructiveness, and of personal crimes among the young. This is a necessary preliminary to social therapies.

It is easy to agree with this. But before discussing remedial measures it is worth looking at parallel problems abroad.

Part Four
INTERNATIONAL

CHAPTER XIX

Europe: The Bourgeois Resistance

THE POST-WAR RESTORATION

As I have said at the beginning of this study, the problem of juvenile delinquency in post-war Britain has to be seen in an international context if it is to be also seen in proportion. British experience is not unique. In different forms—and to different degrees—the Teddy boy problem and a serious increase in youthful lawlessness have in recent years affected a large part of the world. Most Western European countries as well as Communist Eastern Europe, or, further afield, Japan, have all had their share of it, while in the United States the problem has by now assumed alarming dimensions. Clearly, there is something in the spirit of this post-war age of ours which encourages a particular kind of youthful malaise. Travelling through Europe, talking to people specially concerned with youth problems, one gains the impression of something like a near-universal trend at work, though it is also important to realize that its impact is as yet very uneven in different countries. For instance, viewed in the light of British or American experience, the countries of Continental Europe have so far been less troubled by youthful lawlessness than one might have expected.

But then the history of Western Europe since the war has altogether been unexpected. It is already no longer easy to recall the starting-point, the end of the war and its first chaotic aftermath. From the later years of the war, there is one persistent image which has remained in my own mind—a composite image of bombed, jagged ruins flanking dusty roads, along which, as we drove, one overtook groups of numbed, shocked refugees—the picture seemed to symbolize the destruction of a continent. My personal tour had begun in Southern Italy, near Naples, where in the first weeks of occupation hungry, ragged boys from the slums offered Allied soldiers their sisters (or that was the tale) and stole every movable part of a jeep left unattended for a minute. Their sheer pre-datoriness seemed like an echo from life of centuries ago. I can recall many troubled discussions during which we, the uneasy victors, concluded that this lawlessness would be an enduring pattern to be repeated all over Europe, and more especially in the countries which had most directly and most cruelly suffered from the war.

Not a bit of it, of course. Southern Italy, it is true, still represents a special problem. Since the war Italy has remained a state virtually divided into two separate countries with quite different standards of living. Southern Italy is still a museum piece of a region where the classic European extremes of wealth and poverty of a century ago remain disgracefully preserved. With this, not surprisingly, goes a historic tradition in youthful crime. Boys and girls from the most poverty-stricken families still grow up, as it were, in the spirit of an anti-society. A person steals or cheats simply in order to eat; the rich and powerful are always regarded as natural oppressors; if a living cannot be got by straightforward work, it will be got by other means. (Crime figures in parts of the Italian South are, in fact, *six times higher* than in the cities of the North.)

However, in the rest of Italy, especially the industrialized North, and in the other two Western European countries which had suffered the greatest losses, the most extensive dislocation and material damage during the war, France and Germany—the expected did not happen. The surprising development in these countries is not that there should have been a post-war increase in delinquency, but that it was no greater, that the problem should have remained relatively so small.

On the face of it, it would not have been surprising if France, Italy and Western Germany had after the war been troubled by juvenile delinquency on a really large scale. All three countries were for some years catastrophically affected by war; the population of each country witnessed the shock of defeat, the collapse of a régime, occupation by foreign troops; each suffered heavy casualties; vast numbers of men were taken away as prisoners-of-war, families were disrupted, children grew up shocked, harassed and deprived. Yet in the outcome the rise in post-war delinquency in these countries was relatively less than in Britain, less than in neutral Sweden and considerably less than in the United States.

During the immediate period after the war, while chaos still ruled, the relative orderliness and quietism of youth was perhaps not so surprising. The very shock of defeat produced not only numbness but also a positive response. The need to overcome the enormous difficulties in the way of reconstruction, the pent-up desire for normalcy—these things became like an overriding purpose to which everyone in some way subscribed, and which held the fabric of society together. But there was also something else in these three countries. In all of them, I feel, traditional bourgeois culture was more deeply entrenched than elsewhere— the essentially bourgeois society of these countries was therefore not only able to recover more quickly from the ravages of war, but also to offer stronger resistance against the mass attack of the voices of the new society.

This can be seen in the special circumstances of each country— certainly in France. One might have thought that the odds would be against orderliness in everyday French life. For most of the post-war period, the country suffered from governmental instability and general cynicism in politics; the currency was repeatedly devalued; during the 'fifties, one unpopular colonial war was lost while another went on being waged without end. Other aspects of French life, too, might have been thought likely to cause unrest and delinquency. The difference between wealth and poverty in many parts of France remained sharp and provocative. The French housing shortage was particularly acute. By North European standards, French slums, even those bordering on the luxury districts of Paris, were appalling. Overcrowding drove French children into the street and created a peculiarly French juvenile vagrancy problem. In Paris alone, hundreds of children are still annually picked up on this charge. The problem of alcoholism, destructive of family life, was also rather larger in France than elsewhere. In addition, for a rich country, France was relatively deficient in sport and recreation facilities and in youth clubs. Considering all this, French teenagers have been astonishingly law-abiding, and this, to my mind, is due to two things. The first is the resilience of French bourgeois culture, springing from its conservatism. Under the massive impact of post-war industrializa-tion, French life, too, has been affected by the new outlook of the affluent society which goes with mass consumption, mass advertis-ing, glossy magazines and television. Yet the resistance to this outlook in France has also been particularly strong. In this respect, at least, the notorious *immobilisme* of French society may have its advantages. The narrowness of French small-town life, the class antagonisms, the deep-rooted differences between Catholics and anti-clericalists, town and country, north and south, the jealously maintained local attachments, the still living proud tradition of individual craftsmanship as well as that of uneconomic small shops and bars—all these aspects of French particularism, whatever their defects, have also helped to protect the country, and especially French youth against that sense of rootlessness and the anonymity which emanates from a mass consumption society.

In the second place, although this is also changing, French family life is still noticeably different from that of the English-speaking countries, and so is the French education system. Both are still authoritarian, in a bourgeois sense. While French schools insist on intellectual discipline—permissive education is much less known—moral responsibility for the children remains with the parents. By comparison with their British or American counterparts, French boys and girls still live rather less among their own age-group, and are much more at home under the eye of their parents. Like certain old-fashioned touches in French school education, this traditionalism in family life may have its disadvantages, but it also seems a stabilizing influence on youth. Nor is it confined to the Catholic middle class. While the French Communist Party with its millions of adherents may no longer be a dynamic political force, it is worth noting that it remains a powerful social force. In its day, the Party created a whole framework for family and social life, and much of this still remains intact, especially in solid working-class areas. In such areas, boys and girls attend Communist clubs and go hiking in Communist groups, but in a prescribed way and no less under the eye of their parents than bourgeois children.

Much the same applies to Italian youth. In post-war Italy, too, one might have expected a large-scale delinquency problem to arise. The peninsula was fought over for two terrible years, refugees trudged before the Allied armies, families were disrupted and post-war recovery came only slowly. The end of the war also saw the abject collapse of the whole Fascist view of life drilled into the young—the picture of their fathers in black shirts was suddenly ridiculous. The contrast between the booming industrial North and the stagnant, poverty-stricken South remained also as sharp as ever. From this contrast alone, as young Southerners left home to seek work in the North, one might have expected a sharp rise in Italian adolescent delinquency, yet this has not happened. As the Rome correspondent of *The Times* reported, those young Italians imitating their wilder counterparts abroad were more trying to keep up with the spirit of the age, rather than rebelling against it. "What is generally absent is that special kind of delinquency based on a need for self-assertion and a rejection of the limits of conformity. Italian youth is still very conformist."[1]

For most observers who have watched the excited reactions of the Italian authorities and press to relatively small instances of Italian youth kicking over the traces, the reasons are fairly plain. Even in the wealthiest and most industrialized cities of the North, Italian society is still heavily traditional in good bourgeois style. The tradition is, of course, that of centuries of Catholic social and family life, but this is not all—the tradition of Catholic religious observance has proved no bar to rising delinquency in Brooklyn or Boston. The Italian tradition is also that of a most deep-rooted bourgeois culture; even in anti-Catholic working-class areas, no young Italian is as yet so uprooted from family, village, church and local culture as his counterpart in London or New York. The way of life for youth is still heavily prescribed by its elders.

An even more striking example of a bourgeois society resisting change, and so resisting the new delinquency, is that of Western Germany. Even if one takes the atmosphere of continuous economic boom into account, the unexpected and dull tranquility of recent German life has indeed been extraordinary, for quite apart from the psychologically ravaging effect of the Nazi régime and the war, actual physical German casualties were enormous. In as many as three million German families of 1957, one parent was missing, usually of course the father. In addition, very large numbers of young Germans have come over as refugees from Eastern Germany without their parents. If one were to draw a parallel with British experience, one would have thought that such wholesale disruption of families should have produced a steep rise in delinquency, yet this has not happened. Western Germany has indeed been troubled by delinquency, but not more seriously than Britain, even rather less.

[1] "Young Italians Conform", *The Times*, 24th March 1959.

The explanation, I think, lies in the enduring and highly authoritative structure of German bourgeois society. An astonishing aspect of German post-war life has been the outward restoration of this bourgeois look. Travelling through Western Germany today, one might think that the past had never happened. It is not only a matter of the extraordinary physical rebuilding. The terrible instability of Germany society during the inter-war years—the inflation, the mass unemployment, Nazism, the officially encouraged rebellion of children against their parents, the disruptive teachings of Hitler and Goebbels—it might all never have been. Suddenly the old traditions of Germany all seemed to be back in force: the heavy authority of German superiors, officials, judges and industrialists; of professors, teachers and employers; of the German ideal of industrious apprenticeship and of punctual and efficient work; perhaps even, relatively speaking, the traditional authority of the German father over his family. As observers have remarked, there has been something almost unreal about this air of West German social tranquility. It is a bourgeois restoration that goes with not thinking about Nazi days; it has almost brought back to Germany something of the spirit of the old bourgeois days before 1933, or even before 1914. But at any rate, until very recently, German youth seemed content to fall in with this restoration of authority.

THE EUROPEAN AFFLUENCE

The extraordinary tenacity with which the historic values and hierarchies of bourgeois culture have been maintained, or restored, in countries like France, Italy and Germany, despite the upheavals during the years of Fascism and war, is certainly an astonishing phenomenon. Yet this is only one side of the picture. There was also change in the air. True, it seemed to come peacefully. The innocent traveller in Europe some fifteen years after the war might well have received the superficial impression that an undisturbed continent had for generations known nothing except steady advance. Visually, it was an advance towards the life of an affluent society dominated by advertising and mass entertainments, cars and gadgets. As far as the young generation of Europe was concerned, it was an advance towards a youth culture reflecting that of America, a youth culture which went with the new pleasures of jive and rock, fancy clothes, the owner-ship of motor-cycles and scooters, and the espresso-bar life, and which was above everything international. On the level of high-brow jazz, one could walk into Humphrey Lyttelton's club in London, the Caveau de la Huchette in Paris, the Quartier du Jazz on the borders of West and East Berlin, or their Warsaw equivalents, and in each place find what seemed the same attractive-looking boys and girls, either dancing or else listening to the music with the same absorbed and serious attention. On the mass level, the popularity of James Dean in France was matched by that of Elvis Presley in West Germany, of Tommy Steele in Scandinavia and Marlon Brando in Vienna.

All these were signs of far-reaching changes in European life. While the fabric of European bourgeois tradition had so surpris-ingly survived the war, the rising prosperity and the new techniques of the 'fifties were now initiating a social revolution. From *avant-garde* Sweden in the north to traditional Italy in the south, the basic trend was the same: the slow superimposition upon the old bourgeois class order of the less class-ridden and more fluid affluent society. With this, as in Britain and the United States, went the economic emancipation of youth on a large scale, and with this, in turn, a spread of commercial youth culture—and a rise in the delinquency figures. This latter discovery was made in the late 'fifties in country after country; it was also increasingly realized that a section of youth felt discontented and ill at ease, that many boys and girls spent their leisure in utterly uncon-structive ways, that they had nowhere to go, that something ought to be done. In fact, while bourgeois tradition had guided young people through the post-war tribulations of the 'forties, in the prosperous 'fifties it no longer looked adequate as a guide.

THE BROAD PATTERN

Looking at the state of youth in Europe as a whole some fifteen years after the war, and generalizing very broadly, two things could be said. First, the general picture of juvenile delinquency on the Continent resembled the picture in Britain, and could be linked in the same way to the pattern of social change. However, if it is dangerous to generalize too far about delinquent trends in one country, it is even more difficult to do so for a number of countries differing in historic background and in religious, cultural and social outlook. Comparative statistics must be treated with caution. Legal definitions of what constitutes juvenile crime differ from country to country, as do definitions of the age of criminal responsibility. Figures tend to conceal demographic shifts and such changes as a tightening of police vigilance. All the same, if we take six countries like, say, Britain, Federal Germany, Austria, Norway, France and Italy, which were all involved in the war and for which roughly comparable statistics are available (for Italy, at any rate, for the later post-war years), the delinquency figures in all these countries fall into a broad pattern showing three quite strikingly marked phases.

The first phase was immediately after the war when juvenile crime and lawlessness went up in most parts of Europe. In view of the catastrophic effect of the war, this occasioned no surprise. On the contrary, as was mentioned earlier in this chapter, in many places the increase was less than had been feared.

The next phase was that of European reconstruction. At the start of the 'fifties, economic expansion was already under way again in most parts of Europe, food and clothes rationing began to disappear and everyday life returned surprisingly quickly to normal. In keeping with this, delinquency figures also declined steadily from year to year, which again was what the experts expected.

It was the third phase of a renewed rise in delinquency which was as unforeseen by observers on the Continent as in Britain. It was in 1950 that the European economic resurgence began to get properly under way. It was half-way through the decade that, on the Continent as in Britain, economic recovery seemed suddenly to be causing changes in society itself—the direction being a greater or lesser shift from the classic European bourgeois society to the affluent society. The change went with the new pattern of mass consumption; car ownership, for instance, increased in Germany and France even faster than it did in Britain. Television arrived as the new classless entertainment. The new material prosperity drew more married women into work and brought higher pay for juveniles. European life, in fact, was becoming

"Americanized". The mass media came in—in Germany a gigantic glossy-magazine industry was conjured up overnight. Intensive advertising arrived, even if not quite on an American or British scale; so did the new commercial youth culture, and so did a new wave of juvenile delinquency.

In all the six countries, the middle of the decade appeared to be a turning-point when something happened as far as adolescents were concerned. The whole mood of youth changed; new currents of discontent made themselves felt. The post-war decline in delinquency, which had gone with reconstruction, stopped and from 1954 to 1955 the figures began to go up again year by year. Nor was this increase linked with the surviving areas of European poverty and slum life, or exploited regions like Southern Italy, where boys (and girls, too) still took to crime in the struggle for survival. On the contrary, in every country, the new crime wave seemed to go with growing prosperity, with high wages, and apparent new discontents among the young. And a distinct pattern appeared to emerge. This was so striking that the Council of Europe called in 1959 for expert reports from member countries. The cautious study which resulted from these reports[1] showed, for example, that in the years 1954-57 inclusive, industrial production in Western Germany went up by 30 per cent., unemployment fell 40 per cent.—but juvenile offences against property rose by 50 per cent. During the same years in Austria, industrial production rose by 40 per cent., unemployment fell by 30 per cent. and property offences by juveniles rose by as much as 60 per cent. Much the same pattern was revealed in Britain and, with a time lag of two or three years, in France and the industrial north of Italy.

There were also changes in the nature of delinquency. More of the offences were carried out by relatively well-to-do and cynical youngsters. The report to the Council of Europe from Germany noted that the proportion of adolescents convicted for "offences against the person" had in the second half of the 'fifties gone up by over 50 per cent. Though the total was still small, an increase in sexual offences, including violent rape by bands of juveniles, was underlined. In Austria too, though here again it should be stressed

[1] *Juvenile Delinquency in Post-War Europe.* Published by Council of Europe, Strasbourg, 1960.

that the absolute totals were small, sex offences by adolescents increased tenfold between 1946 and 1957. The report from Britain revealed similar trends; so did that from France, which spoke of "a diminution of thefts of a utilitarian character and an increase in gratuitous stealing in which the act of defiance against the social rules seems the most important element". Even in tranquil Norway, figures showed that juvenile convictions had more than doubled during the 'fifties.

Perhaps these figures should not be taken as more than straws in the wind. Still, the experience of countries like Germany, France, Austria and Norway fits by and large into the same pattern as does British experience. So, incidentally, does that of Sweden—indeed, the Swedish experience of unusually high delinquency falls very neatly into the picture. As a fortunate neutral, Sweden had escaped the losses and dislocations of the war. Starting off with a higher post-war standard of living, Sweden consequently advanced towards the pattern of the affluent society rather earlier than other European countries, both in terms of the benefits of this change and its disappointments. The figures of juvenile delinquency in Sweden certainly began to increase earlier than elsewhere. In fact, they have risen steadily year by year through the 'fifties.

THE NEW REBELS

Another indication that the increased delinquency of a minority reflected the wider unrest among European youth in the midst of accelerating social change has been the occasional mass outbreaks which disturbed public order in a number of countries. Characteristically, some of the largest of these riots reflecting youthful discontent have taken place in Sweden, the *avant-garde* country of the European affluent society. The Swedish report to the Council of Europe gave this picture:

Riots dominated by young people have occurred in Sweden, primarily in Stockholm, at regular intervals since the war. The most flagrant episode took place on the New Year's Eve of 1957, when approximately 3,000 individuals, about two-thirds of them under 21 years, collected in the centre of Stockholm. The demonstration was mainly aimed at the police. The policemen, many of them mounted, were bombarded with empty tin cans and other objects. The rioters attempted to frighten the horses with firecrackers. They wrenched off the doors of cars, which they forced to stop. One car was overturned and wrecked. The material damage was relatively insignificant, and there were no serious casualties. Of the rioters apprehended by the police, 63 were under 21 years. The antagonism of the crowd was clearly directed at the police, but the underlying cause is difficult to explain. Animosity towards the police has been expressed on other occasions in street riots in Stockholm. The situation appears to have improved during recent years, principally because the police are better prepared to deal with it, and partly because certain preventive measures have been introduced by the municipal authorities.

It is dangerous to generalize about such collective outbreaks. Just as their motive force is hard to explain, so it cannot be said that their incidence in various countries corresponded to any simple recognizable pattern. When I began this study, the West German authorities were still upset about the *Halbstarkenkrawalle*, the riots of the "Half-Strong", which swept Germany in 1956-58, while the French authorities were confident that similar occurrences in France were impossible. A year or so later the German scene was quiet, while the gang activities of the French *Blousons Noirs*, the Blackjackets, had put France definitely on to the delinquency map.

The German *Halbstarken* riots which from 1956 onwards broke out in city after city were a puzzling phenomenon. They looked like exhibitions of youthful anger and defiance that had no rhyme or reason. Thinking Germans, however, were still haunted by the memories of quite a different kind of violence a generation earlier, and, as a result, these new outbreaks caused considerable alarm and were studied and analysed in meticulous German detail. The studies showed, for example, that a starting-point of the epidemic was a much publicized riot in Hanover in August 1956. On the day before this riot, rumours were running through the city of an arranged fight between the adolescents of two different districts (as New Yorkers would say, a "rumble"), for which reinforcements were being mobilized on foot, mopeds and motorcycles. Even at this stage there was excited talk among the boys that if they were to be "attacked" by the highly unpopular police, they would certainly resist. In the event, the riot became much less of a fight between rival gangs than a hysterical attack upon public order. Groups of assembled youths rushed through the streets of Hanover, stopping traffic and molesting bystanders, smashing windows and hoardings and finally stoning police-cars and struggling in apparent frenzy until an appropriate number were arrested and order was restored.

Spontaneous and destructive disturbances of this type took place in 1956-58 in German cities as far apart as West Berlin, Munich, Dusseldorf, Bremen, Hamburg, etc. The evidence showed them to be much of a type. As a rule some hundreds of youths were involved in the rioting, dozens were arrested, and if casualties were not serious, damage to property was sometimes considerable. In some cases one could fix on the starting-point of the excitement—a rock-and-roll occasion in Berlin, a recital by Louis Armstrong in Hamburg; in others, the hysteria, the smashing and the resistance to the police seemed to arise without any apparent cause. On the morning after, so the German records pointed out, neither the Courts nor the teenagers themselves seemed to know what it had been about. The reports also noted that the participants in the riots were predominantly working-class boys, many of them "provocatively dressed"; that there were few girls among them; that the sensational publicity given by the German press to one riot no doubt played its part in sparking off the next; that the youths turned up for the occasions with extraordinary home-made weapons and with a sense of emotional rancour against the police which puzzled the authorities, as did the cynical disregard of the rioters for public and personal property. In fact, the conclusion was that these *Halbstarken* riots were disturbing not so much in themselves as for the light they threw on the general increase in juvenile lawlessness and the apparent hostility of a section of German youth against any kind of public authority. What was particularly deplored was that two-thirds of this new generation of German teenagers no longer bothered to belong to any youth organization. But just as public alarm became concentrated on these *Halbstarkenkrawalle*, they faded out again, as the British Teddy boy riots had done. Like these, they left behind rising delinquency figures, but this was another matter.

In France meanwhile, at about the same time, I was assured by a wise friend with considerable court experience that France was most unlikely to produce any counterpart to the *Halbstarken* or Teddy boys. Not that French adolescents lacked resentments against adult society, but they appeared to have no impulse to translate these into organized action. On the contrary, the *malaise* of French youth lay in its apathy. In fact, in 1958, with the fading out of the Existentialists, France for the first time since the Revolution was without any Angry Young Men, whether on the intellectual level or otherwise; and my friend thought that the same applied to Italy.

That was in the autumn of 1958. The new young French rebels arrived less than a year later, and in most unexpected guise.

In July 1959, at the start of what promised, and turned out to be, a record Riviera season, a large gang of French youths armed with knives, sticks, buckled belts and bicycle chains (bicycle chains wielded on the Riviera!) staged a pretty savage and boisterous riot on the seafront near Cannes, destroying property, molesting startled campers and stoning the police before scattering and vanishing again. To the alarm of the French "it can't happen here" school, similar wild riots followed in various places along the Riviera in quick succession. A culminating point was reached in a teenage fracas of quite notable dimensions when armed gangs of adolescent toughs from the port of Toulon converged on Bandol, many of them motorized, annoying holiday-makers and noisily fighting each other and the police, and even causing damage to a casino—this last act made international news.

The youths who staged these disorders called themselves by various mysterious code names, such as "*Les Gadjos*". Because of their clothes, however, the public quickly christened them *Les Blousons Noirs*, the Blackjackets (the black leather was usually imitation). And for a few weeks *Blousons Noirs* incidents spread like a rash across France. Organized adolescent gangs under that label appeared suddenly in Paris. In August, one large gang staged a particularly frenzied disturbance right in the Rue Brillat-Savarin, where passers-by were injured, property damaged and the boys tried to fight it out with the police. By contrast with similar British events, many of those arrested were middle-class boys. The Paris newspapers, which gave the disturbance dramatic coverage, reported that some highly respectable parents, on arriving at the police station, could hardly believe their eyes to find their sons under arrest.

By that time, *Blousons Noirs* incidents had become international news, often accompanied by photographs of French policemen vigorously swinging batons. With the biggest tourist traffic in Europe to guard, the French police, as could be expected, reacted with characteristic vigour. A disturbance in the Paris suburb of Drancy led to no less than a hundred arrests. In September the Paris Prefect of Police announced that six large gangs of *Blousons Noirs* were operating in Paris, but that already over eight hundred juveniles (!) had been picked up for questioning. A further sign of public alarm was a series of prominently featured articles in a newspaper like *Le Monde*, with such headings as "It is Urgent to Organize the Welfare of our Morally Endangered Youth" and demanding the provision of more youth clubs and youth leaders. As it turned out, however, with the end of the glorious summer holiday of 1959, the *Blousons Noirs* seemed to have vanished as mysteriously as they had emerged. They made a much publicized fresh appearance in the spring of 1960—French belief in immunity from such "Anglo-Saxon" troubles as youth riots had certainly been shaken.

Italy also, interestingly enough, experienced a relative flare-up of youthful lawlessness during the summer of 1959. By comparison with some other countries, this did not amount to very much. There were a few incidents of the Teddy boy type in industrial cities like Milan and Turin, but on a minor scale. Still, perhaps as a variant from its preoccupation with continuous high society scandals, the Italian press for a time featured almost daily stories of fights and stabbings by young hooligans. One incident above all, in which a peasant girl from Bracciano stabbed to death one of a gang of seven boys who attacked her, had all the right ingredients for nation-wide publicity. It featured not only a youthful gang and an attempted sex crime, but showed virtue triumphant. At any rate, the reaction of the Italian authorities was quick and emotional. In August, the then Prime Minister, Signor Segni, requested the Italian police to proceed with utmost severity against youthful gangsters. (The Italian police, with a tradition of acting against political street demonstrations and a scope their

British colleagues would envy, did in fact not hesitate. In a single razzia in Milan, for instance, five hundred youths were picked up for questioning, many being detained.) A rather absurd Bill put to Parliament to deprive "socially dangerous and exhibitionist young offenders" of the right temporarily to practice their profession did not go far, but indicated the way some sections of Italian opinion were thinking. So did newspaper articles attacking the evil of pin-table machines (whose import was prohibited) and other foreign influences allegedly destructive of Italian morals. This Italian wave of alarm, too, seemed to fade with the summer, and the press turned its attention back to other topics such as, once again, scandals in high society. Still, it had been shown that Italy, like France, was also no longer quite immune to the new mood of defiance and delinquency of a sub-section of European youth.

THE END OF THE LINE

Nor even was stolid Switzerland. Teddy boys, or their equivalent, a friend told me, were even to be found in so clean, prosperous and satisfied a city as Zurich. They were Swiss youths of a new type, he said, who rejected the Swiss tradition of the good apprentice, who refused to learn a trade, worshipped the noise and speed of motor-cycles, hung around juke-box bars and pin-table saloons, imitated American mannerisms learned from films, and got themselves into trouble, who were in fact, Swiss Teds.

I found this hard to believe, for here in Zurich I was back at a familiar starting-point. Through the accidents of the continuous travels of my parents, Zurich had been my first home town, the background scenery of my early school years, and on recent visits this background had looked to me uncannily unchanged. That brooding sense of repression imposed on Swiss youth by parents, teachers and the police, the spirit of cantonal narrowness which went together with the fierce sense of Swiss independence—they seemed as oppressive as ever. Here among the clean asphalt streets of Zurich and the villas which since my time had spread right round the lake, I still felt that bourgeois life had not crumbled, only grown a little stale.

However, following instructions, I walked in the evening along Zurich's street of entertainment, the Niederdörferstrasse, where the strains of alternatively New Orleans jazz and Tin Pan Alley output seemed to flow incongruously from stolid Swiss bars. At a pin-table saloon I drew a blank. The brand-new establishment was brightly lit, shining with Swiss cleanliness; over its rows of polished pin-tables stood Swiss youths, all wearing elegant plastic raincoats and playing the tables gravely and in complete silence. . . . But at the appropriate corner further along the street I found my quarry; youths standing about in large groups, sporting the usual tight trousers, fancy waistcoats and wild shocks of hair above their honest, well-scrubbed Swiss peasant faces. They were standing about, leaning against walls and lamp-posts, waiting, with vacant faces; but as I stopped and they saw that I was observing them, they glared back at me with undisguised hostile challenge. They reminded me of a group of similarly attired youths I had met only a few days earlier in Communist East Berlin. . . . Yet something was not quite right in the picture. Perhaps because I had been a Zurich schoolboy myself, I knew they were not quite the genuine article. Probably they had merely heard or read something of a revolt of youth supposed to be going on elsewhere, and in their adolescent discontent they wanted to join in without quite knowing what to join or how to go about it. And no doubt, something was going on, some sort of revolution in the life of youth was in progress in Europe; only this little group of would-be Teds in Zurich were not the only ones who found it difficult to know where it led to.

CONCERN IN VIENNA . . .

If anywhere in Europe one can feel that history has been as if wiped out with a sponge, it is in Austria. Between the wars, Austria was a seething cauldron of ideological conflict. Social-Democratic Vienna saw civil war, dictatorship, Nazism and war and the vengeful Red Army. In the upshot, by a transformation scene, the Viennese at the end of the 'fifties found themselves citizens of a country in which they had never had it so good but which had evidently opted out of history.

Perhaps for this reason, constant attention was given in the press to the misdeeds of the obstreperous Austrian *Halbstarken* as reflecting a malaise not merely of youth but Austrian youth in particular. They were indeed quite conspicuous in Vienna. Groups of such dressed-up young rebels—the challenging uniform at the time of my visit was black leather or imitation leather jackets, tight trousers and two-toned Milanese shoes—could be met on Saturday or Sunday evenings as they stood about in gangs outside certain cinemas in poses designed to resemble those of Marlon Brando, or mystified their elders by using their mopeds and motorcycles not to reach the country but to drive noisily and endlessly up and down certain streets. And they, too, carried out their antics against a background of rising criminality figures. Perhaps these were not as serious as Viennese newspapers made out, but somehow the outlook of this section of Austrian youth appeared to be changing in a direction which worried not only the press but also the Viennese Socialists (who controlled the municipality), and especially the psychologists and social workers among them.

They were worried, as was admitted in conversation, because against the exciting attraction of high earnings, juke-box culture, the glamour of American films and the motorized life, the special tradition of Viennese socialism and socialist youth organizations no longer carried weight. I was told that some of the *Halbstarken* carrying flick-knives were the sons of active socialist and trade unionist parents living in the famous municipal apartment blocks. It was a sign of the times that to get teenagers off the streets the socialist municipality of Vienna had opened several jazz and jive clubs, with picturesque names like "The Black Panther", or, in English, "Hot Club".

Probably because Social Democratic Vienna had between the wars played such a leading part in laying down new municipal standards in workers' co-operative housing, in social welfare and especially juvenile welfare, I found particularly my younger socialist acquaintances emphatic in the opinion that, valuable as these achievements were, they were no longer sufficient, not for the richer, more demanding and bewildered teenagers of the new society. For these, quite new thinking and town planning was required. An article in the daily *Arbeiterzeitung*[1] criticized the rebuilding of Vienna as having been on wholly wrong lines in not anticipating teenage needs. In the new blocks of standardized labour-saving flats, adolescents had no places of their own where

[1] Franz Kreuzer, "Ersatz fuer die verlorenen Gstettn", *Arbeiterzeitung*, 2nd August 1959.

they could relax, play records, make a noise, nor even cellars or attics for this purpose: they were virtually forced out into the streets. Nor could they find meeting-places there. To a Londoner all this sounded vaguely familiar. The article was accompanied by a map of Vienna with black spots marking the meeting-places of street-corner gangs, and declared that each such area needed a youth centre or youth club. . . .

. . . AND PARIS

In a similar conversation in Paris with French youth experts, the emphasis was on somewhat different lines. They insisted that, with regard to young offenders, French penal methods compared favourably with those of other countries. They also seemed all to agree that the rising rate of juvenile criminality in France was connected with new social trends. When I made the point that the tenacious bourgeois traditions of France had up to recent years resulted in a stable, if repressed, life among French adolescents, they also agreed, but with a sense almost of grievance they refuted the charge that the French political, economic and social structure was still out of date and did not fit into the modern world. Through the uninterrupted industrial expansion of the 'fifties, France, they said, had been catching up rapidly, but, as elsewhere, this change had also brought new social disruption, especially in the case of French youth.

French boys and girls were now far less oppressed by that ubiquitous and censorious demand for social conformity which had been so strong in French village or small-town life: instead they faced the danger of big-city anonymity. The new advance of industrialization was also at last breaking up the traditional, almost clan-like unit of the extended French family, which used to include grandparents, uncles and aunts and remote cousins. Instead, industrialization was producing a new pattern—new in France— of a small isolated family of parents and children only. Especially where both parents were working, this new family, *la famille reduite*, so it was said, offered teenagers an inadequate basis of personal security. Others blamed the unrest on the insidious skill of modern mass advertising, which is more of an innovation in France than in Britain or the United States. This new kind of advertising, they thought, caused unrest by dangling delights before the eyes of boys and girls who could not afford them, and therefore felt permanently discontented and deprived.

Others again pointed to the peculiar difficulties which French life presented for the group activities of youth. By comparison with many other countries, France was deficient in facilities for sports clubs and social clubs. French schools did little in this respect. Investigations in a number of industrial cities had revealed that an alarmingly large proportion of teenagers no longer spent much time at home, but did not know what to do with their leisure, hanging about aimlessly, evening after evening, in courtyards, streets and cafés. Not so much the revolt of the few, like the *Blousons Noirs*, but the apathy of the many was the youth problem which was gradually forcing itself on French public attention and which had to be remedied.

ANOTHER GERMAN YOUTH . . .

In Western Germany, the new youth problem, which made its appearance from about 1955 onwards, has already been made the subject of a series of studies. Post-war Western Germany, to be sure, has been a country full of surprises. The "economic miracle" has been only one of them. Perhaps as surprising has been the dull stolidity of life in the new republic. "Within ten years," Mr Sebastian Haffner[1] wrote in a retrospect in 1960, "it has settled down as an extremely orderly, liberal, humane and almost pedantically law-abiding State with completely unquestioned smoothly-working democratic institutions; it has no real totalitarian opposition either on the Left or on the Right, but only two lunatic fringes. If anything, it is a little philistine, a little Swiss, a little too good to be true."

There were other German observers who felt it was too good to be true and looked on the *Halbstarken* riots as a warning signal. One such warning came from Hamburg. This was a study called "Juveniles Disturb Public Order",[2] written by Professor Curt Bondy and three collaborators from Hamburg University, and to

[1] *The Observer*, 6th March 1960.
[2] Curt Bondy, Jan Braden, Rudolf Cohen, Klaus Eyferth, "*Jugendliche stoeren die Ordnung*", Juventa-Verlag, Munich 1958.

my mind one of the most enlightening brief analyses of the troubles of youth in the affluent society.

Just as the main social developments in Western Germany and Britain during the 'fifties were more alike than generally realized, so Professor Bondy's attempted definition of the *Halbstarken* could equally be applied to the Teddy boys. "Under the term *Halbstarken* we understand male adolescents who move about in larger or smaller groups, who like to dress provocatively and find their main interest in an irresponsible and unconstructive association with others of their age and sex." Going on to discuss the defects of which the *Halbstarken* were accused, such as disregard for other people's property, reckless living for the moment, paucity of experience and emotional superficiality, a lack of basic principles and of a sense of responsibility, Professor Bondy observed gently that all but the first of these failings could be attributed to adolescents in general. The *Halbstarken* only displayed them in more extreme, even hysterical form. Yet this was the significant point. If German society had always had its *Halbstarken*, never before had hundreds of teenagers who hardly knew each other been in the habit of gathering in an excited mood to stage mass riots. If one added the rise in the delinquency rate, this argued that, under the gloss of German prosperity, new social trends were at work which needed watching.

Professor Bondy cautiously enumerated some of these as they affected mainly working-class youth. There was what he called the acceleration of physical maturity. The German teenagers of the 'fifties were taller than their predecessors and tended to look older than they really were. Partly as a result of this, they were too early in their lives put to work rather as though they were already adults. While their working day often brought them high earnings, it often also provided few satisfying personal contacts and little or no scope for the sort of spontaneity which adolescents needed in order to express themselves: they therefore tended to look for it in sensationalism and gang life in their leisure time. Parallel with this went changes in family life. Professor Bondy noted that even in Germany, paternal authority was at last on the decline. In many German post-war families there was no father, and the mother had to play the rôle of both parents. But this was only part of the problem. A new pattern of family life was developing, where the mother, like the teenagers, worked chiefly "to keep pace with the increasing material demands of civilization", and in which many a father tended to become little more than a "discontented lodger". Lack of firm guidance in such families meant that boys and girls were forced far too early into a life of financial and personal independence.

Professor Bondy noted some other factors making for youthful discontent—again they could be applied to the British situation. In the rebuilding of German post-war society, and especially in the actual physical rebuilding of cities, too little consideration had been given to the greater demands of the new generation of adolescents and the greater demands society put on them; for lack of amenities and places where they could meet, too many youngsters were forced into the streets. There was the noticeable decline of traditional morality. Many of the young rejected religious and civic teaching as mere phrases: it was significant that the majority belonged to no youth organization. Lastly, there was the growth— very swift in Germany—of new commercial mass entertainment, much of it in American style. Though its directly harmful effects might be exaggerated, it failed to fill the gaps left by the decline in traditional standards; it provided entertainment but no guidance. All in all, therefore, a new youth problem was emerging in Germany as elsewhere which demanded attention.

SUMMARY

How serious was this youth problem on the Continent? To sum up my own impressions, the chief West European countries had weathered the disturbed post-war years with far less trouble from the young generation which had grown up during the war than one might have expected. By contrast, the social changes of the last few years, leading in the direction of a European affluent society, had led.to a notable and new increase in delinquency and in a number of countries to disturbances of the Teddy boy pattern, and these problems have already caused growing concern in countries like Germany and Austria, Sweden and Norway, France and Italy. In these and other European countries, one also met much the same rather tentative efforts to cope with this situation. There was some public alarm over the apparent indifference of youth in general to traditional standards; it was felt that for want of anywhere to go, adolescents were too much "out in the streets", that purely commercialized entertainment loomed too large in the lives of many boys and girls, and that there was a need for new, modern types of youth organizations and youth clubs. (In France, a new governmental drive in this field was placed under the direction of the famous mountaineer, M. Maurice Herzog.)

At the same time, the incidence of the problem was uneven. In spite of the rumpus created in 1959 by the French *Blousons Noirs*, and a few Italian incidents, the rise in delinquency did not seem as yet so serious in France or Italy as elsewhere. In Western Germany there was perhaps cause for more concern. While the surface of German social life looked calm, German observers themselves were disturbed by a lack of depth, a lack of confident direction beneath this surface. There was, indeed, something strangely empty and purely imitative in the look of the new German commercial youth culture, which seemed completely derived from American films, pop music and advertisements, with nothing new added. In spite of its prosperity, it was perhaps Western German society that looked most exposed to the corrosions of life in the new affluent culture.

As a generalization it could, however, also be said that the problem of juvenile delinquency loomed less large in Continental Western Europe than in Britain (and much less large—see the following chapter—than in the United States). And here I come back to what, to my mind, is the reason for this difference. Even in those parts of the Continent where life outwardly seems dominated as much as it is today in Britain by such things as mass media, cars, household gadgets, mass advertising and other attributes of the affluent society, the traditional bourgeois standards, even if they no longer have their old influence, are still preserved more strongly than in Britain. Especially in countries like France and Italy, the majority of the population has not yet been as much drawn away from these standards towards the new mass culture projected by the advertisers, as is the case in this country. But here the real contrast to Continental Europe is not so much with Britain as with the United States.

CHAPTER XX

America: Advance from Innocence

A HISTORIC CHANGE

THE point has come to turn to a subject which I feel I have up to now almost avoided, because of its rather depressing overtones, namely the juvenile delinquency situation in the United States. This situation has in the last ten years or so had plenty of airing. It has been elevated to the rank of a major national problem, it has been publicized by stories about the formidable juvenile gang warfare in New York, in the reports of Senatorial sub-committees and in challenging films and plays. And the problem appears in fact to have been growing steadily more serious. As Miss Virginia Held put it in *The Reporter*[1]:

> There has probably never been a moment in history when adults were not shocked by what they regarded as an unprecedented wave of bad behaviour among children and adolescents. But in our time reports of gang warfare in the streets, teenage muggings, and senseless killings have turned shock to cold fear. Juvenile delinquency, particularly in the United States, has come to be considered one of the most urgent social problems of the day, and the epidemic of arrogance and crime seems to be spreading so fast that it obliterates the best efforts society can make to control it—or even to understand it.

Control is another matter, but an understanding of the problem should surely not be so difficult.

One first point to note in arriving at such understanding is that, at least as seen from Europe, this specifically American problem of youthful unruliness on a major scale is a relatively new one. The idea which is today put over especially by American films, from those which projected James Dean as a mixed-up kid to more recent tracts like "Blue Jeans", that childhood and growing up

[1] Virginia P. Held, "What Can We Do about Teenagers?", *The Reporter*, 20th August 1959.

impose greater strains in American life than elsewhere, has not always been the popular impression. Quite the contrary—this was a point noted by George Orwell in his nostalgic and memorable little essay, "Riding Down from Bangor". In this essay,[1] written in 1947, Orwell recalled how European boys and girls of his generation, born at the turn of the century or in its first decade, were still very much brought up on the ideas of certain enormously popular American nineteenth-century novels, from which they derived many of their enduring impressions about American life; and these were impressions of a life which seemed both more colourful and more carefree than that which most European children saw around them.

Looking back on his own childhood vision of American life as derived from this reading, Orwell saw it as dominated above all by two pictures. The first was that of a tall, angular man, with a shapeless hat pulled down over his eyes, leaning against a wooden pailing and whittling at a stick. His lower jaw moved slowly but ceaselessly while at long intervals he emitted pieces of folk wisdom to an admiring small boy, at the same time issuing jets of tobacco juice. The second picture

> is of a boy sitting in a whitewashed stone schoolroom. He wears braces and has patches on his shirt, and if it is summer he is barefooted. In the corner of the schoolroom there is a bucket of drinking water with a dipper. The boy lives in a farmhouse, also of stone and also whitewashed, which has a mortgage on it. He aspires to be President, and is expected to keep the woodpile full. Somewhere in the background of the picture, but completely dominating it, is a huge black Bible. . . .

Of the two pictures, one representing the South, the other probably New England, Orwell thought it was the second which had the stronger hold on his imagination. But both pictures carried an impression of childhood in a country where everything was more peaceful, where there was greater ease, than in Europe. The books from which these pictures were derived included the works of Mark Twain and also what Orwell called "good bad books",

[1] Included in the volume *Shooting an Elephant and other Essays*, George Orwell. Secker & Warburg, 1950.

such bestsellers as *Little Women* and *Good Wives*, the *What Katy Did* series, *Rebecca of Sunnybrook Farm*, *Black Beauty*, *Helen's Babies* and the rest; and the general impression which emerged from this reading, said Orwell, was of an American society whose social pretentions might be mildly ridiculous, but which by comparison with Europe seemed still in some way uncorrupted, which had what he thought could best be called "good morale". In making this point, Orwell agreed that these books largely described only that particular nineteenth-century American middle-class society which knew little of the squalor and violence on the other side of the tracks, yet he thought this did not invalidate his point. For instance, the society described in *Little Women* was subdued, bookish and homeloving, while a book like *Life on the Mississippi* told of a crazy world of bandits, gold mines, duels, drunkenness and gambling hells; but in both books he thought one could detect an underlying confidence in the future, a sense of opportunity, a buoyant and innocent view of life. Looking for its causes, Orwell found them in the unique freedom and security which nineteenth-century America enjoyed.

Nineteenth-century America was a rich, empty country which lay outside the main stream of world events, and in which the twin nightmares that beset nearly every modern man, the nightmare of unemployment and the nightmare of State interference, had hardly come into being. There were social distinctions, more marked than those of today, and there was poverty (in *Little Women*, it will be remembered, the family is at one time so hard up that one of the girls sells her hair to the barber), but there was not, as there is now, an all-prevailing sense of helplessness. There was room for everybody, and if you worked hard you could be certain of a living—could even be certain of growing rich: this was generally believed, and for the greater part of the population it was even broadly true. In other words, the civilization of nineteenth-century America was capitalist civilization at its best.

These observations were made in 1947. By this time Orwell was convinced, and this was really his impulse for writing the essay, that American capitalist civilization was in many ways no longer at its best.

English children are still Americanized by way of the films, but it would no longer be generally claimed that American books are the best ones'for children. Who, without misgiving, would bring up a child on the coloured "comics" in which sinister professors manufacture atomic bombs in underground laboratories while Superman whizzes through the clouds, the machine-gun bullets bouncing off his chest like peas, and platinum blondes are raped, or very nearly, by steel robots and fifty-foot dinosaurs? It is a far cry from Superman to the Bible and the woodpile.

And it is still further from the Bible and woodpile to the Shook-up Generation. In suggesting that the consequences of un-trammelled American capitalism were likely to be not so much economic hardship as moral and cultural dislocation, Orwell was only anticipating the American sociologists of the 'fifties. Economically, the affluent society brought the Americans those vast material benefits, which have spilled over into Europe and the rest of the world. But the same system has simultaneously brought a whole crop of new social problems, ranging from excessive status preoccupation to corruption in mass entertainment; and whatever else one may say about it, it is surely as one such direct aspect of the American affluent society that the current American juvenile delinquency problem has to be understood and studied.

HOW BAD IS THE PROBLEM?

Viewed from Europe, the present youthful lawlessness in the United States seems both more widespread and a more intensive kind of lawlessness. For instance, the violence of the teenage street gangs in Manhattan suggests what the Teddy boy problem might become in another twenty years, *if* the problem grew worse (and the Teds more sophisticated) year by year. What also strikes a European observer is the evident inability of the New York authorities to take really effective offensive action against these gangs, even though such action was several times promised jointly by Governor Rockefeller, Mayor Wagner and Police Chief Kennedy. In 1959-60, after every kind of attempt to put them down, it was estimated that 150 juvenile gangs with about

7000-8000 members were still "operating" in New York. "Only the police blotters and the hospital files and the morgue records tell the story," indignantly wrote Mr Douglass M. Allen, Associate Editor of *Newsweek*[1]:

> And what they say is that sizable areas of the world's foremost metropolis are splintered into feudal enclaves, run in effect by gangs of ruthless, amoral teenagers. . . . Between them, they rule over the slums and drab housing projects of Harlem and the Lower East Side; the Bronx; the Bedford-Stuyvesant and Navy Yard districts of Brooklyn, and South Jamaica and Ozone Park in Queens. They reign by terror, and strangers enter their demesnes after nightfall at their peril. Some of the gangs are bigger and more powerful than others, with 250 to 300 members; some have alliances; they can field a battle order of 1,000 troops or more.

This passage may sound somewhat dramatic—the average New Yorker only *reads* about delinquents—but it brings home the point that by 1959-60 adolescent gang life in New York had developed into something well in advance of what could be found in any other big city in America or elsewhere. The situation was that sections of New York were dotted with organized gangs of lawless teenagers—lawless in recognizing little authority beyond the rules of initiation and discipline they drew up for themselves. The most recognized uniform was a black leather jacket. Each gang had its territory, or "turf", recognized as such by other gangs, and which each gang was ready to defend against intrusion by armed violence in the streets. The gangs had their colourful names, like the Chaplains, Sinners, Bishops, Cheyennes, Demons, Imperials, Viceroys, Jokers, and so forth (unlike the London Teds who rarely rose beyond geographic appellations like the Elephant Boys, the Angel Boys, the Highbury Corner Boys, etc.). The 25,000-strong police force of New York, which in any case had its hands full in this city of skyscrapers and slums, of teeming immigrant quarters and taut race relations, was quite unable to put down these teenage gangs as a whole—as some were disrupted by the arrests of members and some dissolved, others sprang up again like weeds.

[1] *Newsweek*, 14th September 1959.

The enormous efforts of social agencies to "reach" the adolescent members of these gangs, to divert their energies and desire for adventure into "constructive" channels, for instance by providing street-corner youth leaders to work with them, also appeared to have little lasting effect. The biggest New York press headlines were usually accorded to organized armed clashes or "rumbles" between rival gangs, of the kind glamourized in that well-known musical, *West Side Story*, but which were really pretty ugly and bloodthirsty affairs—the knowledge that two large adolescent gangs in an area were feuding was enough to keep the police detachments in that area in a state of perpetual alert. What was probably worse, however, was that by perpetrating assaults, muggings and robberies practically in the manner of adult gangsters, some of the gangs were definitely making a few areas of New York unsafe after dark as they had not been for many years. At the same time, through this education in delinquency, the gangs provided a steady stream of recruits into the world of American adult crime.

Socially, most of the teenage boys in these gangs were drawn from the lower working-class income groups of New York, from the slums of the city or from slum families recently moved into new housing developments. They were particularly concentrated in areas where antagonistic racial groups overlapped. In actual fact, young Negroes and Puerto Ricans formed a much larger proportion of young gangsters than one would imagine from the carefully censored American official statistics on this question. The claim sometimes made that the majority of the most violent young delinquents came from the one per cent. of known problem families in New York (about 20,000 out of 2 million families) was probably roughly true. In this respect, in being big-city adolescents trying to push their way up from family life in the "submerged tenth", the young members of the New York gangs were rather like the original London Teddy boys. But there were also notable differences between the two sets of adolescents—to compare the London Teds, or for that matter even the members of the Chicago street gangs of the 'thirties, with the sophisticated New York fighting gangs of today is like turning from an old-fashioned detective story to the tautly constructed American thriller of today, with the usual touch of mental illness thrown in.

There is, first, the marked difference in the degree of habitual violence. The weapons used in New York inter-gang fights consist not only of knives, clubs, torn-off car aerials, home-made zip guns and the like, but of such savage weapons as wire whips and regular firearms; and, in fact, gangsters did not stop short of murder. The toll of one single black week of running fights between Puerto Rican and "White" teenagers in September 1959 was four youngsters killed and fifteen in hospital with gunshot and knife wounds. Of the four killed, two were boys of 16, one a boy of 14, one a girl of 15 shot by mistake. Casualties on this level are of course not imaginable in London. Commenting on the fact that the figures of grave acts of juvenile violence in the United States were so many times higher than in Europe—in 1957 there were 133 arrests of youngsters under 18 for murder and non-accidental killing, an authority like Dr Melitta Schmideberg (Director of the Association for the Psychiatric Treatment of Offenders) has observed[1] that when all immediate causes had been discussed, there remained the conclusion that a society must expect the sort of crimes that were apparently tolerated by popular attitudes. The evident trouble was that American society did not sufficiently *abhor* the many acts of violent brutality and destruction in which youth indulged, acts whose very thought would in many European countries be at once suppressed. In other words, at this point of violence, the aggressive fantasies of the New York teenage gangsters appeared in line with the ideas of violence given such constant expression in American popular culture.

Another difference is that the New York teenagers appear to be much more emotionally involved in their gang life. A mob of London Teds usually included a few psychopathic youths who led the others on occasional wild destructive raids. In New York, similar psychopaths are often the automatic gang leaders who rule over a whole fantasy world of violence, ruthlessly enforcing their discipline on younger and weaker boys. Again, it was common for gangs of London Teds to be driven by their underlying feeling of anxiety or a sense of grievance into defending "their manor" but the attachment of the average New York gang to its "turf" is evidently far more intense. Such a "turf" might consist of no more than a few drab blocks of streets, a drugstore counter or two, a few back yards, a strip of parkland. However, whether the reason

[1] Quoted in *The Reporter*, 20th August 1959.

is that the plight of being a problem family in New York is a more dramatic one than elsewhere, so that the teenagers from such families feel more anxiety-ridden, more fiercely resentful, the fanaticism with which they will defend their "turf", as if it were the only thing they can cling to in a hostile world, is something quite exceptional.

At the same time, the New York gang members seem also to have advanced a good way towards sophistication. It has been remarked that unlike, say, the English Teds, who are still easily cowed by the authority of the Courts, New York delinquents on arrest often reveal little sense of guilt; they will put their conviction down to the unfairness of lawyers and judges and appear to be genuinely without a sense of the wrongness of brutality and violence—what has pushed them into crime seems often not an uncontrollable impulse but simply an uncontrolled one, which brings one back to the influences of contemporary American culture which plays on the minds of these boys. Another striking feature is the early age of some of the New York gang members and delinquents. Arrests of boys of 13, 14 and 15 after gang fights are not uncommon—there was a widely reported incident in 1957 when one young killer of 14 calmly told New York detectives how he had stabbed another boy in the back to "get the feeling of knife going through bone".

As I have said before, one should not exaggerate. In the vastness of a metropolis like New York, these juvenile gangs represent only a marginal problem. American life has a tradition of turbulence, and an immigrant city like New York with its racial ghettoes has its particularly rough edges. Much juvenile violence arises from the larger problem of tense race relations, and some of the most dangerous adolescent gangs are all-Negro or all-Puerto Rican in membership. Considering the devastating psychological effects of race and colour discrimination, it is, for example, not surprising that the delinquency rate in an overcrowded Negro ghetto like Harlem should be as high as seventy-six per thousand. Even so, racial antagonisms are only a partial explanation of the gang life. For instance, while in segregated areas juvenile gangs tend to be all-white, all-Negro or all-Puerto Rican, in the growing number of integrated neighbourhoods the gangs also tend to become mixed, which shows that geography rather than ethnic origin is most important in gang formation. Secondly, the half a million very new Puerto Rican immigrants in New York may in some ways be a fairly primitive community, yet in Puerto Rico itself delinquency rates are exceptionally low; it evidently takes several years of life at the bottom of the American social ladder to create the new resentful and delinquent outlook among Puerto Rican youth. Thirdly, as populations are cleared from the slums, some gangs break up but others simply continue their criminal activities in the new housing developments. All this indicates that while all kinds of special factors may have intensified the juvenile gang life of New York, basically it has to be regarded as a result of the general pressures of American social life of today.

EXTENSIVE DELINQUENCY

If the teenage gangs of New York with their addiction to *intensive* violence provided the most sensational material for American press headlines, the 1950s also brought evidence that juvenile delinquency was growing more *extensive* in American society as a whole. The period was one of dynamic suburban growth, and in 1957-60 delinquency in the small towns and also in the new suburbia increased faster than in the big cities—the move to the quiet tree-lined avenues proved evidently no barrier. Much of it, to be sure, only consisted of petty misdemeanors, youthful drunkenness, motoring offences, the usual larceny and breaking-in. Since youth must go joy-riding and many young Americans are accustomed to have what they want, it was no surprise that juveniles under 18 should be responsible for more than half the reported automobile thefts. It was, however, more alarming that they also accounted for 20 per cent. of the known cases of rape—this was indicative of a generally growing mood of violence. In Washington, 150 cases of assault against police officers were reported during the first six months of 1959, the majority committed by teenage thugs who vanished again into the night. The new insecurity in the Federal capital was partly, but only partly, linked to the rapid increase in its Coloured population. Reports in 1959 from cities like Baltimore, Detroit, San Francisco, Los Angeles and Philadelphia brought news of special emergency measures against juvenile crime, such as strict curfew hours for young people, laws against groups assembling on the pavements after dark, or the selective arrest of known gang leaders at the first sign of trouble. In short, if in 1960 one could still say that 95 per cent. of all young Americans grew up without *serious* trouble with the courts or the police, the lawless minority has also grown uncomfortably large; sections of American cities and even some suburban areas had been rendered unsafe after dark; the recruitment of youngsters into the world of adult crime, which in 1959 cost the United States the fantastic sum of 20 billion dollars a year, had been steadily going up; and if one talked of the points where United States culture was failing in the ideological struggle against Soviet Communism, the prevalence of juvenile delinquency was one of them.

THE REAL INCREASE

Yet apart from the increased publicity given to it, was the problem really so much larger than in the past? The question is worth asking because some American writers have thrown doubt on the idea that crime and especially juvenile crime were in 1960 sensibly worse than at previous periods in United States history. The change, according to this argument, is simply that today far more fashionable attention is paid to neurotic behaviour in every form, and juvenile delinquency is one of these forms. This point was recently made by so knowledgeable an American sociologist as Dr Daniel Bell,[1] who argued, though only on the basis of statistics up to 1957, that the fluidity of the American social situation made these statistics deceptive, and that many types of crime were actually on the decline.

I think it is possible to go some way along with this argument, or perhaps it was possible to do so until a few years ago. For the purposes of comparison with other countries, American juvenile crime statistics are not easy to disentangle, because in the United States the majority of less serious cases are referred by the police directly to the social agencies and only a minority are handled by

[1] Daniel Bell, *The End of Ideology*. Free Press of Glencoe, Illinois, 1959.

the juvenile courts. Definitions of what constitutes a serious offence vary from state to state. So does the attitude of different police authorities, who in the United States are subject to different political and electoral pressures. It has been said that a sudden increase in reported cases of juvenile crime in an American city may simply reflect the sudden activation of the local police force or a politically-inspired order to bring in more convictions against young hoodlums. Furthermore, since so many juvenile crimes concern automobiles, their increase may merely reflect the fantastic motorization of the American nation. Again, it is said that the statistics have been distorted by the great movement into the suburbs. The tolerance accorded to young law-breakers in a tightly-knit slum community, where everyone is against the police, disappears the moment the slum-dwellers settle in suburbia and acquire the censorious outlook of their new surroundings, where a mere stone thrown through a window can become a case of vandalism reported to the police, and so on.

All these arguments have some weight, but I think in 1960 they can no longer be regarded as affecting the general picture. The trend towards an increase in juvenile crime has in recent years become quite unmistakeable and alarming. Between 1947 and 1959, cases handled by the juvenile courts, after adjustment to the increase in the United States population between 10 and 18 years, have gone up about $2\frac{1}{2}$ times; cases handled by the police have gone up 3 times; so have murders and accidental killings in this age-group; burglaries have increased about 4 times and cases of assault about 7 times. In other words, the truly nation-wide trend towards a new high plateau of juvenile crime in the United States seems beyond doubt, and it has been a regular trend. The following figures show the percentage increase in juvenile court cases from one year over the preceding year:

	%		%
1949	7	1954	6
1950	3	1955	9
1951	6	1956	21
1952	11	1957	16
1953	13	1958	17

These figures are taken from a cautious study[1] by Mr E. Richard Perlman, Chief of Juvenile Delinquency Statistics at the Children's Bureau of the U.S. Department of Health, Education and Welfare, who has no doubt that they illustrate a real, alarming increase in lawlessness:

> It cannot be accounted for by better reporting or better law enforcement. It cannot be attributed solely to the recent increase in the child population, since the increases in both police arrests and court delinquency cases have far outstripped the increases in the child population. And the prospect for the future looks even worse. The Bureau of the Census predicts we shall have 35 per cent. more boys and girls in the 10 through 17 age-groups in 1965 and 48 per cent. more in 1970 than we had in 1957. This is due to the large sustained birth rates that occurred during and after World War II. Should the number of delinquents increase only at the same pace as the child population increases, the problem will be much bigger than it is now. Should the number of delinquents increase at a faster pace—as it has been doing in recent years—then the problem may become staggering.

It is probable that even as things are, within two or three years the number of juveniles in the United States annually picked up by the police will approach the two million mark. Or to draw another comparison: bearing in mind that young delinquents in the United States are still only a small minority, if one goes by such things as the total of American juvenile court cases or the number of boys and girls annually sent to training schools (corresponding to British Approved Schools), then this delinquent minority seems roughly about three times larger than in Britain. The situation seems certainly a far cry from the days of the wood-pile and the Bible.

[1] Published in *Annals*, Journal of the American Academy of Political and Social Science, March 1959.

CHAPTER XXI

America: The Receding Super-ego

WHAT IS BEING DONE?

THE answer to this question is that plenty is being done in the United States to try to cope with delinquency and, at the same time, whatever is being done does not seem enough. A vast country like the United States is, of course, not really comparable to a small tightly-knit European state, but what strikes the European observer who looks at the American penal scene is the enormous amount of research which is continuously being produced on juvenile delinquency, and the confusing variety of American penal, social and community agencies which in different places and different ways are all trying to deal with the problems of American wayward youth. Yet it is hard to feel that many of these efforts are directed at the basic causes of the problem, and many American experts themselves seem to share this view. "A fairly substantial proportion of delinquency," write two such reasonable authorities as Herbert A. Block and Frank T. Flynn,[1] "reflects strains in the American social structure affecting families in myriad ways. Despite its roots in individual differences, delinquency as a cultural problem means that society is the patient. Unfortunately the American social structure has a deceptive kind of rigidity and resistance to social change, so that anything that smacks of social planning is likely to be regarded as radical socialism."

This is surely the crux. When one looks at the huge array of American academic and practical fieldwork studies on delinquency, one feels that the required research on practically any aspect of youthful crime has already been done, much of it some time ago, and some of it research on a scale to which there is no equivalent in Britain. There seems relatively little to add to Frederic M. Thrasher's classic study of the swarming Chicago street gangs of the inter-war years, or the graphic descriptions by Clifford R.

[1] Herbert A. Block and Frank T. Flynn, *Delinquency*. Random House, 1956.

Shaw and H. D. Mackay of all the disruptive social pressures which were impelling the children of new immigrants in Chicago towards lawlessness. The problem in America today is not that not enough is known about delinquency but that remedial action presents the difficulty—which is why there is a certain unreality about even the best of such American research.

One of the most prominent examples of such work has been the monumental investigation into the causes of juvenile crime by the Drs Sheldon and Eleanor Glueck.[1] On the basis of long-term and most elaborately detailed observation of 500 young delinquents, scrupulously matched with the same number of non-delinquents as controls, the Gluecks concluded definitely that the delinquents tended to belong to certain recognizable physical and psychological types, and could be identified at a much earlier age than had been supposed, at 10 or even 8 years of age. The Gluecks therefore recommended that the potential juvenile delinquents should be picked out at this early age for special remedial treatment and education. Although hailed in certain American circles as setting new perspectives in the treatment of young offenders, these views about their earlier selection are perhaps not so unique: they are, for instance, today largely shared in British Approved School circles. Yet the crucial question is surely what appropriate methods of remedial treatment would in practice be available for the larger number of boys and girls who in the view of the Gluecks are in need of it; or at any rate how much of it could be provided without some fairly comprehensive social re-planning of the American penal system. Could the existing network of training schools and the already shockingly overburdened probation service in many American states and cities deal with any additional influx of young offenders without some pretty decisive expansion of these services, and would the cost of this be voted for? Or again, where the discipline in certain New York schools in criminal areas has already broken down to the extent of creating a "blackboard jungle", could one even think in such schools of a special curriculum for young delinquents? These are surely not only penal but social and political questions.

Viewed from Europe, many of the American voluntary com-

[1] Dr Sheldon and Dr Eleanor Glueck, *Physique and Delinquency*. Harper, 1956.

munity efforts to attack the delinquency problem seem bold and imaginative. One could say this about the "area projects" directed by Mr Clifford Shaw and his colleagues in Chicago, in which the resources of every relevant social agency were with significant success concentrated on certain of the worst criminal areas in the city. Again, there is much to be learned from the determined efforts made under the direction of New York City Youth Board to "reach" young delinquents through special workers who bravely and sometimes thanklessly try to contact the gangs themselves at their street corners, while simultaneously squads of other case-workers endeavour to "reach" the families involved. Many such American efforts are admirable, but they have to be set against certain crass and continuing inadequacies in the American penal system, which may have their explanation in the special circumstances of American federal and state history, but which cannot at the present day be any longer justified. To give one illustration, American films about youth have popularized the alarming picture of frightened youngsters, arrested for stealing, or perhaps drunken driving or a sexual offence, looking terrified or defiant as they are hustled behind prison bars. The picture is not so far from the facts. Figures indicate that for want of other places of detention, between 50,000 and 100,000 juveniles are every year clapped into city or county jails, even though thinking people realize that this is a reprehensible practice.

Again, as in Britain, the penal apparatus in many parts of the United States has been administratively almost swamped by the recent juvenile crime wave. Juvenile courts in many places have been working without the regular services of probation officers. The reason given for the acute shortage of probation officers is the obvious one of inadequate pay and prospects of promotion in the profession. Seeing that probation was a penal method very much pioneered in the United States, this throws revealing light on the confusion of social priorities in the American affluent society. Or to take another point, like British Approved Schools, American training schools for the 10 to 17 age-group vary greatly in their efficiency. Some, indeed, are very modern, but to a European observer the total number of places in American training schools seems far too small for such a vast country with so large a delinquency problem. The American penal system as a whole also lacks a national equivalent to the British Borstal system for the detention and re-training of young adult offenders in the 17 to 21 age-group. Though reforms have often been discussed, young offenders of this age are in many states still accommodated under demoralizing ordinary prison conditions, for the simple reason that money for anything else has not been made available, though here again thinking people know that this is wrong. These and other glaring shortcomings in the American penal system need no elaborate research in order to establish how much harm they cause. They have been continuously exposed, criticized and written about by American authorities. Any discussion of them leads one back to the central problem—the resistance of the American social structure to certain types of effective public action, of whose benefits few individual people would need to be convinced. In fact, in the whole discussion of American delinquency and penal problems there is one basic puzzle: the *degree* of social unbalance which has already been permitted to develop in the American affluent society. That is, since this society has produced such staggering achievements in raising the general standard of living, and seeing that increasing juvenile delinquency has become a major American problem, why are American penal efforts to tackle it often so shabbily neglected or even starved of adequate finance?

The inevitable answer is that in the American affluent society, more than anywhere, it is the same social forces which have been encouraging juvenile delinquency, which are also the forces that obstruct comprehensive penal reform by determined public action.

AFFLUENCE—AND ITS REVERSE

Trying to discover what precisely is going on in American society—or rather, what is going wrong—has become something of a fascinating pastime. We have in the last years been treated to sharp criticism of the current American drift from some of the most persuasive American economists, sociologists and journalists. Because so many American trends of today are the European trends of tomorrow, their books have been read with avid interest abroad. The pastime is infectious. I myself, during an American tour some years back, found myself continuously trying to gather my confusing impressions of American society into a coherent picture of the direction in which it might be heading. There was the initial, overwhelming impression of American space and vastness, the equal impression of bounding youth and vigour, of friendliness, sociability, and easy, democratic mixing, but there were other impressions, too. In each hotel room, from coast to coast, a radio set was fitted beside my bed; I had only to press a button at random and the room would be filled with idiots' voices projecting advertising slogans or mouthing pop lyrics—how could one help wondering what would be the long-term effect of this drip, drip, drip on American life? As a result of the explosion of American cities in the automobile age, there was the depressing sense of blight and disorganization at the city centres—in Chicago, in Detroit, in down-town Los Angeles: in these places some of the essence of urban culture seemed to have been lost, and I did not feel it had been replaced in the new landscape of interchangeable suburbs, country clubs, golf courses and filling stations into which the city dwellers were moving. The purely material concept of home ownership was no substitute for urbanity. Driving through the monotonous suburbs of a sprawling city like Detroit, in area as large as London, I thought I could sense why people there reputedly talked so much about "roots", and at the same time were always on the move, and also why juvenile delinquency was rife.

It is important to see this restlessness as something new and contemporary. To blame American capitalism is not enough. We have already seen several stages of capitalist culture. As George Orwell has said, it could be argued, especially if one talked about the surroundings in which children grew up, that the spacious, optimistic spirit of nineteenth-century America represented capitalist civilization at its best. Deterioration probably set in towards the end of the century as the scale of American industrialization quickened, to become gigantic; but only after the Second World War did it begin to be realized that in the American affluent society something of a new *kind* of capitalist society was being produced. By now, however, the analysis of this new society is very much the vogue. The endeavours of writers like Riesman, Warner, Galbraith, Whyte, Wright Mills, Fromm and others to elucidate its mysteries have already been widely studied, not only in the United States but also in Europe, where it is felt that many similar social forces are today at work.

Perhaps this similarity was at times obscured. To talk of the advance from an American bourgeois society to an affluent society may sound far-fetched if "bourgeois" is associated only with the stuffy class structure of Europe. Yet in the broader sense of the word the analogy holds. The canvas of American life of fifty years ago might have been enormously varied—that of a class-and-caste society in New England and the South, of newly-rich boisterousness in the Middle West, and beyond this yet newer states where a frontier spirit still flourished. Yet in overall terms the United States could be described as bourgeois—as a very open bourgeois society, dominated by independent entrepreneurs and professional men and farmers, whose direct personal contacts created the tone of American life. But that is already the past. The present change appears to be that American society has already to a considerable extent been taken over by the big corporations, whose top executives have crystallized into a new social power elite, buttressed by the high barriers of exclusive clubs, colleges and residential areas, while their employees are being graded into increasingly rigid classes, and at the same time a new spirit of impersonality has entered American life.

Much the same social transformation has also begun in Europe, but there are three special American developments which ultimately, I think, all have their bearing on the problem of delinquency.

First, in the United States, one is reminded much more ruthlessly that Western capitalism is not a static but a dynamic economic system, making for continuous technical and social change, and one can see more clearly that the present concentration of production in giant units is tending towards the disappearance of the older bourgeois social order as surely as country lanes are yielding to motor highways.

Secondly, it appears that once mass manufacture has reached the size attained, for example, by the American motor industry, it *does* generate a trend to divide its customers by advertising into convenient fixed market grades—a Chevrolet grade, a Buick grade, a Cadillac grade. One can also see the advantage to manufacturers of using high-powered advertising to keep customers firmly in these grades by associating them with social status—but this means that both the consumer and the consumer's goods carry a common label.

Thirdly, there is the new fact in American life of the mass manufacture by large-scale enterprise of actual homes. One can see how, once this technique of house and suburb construction has been introduced, the most profitable method for entrepreneurs —with houses as with cars—is to construct standardized one-community suburbs which are either all-white, or all-white-collar-middle-class or working-class, all-Gentile or all-Jewish. This means that Americans are increasingly divided into separate social groups not only horizontally by income and education, but vertically, according to religion or ethnic origin.

UNDERPRIVILEGE AND DELINQUENCY

These special developments of the American affluent society have all had an effect on delinquency, both in making it more intensive and making it more widespread, and in the first place among the underprivileged in this society. For example, one effect of the new class stratification imposed on the American people has been to make it appear as if the escalator along which new immigrants in the United States have for so many years been carried upwards had today been suddenly stopped, or at least badly jolted. For instance, the American Negroes have in recent years achieved some advance in employment, in the armed forces and in integration of schools and colleges. But in the image of American life projected by advertising, such desegregation still simply does not exist—in the image projected to sell the project, the ideal American family always appears white, Nordic and middle class. This has always been pretty well the case, but when, as today, American advertising has become a super-industry with an inescapable impact, one can see why this impact should simul-taneously set more precise cultural standards for the majority who can keep up with them, and arouse permanent feelings of rejection among the excluded. And among the young, above all, such a sense of rejection is a powerful incentive towards lawlessness. The reaction of many young Negroes and Puerto Ricans illustrates this situation.

The exclusion of minorities is also being made very real by the present American mass movement into new and variously "restricted" suburban residential areas. Personally, I found the picture of race segregation in, say, Chicago, a more disturbing one and visually more depressing than that of the cruder race conflict in the South. The latter might be more savage, but it seemed something like a colonial problem within the United States which time might be expected to cure. On the other hand, the residential race barriers in Chicago, which keep the Coloured population crowded into a few mid-town areas, are discouraging precisely because they belong to the American present. The prime cause has become the fear of white residents that the arrival of Negroes would cause the capital value of their houses to fall, which was in turn due to the idea that through such association their status would suffer—that is, race segregation had already become part of the particular mythology of the affluent society, with its advertisers' values: no one was wicked, but everyone followed the rules. But this very impersonality makes the new segregation harder for those excluded to bear, and especially for the young who need to feel that the world is open to them—young Coloured American adolescents as much as anyone else. Again, it should cause no surprise that, as these more impersonal race barriers have in the last ten years *appeared* to harden in the United States, so there should have been a sharp increase in delinquency among Negro and Puerto Rican youths.

The poor of any race also seem to have become something of a sharply defined minority in the American affluent society. American sociological studies suggest that there has been a significant recent change in the whole American outlook upon poverty—it is no longer just a misfortune, as in the past, but a kind of moral stigma, a sign of failure to make the grade, or in the case of a young person, the failure of the parents to make the grade. This shift in ideas is important. To be sure, in bourgeois society, too, the majority of the urban population, especially the industrial workers, had little direct share in the dominant middle-class culture. But against this the working classes had their own class culture, with a traditional way of life that made sense, with its warmth and solidarity, and often a defensive pride in being working class—in this solidarity there was reassurance for the individual. But in the affluent society the idea is increasingly propagated that below the culture of the majority, below the material standards prescribed by the advertisers, there is no culture, just nothing—if you can't live up to these standards, you're nobody, you're out. In this sense of cultural disintegration below a certain income line one can probably see reasons why the teenage gang members in the slums of New York build up such an intense fantasy life round the possession of their "turf", and their gang loyalty: the fantasy life, like their violent attitude against society, is a defence against the terror of having nothing. In general, it appears that in the American affluent society it is already harder than almost anywhere else for those who cannot follow the advice of the advertisers, those below the majority standards, to lead any life which is psychologically secure and dignified. This increased cultural isolation and frustration looks like a basic cause of what Mr Vance Packard has called "the fantastically high delinquency and crime rates among the younger poor of America".[1]

Another point must be added. As in Britain, but rather more so in the American affluent society, the existing disadvantages of being underprivileged are exacerbated by the relative decline of the public sector of society. American slums have a peculiarly dispiriting look, not only because what might be called "lower-class culture" has been destroyed, but also through the contrast between their drab squalor and the surrounding dynamic power and affluence: the magnificently efficient modern factories, the lavishness of cars and highways, the vast consumption of hand-somely packaged goods displayed in the new suburban shopping-centres. All this underlines what appears to a European an often striking neglect of American public services. As Mr Galbraith has put it, this neglect is also common knowledge.[2]

In the years following World War II, the papers of any major city—those of New York were an excellent example—told daily of the shortages and shortcomings in the elementary municipal and metropolitan services. The schools were old and over-crowded. The police force was under strength and underpaid. The parks and playgrounds were insufficient. Streets and empty lots were filthy, and the sanitation staff was under-equipped and

[1] Vance Packard, *The Status Seekers*. Longmans, 1960.
[2] J. K. Galbraith, *The Affluent Society*. Hamish Hamilton, 1958.

in need of men. Access to the city by those who work there was uncertain and painful and becoming more so. Internal transportation was overcrowded, unhealthful and dirty. So was the air. Parking on the streets had to be prohibited, and there was no space elsewhere. These deficiencies were not in new and novel services but in old and established ones.

Such discussion of this public poverty, says Mr Galbraith, had to compete in the press with stories of ever-increasing opulence in privately produced goods: the gross national income of the United States was rising steadily, so were retail sales, so were personal incomes. And by and large this is still the pattern.

This social unbalance of the American affluent society affects larger issues than delinquency—such as the whole level of American education—but on the special problem of its effects on delinquency two points can be made. As in Britain, but even more so in the United States, it is the children and adolescents of the underprivileged minorities who are most acutely affected by the inadequacy of public services. In the American affluent society these groups are the majority of the Coloured, the new immigrants, the poor in general: it is the boys and girls in these groups who suffer if classrooms in old schools are overcrowded, teachers lack authority, the police is under strength, there are too few parks and playing fields, slum clearance is delayed; if there are too few probation officers and a lack of special detention facilities for adolescents. Among such young people, the inevitable sense of public neglect must both diminish their respect for society and intensify their attitude of social defiance—the outcome again is increased juvenile crime and delinquency.

As Mr Galbraith has also observed, if American society, through inadequate public services, neglects these youngsters, other and not at all public-minded interests are quick to exploit them. In a balanced community, where an efficient school was surrounded by good recreational opportunities, "the diversionary forces operating in the modern juvenile" would do little harm. Comics and the violent modes of television, films and advertising would have to contend with the intellectual discipline and social attraction of the school. But in a society where "private opulence" goes with "public squalor", the schools often cannot compete at all—not against the impact of ubiquitous television or against an output of 100 million copies of questionable comics a month. Some recent interrogation of hardened young New York delinquents have shown how deeply they were influenced by the fantasy crime world of television, and how little by school. Again, one can see a reason for the sharp increase in juvenile crime on the lower rungs of American society.

However, as soon as one speaks of the cultural impact of the American affluent society, it has to be realized that this does not, of course, affect only the underprivileged minorities—at this point one must turn to generalizations about American youth as a whole.

THE RECEDING SUPER-EGO

To use a loose phrase, some of the cultural troubles of the American affluent society—such as the greater confusion among its adolescents—seem to me to stem from the fact that the voice of advertising has become that of the super-ego—a rôle which should be played by society itself.

That advertising is inadequate in this rôle is self-evident. Whatever may be the wording of its message about vital matters like family life, friendship, social status and getting on in life, this is only a cover. The real aim of the images projected is always merely to sell the product. If advertising therefore looms too large in social life, all popular culture will take on a gloss of double-think, and society will advance that much further towards Huxley's brave new world.

This may appear a trite observation, but because angry American critics have inveighed so fiercely against the social havoc wrought by the morals and methods of Madison Avenue, it is surely important, even in order to see a problem like juvenile delinquency in perspective, to reiterate that the whole advertising industry is itself only an instrument. The primary forces which shape the affluent society arise from its economic structure. Such a primary force, to quote the example again, is the requirement of the gargantuan American motor industry that American families should always continue to buy new cars, that American life should always be automobile-dominated. Intensive advertising which never lets up is only the instrument by which the automobile producers, like the other big American producers, achieve this purpose. Yet if the instrument of advertising is used on too large a scale, then it is true that it acquires a life of its own, that its persuasive commands become like those of society itself; and when this happens, the result is likely to be a state of cultural confusion which can be especially devastating for the young.

American sociologists have recently been busy in analysing the various ways in which this is already happening. There seem to be growing indications that one effect of sustained mass advertising on culture is to weaken the bonds of family life and lessen the authority of parents. Some aspects of life in the new American suburban communities provide a good illustration of this. Leading American investigators have written pretty scathingly about what goes on among those labour-saving little homes among the tree-lined avenues. Where a passing European visitor may carry away an impression of material ease, of hospitable and sociable people, of attractive and remarkably independent children, American researchers into Plywood Estates have painted an almost uniformly black picture of suburban families living in a state of social isolation—of competitiveness between neighbours, artificiality in friendship, anxiety over status, always anxiety.

This picture may well also be overdrawn, but one thing is probably true. There *is* something in the whole look of the American suburban landscape which carries a suggestion of rootlessness and of a social life which is not quite complete. The highly organized lobbies of the builders, salesmen and advertisers of American homes *have* succeeded in implanting the idea that the social status of a citizen is linked closely to the size and position of his house. It follows that as a man rises in his career, the voice of the advertisers is also persuading him that he must move house. (It cannot be mere native American restlessness if one suburban family in four or five is on the move each year.) But each move means tearing up roots and usually a complete change of friendships and neighbourhood attachments, both for the parents and the children. The result must be at least a measure of insecurity for the whole family, and insecure parents have less authority over the young. It has been said that some of the newer mass-produced American suburbs, where each house is scarcely distinguishable from its neighbour, are pre-eminently communities where home becomes regarded as a place where the members of different generations belonging to a family seem merely to be living together for a certain time. The result is that teenage boys and girls live much more within their own age-group, without much guidance. The result, in turn, is more of those incidents so often reported in American case-studies, newspaper articles, books and films—of teenage boys and girls who stray through ignorance into delinquency, of cases of reckless driving, accidents, youthful drunkenness and early sexual disorder, with parents nearly always largely unaware of what goes on in the autonomous teenagers' society. These incidents only affect a minority of American adolescents, but if it is argued that this minority is too large, that there is something unsatisfactory in the structure of American suburban life, that it lacks the sense of permanency and focused authority which young people need, and which the American small town of the bourgeois age possessed, then to see the trouble clearly one has to go back to the starting-point of the process, namely that it is enormously powerful economic interests which are today creating the American suburbia in its particular shape. And this process is not easy to change.

In recent American sociological literature one comes also surprisingly often upon the assertion that the conflict between the generations finds sharper expression in the United States than elsewhere. Above all, older people in the United States are more noticeably hostile towards adolescents. This observation has been put forward by writers like Margaret Mead and Kingsley Davis; it corresponds with the first-hand conclusions of American teachers who have studied European schools and family relations. To the extent that this intensified American conflict between harassed adults and demanding adolescents is a fact, it is again surely no accident, but something which goes with the forced development of a separate, commercialized teenage culture. This development has been pushed further in the United States than anywhere else—by the standards of any European country, the specialized teenagers' consumption market in the United States is of staggering dimensions. And the interests of the suppliers of this market certainly run counter to ideas of parental restrictions. If American girls use cosmetics when hardly in their teens, if schoolchildren go in precociously for competitive dating, if teenagers as early as possible feel entitled to cars and expensive outfits and amusements, the overriding reason is that large commercial interests, including some of the biggest corporations, are interested in fostering these fashions of teenage consumption and the idea that American adolescence should be prolonged as much as possible. "Don't keep them back. Don't frustrate them. Let them be buyers and consumers, just like you!" This has become the basic message conveyed by the American advertising industry, whose most advanced practitioners seem today increasingly to portray teenagers as sexually precocious pseudo-adults. (This trend is already also becoming marked in British advertising.) It is hard, and sometimes impossible, for parents to oppose these forces. But not all boys and girls are suited to this life of precocious teenage independence, in lavish consumption and spending which here and there takes its toll in delinquency.

The same observation could be made about the excessively "permissive" character of much American education, whose effect in lowering educational standards has been worrying many authorities. For this "permissiveness", critics have blamed various influences, from the philosophy of John Dewey to Freudian precepts accepted in distorted form. Again, I think these are minor factors. Fundamentally, "permissiveness" in schools seems a logical outcome if certain trends in the affluent society are allowed to go on unchecked. It is in the direct interest of American consumer industries that school discipline should impose no irksome restriction on the social life and the spending of teenagers. The whole impact of their advertising is implicitly directed towards projecting this idea. But again—like the economic pressure against the authority of parents—so this economic pressure against discipline at school appears to create its proportion of "mixed-up kids" and delinquents. As has always to be said, not a large proportion. The majority of ordinary American boys and girls can cheerfully take the affluent society in their stride (as normal adolescents take anything in their stride); but still, it is a larger proportion than in a more directly disciplined society: this seems a price that has to be paid for the maintenance of a special teenage culture with high standards of consumption.

Lastly, in talking about the problem why the process of growing up in the United States has become so much more difficult than it was in the past, one comes to what is probably the most important reason of all—that young people in the affluent society are subjected to a constant and very special confusion of values all around them.

American bourgeois morality of the past was no doubt also a highly confused amalgam, composed of the traditions of bourgeois individualism, the American democratic ideal of independence, some genuine religious beliefs, mixed in with all kinds of sentimentality and hypocrisy, with class and money barriers, race prejudice and the rest. Yet in some way all these elements added up to the genuine sentiments of bourgeois America. On the other hand, in a society dominated by mass advertising, the values imposed on the individual are not only "outer-directed" in Mr Riesman's term. What I think more important is that from their nature they represent sentimentality and not sentiment. Because the advertisers themselves are concerned with something quite different, whatever they have to say about family life, social life, social status and the rest cannot be based on sentiment; it must be manufactured sentimentality. Obvious enough: but the danger is that when the affluent society has reached a certain stage, the advertisers' substitution of sentimentality for sentiment becomes more and more the pattern of all popular culture, especially when the bulk of mass entertainment also becomes subordinated to selling the product. The views put forward by a writer in even a good magazine may be his perfectly genuine opinions, but they are never put out for this reason alone, but always also in the light of how they will help sell the magazine and what the advertisers will think.

In the true affluent society, this substitution of sentimentality for sentiment also appears to be a steady process; it encroaches on social life; it invades democratic politics—when elections become in effect campaigns waged by business interests through advertising agencies and advertising methods, politics are no longer the same. And at this stage, society also ceases to be adequate in its rôle of collective super-ego, as far as the outlook of the young is concerned.

There are various indications from the United States how this contradiction between accepted sentimental precepts and the realities of life makes it harder for young people to know what they should think. American sociologists have pointed out how advertising is constantly urging people to upgrade themselves socially through increased consumption just when a certain hardening of class barriers actually makes such upgrading more difficult. Critics have recently stressed another point where the realities of the affluent society clash with its precepts. It has been the long-accepted ideal of the American boy to tinker with machinery. Only a short time ago, the ambition of an individual boy might have been to become a motor mechanic working in a garage—to take pleasure in dismantling, reassembling, repairing the engines of cars. Today such a boy soon learns that this ambition, too, has been relegated to the realm of sentimentality: the last thing the big manufacturers want is that any but the most superficial repairs should be effected on their cars—for some models, indeed, no spare parts are issued after five years—and that the minimum service or even shoddy service does as well as craftsmanship. Naturally he soon falls into line; but, with craftsmanship, another set of once traditional values has disappeared. (Probably one should make this observation with caution. Although American writers have written much about the current "alienation" of Americans from meaningful work, European missions of trade unionists still find that many ordinary Americans still take greater pleasure in the sheer efficiency of their work than their European counterparts. But the significant word here is "still".)

To turn to another contradiction—since the stern old days of the woodpile and the Bible, American religious observance has also undergone a transformation. In the new suburbs one meets with a surprising amount of regular church-going (far more than, say, in England), but from all accounts this serves a mainly social need. The manifest aim is to turn the suburban church (or synagogue) into a new focus of social life. There is nothing wrong with this aim, which corresponds to the spiritual hunger of people genuinely anxious for roots, but the point is that a young American must soon see that this increased church-going (or synagogue-going) has apparently little link with the other sides of American social life. For example, the bulk of American mass entertainment (always with laudable exceptions) seems devoted more than ever before to the cult of violence. An investigation by the National Association of Educational Broadcasters in 1953 revealed that American television shows averaged 6·2 acts or threats of violence per hour, and as Block and Flynn write,[1] "it is likely, though not proved, that a demoralization of our youth, seen in its broadest terms, results from the continuous exposure to the spectacle of untrammelled sex and violence in our recreational media". As everyone knows, this slant stems not from wickedness in the entertainment industry, but from the general conviction that this represents the best way of selling the product, that is, the entertainment itself and the advertisements it carries. Yet acceptance of this priority precludes other moral values. Because of it, the sensational revelations early in 1960 about straightforward corruption in the American television industry, the faking of quiz shows, the payola racket among disc-jockeys, proved only the briefest sensation. Yet what should young American boys and girls think about it?

Or again, what should they think about the American comics industry, the worst of whose productions—I quote from the Senate Sub-Committee of 1955—offer "short courses in murder, mayhem, robbery, rape, cannibalism, carnage, necrophilia, sex, sadism, masochism and virtually every other form of crime, bestiality and horror". Well, American educational authorities (like those of other countries) are divided about the direct effects of horror comics on young readers. One need not, perhaps, worry too much about their effects on normal, balanced children. But there is some good evidence to think that to the disturbed, the delinquency-prone and suggestible child they can provide both stimulus and documentation for delinquency. Even so, I think this direct effect is relatively only a detail. The real trouble and cause for alarm is that in a society which places such stress on increased church attendance, this flood of horror comics should even exist, just as it is cause for alarm that the juvenile gangs of New York should even exist. The real trouble, in fact, is the constant confusion of values which goes with the affluent society. In this context, the case of the large number of young American prisoners-of-war in Korea, who put up only weak resistance against Chinese brainwashing—something which came as a shock to American public opinion—was, I think, not only significant but also understandable. Such over-exposure to the advertisers' message, which is never what it seems, has to cause a confusion in the minds of young people, in which the ideas of democracy and

[1] Herbert A. Block and Frank T. Flynn, *Delinquency*. Random House, 1956.

freedom become hardly distinguishable from the slogans in car and toothpaste advertisements, and can therefore be as readily discarded. Much more than anything else, this constant confusion between moral values and advertisers' values is surely the reason why in 1960 about two million American boys and girls were involved with the police or the juvenile courts for petty or more serious acts of delinquency. To put it in a simplified way, one feels that the voice of American society, as it is heard by adolescents, is no longer adequately that of the collective super-ego.

SEEING THE PROBLEM IN SCALE

From what I have written in the last pages, it can be deduced that I have no great liking for some of the latest cultural developments of the affluent society in the United States or anywhere else. My observations are on the whole in line with the remarkable warnings about these developments which have recently come alike from professors at Harvard, Yale and Chicago, and journalists in Washington and New York. Reading these alarmed books one after the other, one can almost get the impression that, just as the totalitarian society pictured by George Orwell in *1984* was divided into the Inner Party, the Outer Party and the Proles, so the society of the United States has already been equally transformed, with on top the Power Elite, below this the Organization Men, and below these the Lonely Crowd. Of course, there is a danger in such generalizations. Perhaps the trends described are all going on, but so are others—there is always the reality of America as a giant country of—soon—two hundred million people of every kind, most of them living at a very high standard; a country of dynamic vigour and technical achievement, of wealth, of teeming and optimistic youth. Yet it is difficult to read the warnings of American writers and not to feel that all is far from well. The life of the affluent society exacts its price, and this seems clearly illustrated in the United States today. Part of this price is evidently an increased delinquency problem, which in special circumstances of life in the United States has two aspects: a very noticeable—and understandable—increase in violent juvenile crime among the underprivileged minorities, and an increase in the number of "mixed-up kids" among the population in general.

It has to be said straightaway that this is a price which a country as rich and powerful as the United States can go on paying. Even if the minority of American juvenile delinquents goes up another one or two per cent., they will still remain a small minority among American youth. Yet the existence of this high plateau of juvenile delinquency is surely important apart from its direct cost. It is important because it illuminates dangerous weaknesses in the American social structure, and for this reason it is of major interest to see how much will follow from the countless proposals being put forward to attack the evil. There is no shortage of such proposals. Some critics see the best hopes in drastic penal reform—in the establishment of a Federal Youth Authority with powers to overhaul the whole American penal system, to provide training and reform schools on a far more lavish scale, to recruit more and far better paid probation officers and social workers, and so on. Others place stress on such familiar needs as better schools, accelerated slum clearance, more parks and playing fields, or an attack upon race segregation in public housing.

No doubt many such measures are urgent. However, if the analysis I have given is at all valid, then what surely makes most sense is to regard high delinquency—as foremost American social critics have begun to do—as the outcome of *fundamental* unbalance, a *fundamental* confusion of social priorities and values in the American affluent society, and so only to be solved—like other contemporary American problems—by rectification of this unbalance, that is, by an offensive against this society itself. And here we come to a vast problem indeed, for this social unbalance is conditioned by the same structure of the gigantic United States economy which also provides the majority of Americans with their standard of living.

And this thought brings one to President Kennedy, who during his first spirited months in office has already launched a direct attack upon the values of the affluent society. Should it succeed, even the problem of juvenile delinquency may be brought within manageable bounds. Yet the sheer size of the task of carrying through political reform in the U.S. still poses a giant question mark. Specific political measures against delinquency can probably be envisaged more easily within the smaller, tighter confines of Britain. But before considering these, there are good reasons for taking a look behind the Iron Curtain.

CHAPTER XXII

Moscow: Youth under Authority

WHAT CAN WE LEARN FROM THE RUSSIANS?

BACK in the days when the Soviet Union was still regarded as an experiment, the question what we could learn from Soviet methods of training young people was one which featured frequently in Western discussions on education. It may seem paradoxical that the question is heard so much less today, when the results of Soviet technical education are startling. The probable explanation is that we are today also aware of all the differences in past experience which divide us from the Russians.

How, for instance, would the Soviet security police and peoples' courts at the height of Stalin's dictatorship have coped with a problem like that of New York's armed juvenile gangs? The answer is easy. Had Stalin ruled from Washington, the thousands of juvenile gang members would simply have been rounded up and flung into jail. The leaders would have been shot and the rest of the boys sent to labour camps in Alaska, some eventually to come back, many others never. Any youngster with the slightest doubt about him, any relative or friend who uttered the slightest criticism, would have found himself in Alaska, too. The censored New York press would have produced paens of praise about this merciless cleansing of American life from young bandits and parasitic elements—and with enough grim militiamen on patrol, there would have been deadly stillness on the Manhattan front. . . .

Agreed—in the Soviet Union of today, such Stalinist severities are a matter of the past. Yet what seem to us the deep contradictions of present-day Soviet life—of a society still run by censorship as a monolithic one-party state, but where at the same time the TV aerials sprout on the kolhhoz roofs around Moscow, students are jazz-mad and a race-course fixing can become national news—these contradictions pose fresh puzzles for the Western observer. To write about subjects like education, the state of youth and juvenile delinquency in the Soviet Union without being carried too far into analysis of Communism and Soviet society is extremely difficult. If I am nevertheless going to attempt to write about these subjects in isolation, it is because I believe that recent Soviet experience holds one or two important lessons for the West. For quite clearly, like the West, so the Communist countries behind the Iron Curtain have been affected by the wave of youthful unrest of the 'fifties.

This coincidence in time is, I think, not accidental. For instance, it is interesting and significant that on this side of the Iron Curtain and the other, the cult of jazz should have become a symbol of youthful revolt. At the same time, we should also recognize some basic differences in the two movements. In the West, sections of the young have rebelled against moral confusion, too little guidance: they have reacted against having too much easy money and not enough money for special purposes. In Eastern Europe the young rebelled against drabness, against regimentation, against political unfreedom and oppression: this was a revolt on quite a different intellectual level from any movement in the West. In the satellite states, and especially in Poland and Hungary, this revolt expressed itself in a remarkable mass repudiation of Communism by the young people living under it—one might almost call it a teenage counter-revolution. This passionate defiance of Communism by Polish and Hungarian youth was one of the astonishing phenomena of the mid-century, about which not enough has yet been written. It not only created its heroic legend in the Warsaw and Budapest risings of October 1956—it probably decisively influenced the ultimate course of Communist rule in Europe. Since Poland and Hungary were, in effect, countries under foreign police-state rule, the special circumstances which led to the risings of 1956 are really outside the scope of this book. Even so, the discontent, the defiance of East European youth falls into the pattern of our time, and what should be noted is that, in a less tangible way, Soviet Russian youth has also been infected by the unrest of today—it has not escaped this infection. Even Moscow, with its *stilyagi* in Gorki Street and its hooligans in the workers' suburbs, has its rebels without cause. And on another level its angry young writers: the more serious disenchantment of young Russians with the inequalities, the cynicism and hardships of current Soviet life is reflected in novels like Dudintsev's *Not by Bread Alone*. How far this disenchantment can have political consequences in a country under Communist dictatorial rule is hard to say. To speculate on this would lead me beyond my theme, but I think that the state of mind of youth which the Soviet system has produced, is an interesting subject in itself. For obvious reasons, one can here only deal in very general impressions. But it might be useful to start with the top Soviet achievement.

ALL PROBLEMS SOLVED?

A visit to a top-grade Soviet school is usually a rather startling experience which an English or American writer especially finds hard to reconcile with preconceived ideas. The picture has been made familiar to us by a host of Anglo-American correspondents, from Mr John Gunther downwards. Our correspondent would be taken to visit Moscow public school No. 315 or perhaps No. 151 (to judge from the published stories, No. 315 is a favourite show-place), and if he is an intelligent middle-aged observer, he would feel at once alarmed by the standard in education achieved and puzzled by something nostalgic in the whole atmosphere of the school.

From the entrance hall onwards, our observer would notice on all walls large, patriotic portraits of Tolstoy, Lenin and Gorki, of Marshal Suvorov and other Russian military heroes, and might ponder about this touch of old-fashioned authority. Starting his tour with the younger pupils, he would find himself in a classroom full of surprisingly attractive children ("The children were entrancing, bright as fireworks," John Gunther) sitting at old-fashioned double desks with inkwells; they would be neatly and uniformly dressed, the girls in black or brown pinafores with their blonde hair in plaits, the boys in their little semi-military belted uniform (rather like German or Scandinavian schoolboys of 1910). Boys and girls who were in the Pioneers, the Communist equivalent of the Scouts, would be wearing bright red kerchiefs round their necks. All the children would seem responsive, spontaneously natural and yet polite, with that impressive look of bright eagerness which a sense of purpose together with tight discipline can give to youngsters. (I myself noticed this with a shock in the Hitlerjugend in Berlin in the summer of 1939.)

Proceeding to the classes for older boys and girls, our writer might well feel that the curriculum in this Moscow school for *all* children appeared to be equal to that of the best Central European schools for selected upper-middle-class boys and girls. A British journalist, if imaginative, would note with, one hopes, a certain shock, that the Soviet school system was managed without any 11-plus test. The basic theoretical arrangement was for *all* Soviet children to receive ten years of strenuous, purposeful academic education. There was nothing like the British idea of segregating a middle-class minority of children who received a similar education from the working-class majority who did not; nor any hint of the resistance to middle-class culture often found in British secondary modern schools. This difference between British and Soviet schools in the matter of class outlook would alone be enough to make a British visitor feel thoughtful.

Again, an American visitor comparing the schools of Moscow and New York would be struck by the apparent total absence in Moscow of any distracting commercial youth culture: he would find no 12-year-old girls prematurely occupied with dating and cosmetics, no exaggerated cult of athletics, no commercial television, no horror comics. Above all, among all these serious and attractive Soviet children he would be impressed by the unquestioned authority of the teachers and the respect accorded them. (He would be told that there was no shortage of teachers; at an average salary of 800 roubles a month, they were relatively well paid by Soviet standards.) In this respect, our American might feel uneasily, a Soviet school of today was rather like the ideal of an American school of the bourgeois past, before big advertising and the teenage market had been invented. . . . Yet the Soviet school system appeared simultaneously to provide a purposeful preparation for the scientific world of tomorrow. Every child took four years of chemistry, five of physics and six of biology. The average Russian boy or girl, Mr John Gunther reported, got more than five times the amount of science and mathematics stipulated for entrance even to such a specialised American institution as Massachusetts Institute of Technology.[1]

Moreover, according to what our visitors were told, there would seem to be little difficulty in pushing all ordinary boys and girls through this curriculum. If our visitors asked the headmistress of

[1] John Gunther, *Inside Russia Today*. Hamish Hamilton, 1958.

such a Moscow school whether, as they had been told, some pupils did indeed leave at the age of 14 or 15, the answer would usually be that a certain number did go, but only to receive the practical, specialized technological training of which the continuously expanding Soviet economy was in such need. And, as compared to this drive for scientific and technical knowledge, problems of occasional indiscipline at school caused evidently only very minor worries. The headmistress would clearly not be very interested in this question; or she would reply that the children had naturally already acquired the habits of spontaneous discipline and the desire to learn at one of Moscow's 2,000 kindergartens. Our visitors would meet the same atmosphere of youthful zest and discipline when they went to a Pioneer institution, say the Central House of the Pioneers in Moscow. Here, in a vast club-house with a wealth of wonderful equipment, they would meet boys and girls every one of them absorbed in "constructive leisure": spending their free time being taught crafts and hobbies; studying literature, dramatics, the arts (the latter in a good bourgeois way—girls would be embroidering, painting water-colours, playing piano *études*, as schoolgirls in the West did a generation ago). And if our visitors in their tour of Soviet education passed on to, say, Moscow's skyscraper Lomonosov University with its 2,000 laboratories and 5,000 rooms (costing 5 times as much as Chicago University), if they were overwhelmed, as they usually would be, with Soviet educational statistics and watched the serious, mature-looking students swarm in and out, they might be pardoned for feeling a little dizzy. Since most visitors would be unaware that this stress on more and more education had been maintained even during the worst severities of the Stalinist days, they would feel themselves faced with puzzling contradictions in the Soviet system. An American visitor, particularly, might by reaction feel that the Soviet leaders had solved one of the great problems troubling America; that, however repellent their political system might be, they had somehow inculcated such a drive for knowledge and culture among Soviet youth that questions of indiscipline, youthful disaffection and delinquency simply solved themselves. . . .

One could put it another way. I have earlier mentioned George Orwell's picture of the American nineteenth-century romantic ideal: of a barefoot boy sitting in a whitewashed schoolroom dominated by a big black Bible, who aspired to become President, but had first to attend to the woodpile. After a tour of a showplace Moscow school, our American observer might imagine that Soviet education had simply progressed from this same ideal. The authority of the black Bible—in its place one had that of Marxist-Leninist teaching. The woodpile—from the start, the notion of social duties was drummed into the head of every Soviet child. And the dream of becoming President—this was embodied in the enormous opportunities for young Russians of today to lead cultured lives their parents had never dreamed of. In fact, it might seem as if the Russians had done a very simple thing: maintained the ideals of the bourgeois age, broadened them to include every social class, and carried them forward into the scientific age: how unlike the West.

APPEARANCE AND REALITY

This, roughly, is the rather alarmed impression of Soviet education one can gather from the accounts of a number of British and American visitors, usually short-term visitors, and especially from American visitors arriving in the Soviet Union with superficial pre-conceived ideas and with worries about American commercialized culture back home. But just because this idealized picture of Soviet youth is in some ways valid, it is equally important to know where it does not tally at all with Soviet realities.

To give just a few points: *Item:* It is British and American observers who are most startled by the educational standards of picked Soviet State schools. Visitors from Germany or Scandinavia, where the school system is not very different, would be much less surprised. *Item:* Soviet higher education is not free from the disorders troubling the West. The competitive rat-race to get into universities is so fierce that a Soviet enquiry in 1958 found that a large number of 17- and 18-year-olds were working themselves into a state of nervous and physical illness. *Item:* As almost all foreigners find out, most Soviet young people are enormously attracted by the Western youth culture which is officially attacked and derided by their propaganda. Students make and trade "black tapes" of Western jazz, recorded from foreign broadcasts. After an international youth congress, fortunate

Russian girls eagerly display acquired Western clothes. *Item:* Boys and girls who do not pass their examinations into higher education suffer from an acute sense of social failure, of not getting into the superior social class. They are, indeed, often impelled very ruthlessly into jobs in factories, mines, in agriculture or clerical work, wherever the Soviet economy needs them and whether they like it or not—hence, the noticeable cynicism of many Soviet adolescents who have left school. *Item:* The universal 10-year education is still only a theoretical ideal. In 1958, Khrushchev admitted that only 80 per cent. of children in the Russian Soviet Republic (and certainly l s in the outer republics) completed even the full 7-year school. *Item:* The Soviet Union has a hooligan and delinquent problem large enough to feature in the national press. Some districts of Soviet towns are also not safe at night. In cities like Moscow, Leningrad and Kiev, squads of young Communists have been detailed to help the militia patrol parks and streets as guard against youthful gangs. *Item:* Until quite recently, the Soviet penal code towards young offenders was incomparably harsher than in the West. Juveniles could be, and were, sent to prison or labour colonies for five years or more. And if innocent people in the West imagine that anyone who is "Left", like a Communist, must also be an enlightened penal reformer, they can be sorely disillusioned from the Soviet press. Thus, not long after the Supreme Soviet's penal reform act of summer 1958, in fact, already in October 1958, one had the Communist youth organisation's newspaper, *Komsomolskaya Pravda*, inaugurating a campaign for the introduction of the death penalty for killings resulting from so-called "acts of youthful hooliganism"—and not only for the actual assailant but for any member of the gang found with weapons. Similar demands for harsher penalties could be found in the Soviet press at steady intervals during 1959 and the early part of 1960. There must have been good cause for this.

On a closer look, these are some of the contradictions of the present Soviet social scene: above all, an intense educational effort in which the young are kept under tightest authority, side by side with what is quite a large delinquency problem, quite possibly larger than in many countries of the West. How have these contradictions come about? I think that to see both the Soviet educational drive and the problems it has encountered in perspective, one has to go back to the starting-point of it all—and this means to Lenin. This may seem a towering name to introduce into my limited theme, but there is no help for it.

EDUCATION AS PRIORITY

I am aware of the difficulty of writing about any single aspect of the Soviet system in simple and unpolitical terms. As an expert with first-hand knowledge of Soviet life like Mr S. V. Utechin has observed, Western writers who try to isolate one aspect of Soviet education, now the narrowness of indoctrination, now the spectacular scientific advance, usually go wrong. "The truth is that vandalism and outstanding scientific achievement, totalitarian aims and experimentation, have always been and are there, co-existing with each other."[1] Even so, even if in over-simplified terms, I feel there is one point to pick out in Soviet educational history which is of vital importance to the West, namely the vision of Lenin and his colleagues (to use this simplified phrase) of raising the education of every single citizen in Soviet society to a level previously thought appropriate only to the middle class. This aim has in the course of forty years' practice not been achieved, but as far as it has gone, and from the standpoint of the education which in our affluent society we could well afford, the Soviet educational drive holds important lessons for the West.

The purpose of the Bolshevist revolutionaries in starting their educational drive was a very concrete one: to make the Soviet Union powerful. At the same time, however, the Bolshevik revolution also engendered the vision of an ideal education, and it is important to see what elements went into this. First, even long before Lenin, education in Russia had that special social prestige it often has in under-developed countries—the technical know-how and learning of Germany had in particular always exerted a powerful attraction on the Russians. The Czarist Russian education system before Lenin was, in fact, modelled on that of Imperial Germany, from State primary school up to the *Gymnasium* and *Realschule*, with due bourgeois stress on discipline, hard work and learning. This was one starting-point. Proceeding from it, the Russian intelligentsia had in its revolutionary struggles steadily

[1] *The Political Quarterly*, London, October-December 1958.

developed the theme that the spread of education was *the* key to the new society. The concept had undergone changes. The nineteenth-century Populists had hoped to achieve such universal education from below. The Communists, who came after, were on the contrary determined to impose it from above. But about the shape of this envisaged education, one could say, roughly, that the vision in the minds of Lenin and his colleagues was that every citizen of the future Soviet Union was to be educated up to the level of, say, the Central European intellectual middle class. This ideal was fairly clearly formulated in the original Communist Party programme of 1919, which proclaimed that every Soviet child should have ten years at school. This was the theory—since immediate achievement was not possible, for a start the minimum for every child was to be seven years. Even this minimum has not yet been attained, not completely; but if we look at Soviet schools of today, we can see how this *ideal* of giving every Soviet child something like the educational standards of the European middle class has been pursued all the time, in theory at least, even if in nothing like universal practice: and it is one aspect of the Revolution which has drawn a powerful response from the Russian nation.

But Lenin and his colleagues also added another element to their educational drive. Their political purpose was ruthlessly single-minded: to destroy the old order and build a new one on its ruins. One of their means to this end was by harnessing the enthusiasm, the energy and the emotions of the young completely to the purposes of the Soviet State. (Lenin had already announced this in 1905: "We are the party of the future, and the future belongs to the young. We are the party of innovation, and it is to the innovators that youth always gladly gives its allegiance. We are the party of self-sacrificing struggle against ancient rot, and the young are always readiest for sacrificial combat . . . we shall always be the party of the youth of the advanced class.") The Communist leaders also had another motive for seeking total control over the minds of the young. Ruling as they did by dictatorship and police methods, they felt they could not trust the older intelligentsia. Their explicit aim was therefore to train a new Communist generation, of their "own flesh and blood", loyal to the State. This was to be achieved not only through the schools. Indoctrination was to be carried out by organizing the out-of-school activities of children through the controlled Pioneer organization, while older boys and girls were to be shepherded or forced in the right direction by the dedicated revolutionary "vanguard" of the Young Communists, or Komsomols.

For over a decade, therefore, Soviet boys and girls were deliberately educated to a wholesale rejection of the past—this often meant a rejection of all that their parents stood for and often of the actual parents themselves. This was the phase of the great flush of Soviet experiment in literature and the arts, in such things as easy divorce and abortion, and the Soviet education system in this stage also tended to be strikingly *avant-garde*: the Dalton plan, the Montessori plan, children's self-government in schools—it included the lot. This phase in the 'twenties was also the time when Western observers talked most of what could be learned from Soviet education. It is therefore important to note that this experiment of teaching boys and girls to reject their parents and tradition, but without putting them under an equivalent alternative authority, ended in failure. The authority of the Russian family was broken by the Revolution—but one outcome was disorder. Indeed, as one could read from admissions in the Soviet press, one result of the Revolutionary vision of youthful emancipation was widespread inefficiency, delinquency, promiscuity and a sharp fall in the birth-rate, or as the Soviet leaders saw it, "a loss of cadres".

As a result (for other reasons as well, of course!) Stalin went heavily into reverse to clamp down on youthful freedom. The formal traditions of family life were restored and puritanism swept back; out went easy divorce, grants for unmarried mothers were abolished, abortion became illegal. The new concept was called "Communist morality", but it looked remarkably like Victorian morality. In schools, the return was to Czarist discipline, and it went all the way; out went co-education, uniforms came back, children stood up when an adult entered the class, there was no more nonsense about children's self-government. Out of school, puritanical standards were by order of the Government, i.e. of the Communist Party leadership, imposed through the Pioneers and the Komsomols, based on collective responsibility of children for each other—a system of collective informing and shaming, with harsh penalties. It looked as if the clock had suddenly been turned back. This was the time when, in surprised disillusion, Western intellectuals stopped asking what could be learned from Soviet education, for in undergoing her industrial revolution Soviet Russia seemed to have turned back to the puritanical morals of the nineteenth century. The very appearance of the new Soviet art and architecture and life had suddenly a Victorian air.

Yet I think this loss of interest was a pity. True, Stalin's counter-revolution was directed sweepingly against the whole message of emancipation of the Revolution, especially the emancipation of youth: brutal authority and not freedom was now the watchword. But behind the "Victorian" façade, it was not the authority of parents, of the bourgeois past, which was restored. On the contrary, the authority now re-imposed on the young as well as on their parents was completely that of the State, represented by the Communist Party, which, whatever its words, in reality spoke not of freedom but of work, of duty, of submission to the demands of State authority. Here, in this counter-revolution, we have the start of the problem how far a young person's life can be influenced by, respectively, his own wishes, those of his family and those of the State, a problem which is still completely unsolved in the Soviet Union of today, and certainly a cause of large-scale youthful malaise.

For a time, however, this reality behind the Soviet "Victorian" look was hidden by Stalin's rule of terror which for some years reached such a pitch (with greater oppression as the Soviet Union grew stronger and with millions of people done away with) that the whole of Soviet life was shrouded in impenetrable mist. During these years, face to face groups were afraid to talk; under the terror, society seemed atomized. Yet it was striking that during these same years the Soviet education system went on expanding steadily—the drive went on and on.

In retrospect one can see reasons. The over-riding aim of the Communist leaders was to make the U.S.S.R. economically and militarily strong, which meant promoting technical know-how and mass literacy—during all their political phases the Communist leadership never wavered from this aim. But there were also other reasons for the uninterrupted expansion of education. Because planted in receptive soil, the idea of social betterment through universal education remained the one concept of the Revolution eagerly accepted by the Russian people. Moreover, as the early

Bolshevik leaders had done, so Stalin now aimed to create a new, indoctrinated generation of intellectuals and technicians entirely loyal to himself, and so, even during the harshest days of his tenure, technical education was given priority in resources. Again, amidst the austerity of Soviet Russian life under Stalin, education stood out as the one supreme avenue through which young people could better themselves and achieve social advance, all the more so as the alternative avenue, that of becoming a member of the Communist Party aristocracy, had now become highly dangerous.

For all these reasons, schools and colleges in Soviet Russia continued to be given first priority. And something else happened, too. In the West, the bourgeois educational ideals of fifty years ago, with their stress on discipline, on formal good manners and the notion of the good apprentice, have been very much changed by all the influences of our commercialized culture, with its advertised hedonism. But in Soviet Russia, where for years there was no such consumers' culture, the pattern of this bourgeois education of fifty years ago has been curiously preserved, right to the present day. The more I read about the atmosphere and appearance of Soviet schools of today, the more it reminds me of that sound Swiss-German school which I myself attended many years ago.

GUESSES ABOUT RUSSIAN YOUTH

And so to the present day. Most Soviet Russians over 30 or 35 appear agreed that, whatever present difficulties, by comparison with the days of Stalin's terror and those of the war, they have emerged from the shadows. Recent years have at last seen an advance towards greater amenities in Soviet city life: new apartments, more television, an enormous boom in every single kind of sport. The promise no longer sounds so unreal that there will soon be far better and brighter goods in Soviet shops and that, just as in the West, such possessions as cars, washing-machines and refrigerators will be available on hire-purchase terms in real quantity supplies. For the overwhelming majority of ordinary Russians, these material benefits, and not politics, are the things that really occupy their minds. Angry young Soviet novelists have already written scathingly about the evidently pretty ugly scramble for jobs, possessions and status which this new material advance has unloosed—stressing that all the old Communist romanticism has vanished. However, for the young, this post-Stalinist Soviet world of rising living standards, ruthless competition and vanishing ideals is the only reality they know. From the reactions of Soviet young people we now also know more about their worries. At the first glance, American and Soviet society seem like precise opposites in their youth problems. American complaints are about lack of drive in schools, insufficient authority over adolescents and an overdose of commercial youth culture. By contrast, Soviet education is tight and disciplined, but out of school youngsters feel repressed by rigid authority, while the lack of spontaneous teenage culture is a major social problem.

If one talks about youth in the Soviet Union, one still has to begin by talking about the Soviet State education system. The historic message transmitted from the revolutionary intelligentsia to the Russian masses, that learning can give a social status higher than anything else, still evokes a passionate response. But in the changing Soviet society of today, the drive for education has already also come up against new limits and produced some social problems familiar to us. For instance, in keeping with the Party programme of 1919, the Soviet leaders in 1950 decided to raise the length of school attendance for all children from seven years to ten years, the change to be effected by stages by 1960. In this form, however, the scheme was abandoned half-way. If one takes the figures both for the towns and the schools in the countryside, it had in actual practice been nothing like fulfilled. Even so, in urban areas, this extension of secondary education created new troubles because it touched on a sore spot in Soviet life—the gap in status between those who passed via school and higher education into the new class of Soviet administrators and technicians, and those who did not and were consequently relegated, perhaps to manual work. For many secondary school pupils this was a sufficiently frightening prospect to make them feel social failures, "also rans". The result of the new policy was to create a whole class of adolescents who, on failing university entrance, did not go into jobs but tried despairingly to take the examination again and again.

The first response of the Soviet authorities was official pressure to compel these dissatisfied youngsters to take ordinary manual jobs in industry and on collective farms, or to go out as pioneers into the virgin lands to the East; as especially Mr Khrushchev demanded in his orations. The pressure was accompanied by rather strident propaganda against *beloruchki*—literally, those with "white hands"—that is, adolescents who did not care to go into manual work and so, in Soviet parlance, were shirkers who refused their patriotic duty. However, as these methods of persuasion proved inadequate, the Soviet leaders—and this is interesting—in about 1954-55 put their whole education policy into reverse. The first measure was to introduce a sharper division, usually made at the age of 14, between those secondary school pupils who were to continue with academic education and others who were to proceed straight into some form of practical and technical training —a kind of British 11-plus test, if at a later and more suitable age. The next step, proclaimed in detail at the 20th Party Congress in 1956, was a call for the "polytechnisation" of the entire Soviet secondary education system. All secondary school education was now to include some periods of practical training in industry and agriculture. A third innovation was the introduction of boarding schools for boys and girls, of which a considerable number have already been set up. Their slant as compared to day schools is still uncertain, but one thing is clear: one main purpose of introducing boarding schools is to give the authorities—that is, the Communist Party leadership—greater physical control over Soviet adolescents, presumably in an attempt to achieve greater social and political control.[1]

[1] Boarding schools were quite well known in Russia before the Revolution, either as privileged schools on English public school lines like the famous Lycée in Tsarskoye Selo, the Pages' Corps and the Institute for Noble Girls, or as professional institutions like theological and teachers' seminaries and military schools. After the Second World War, the pre-Revolutionary military cadet corps institutions were resuscitated in the new Suvorov and Nakhimov schools. It may be of surprise to some readers that at the time when the boarding school reform was introduced, the merits of the English public schools were discussed at some length in Soviet journals (*Sovietskaya Pedagogica*, June 1956; *Uchitelskaya Gazeta*, May 1956). And some of their features, such as the house system and the arrangement of the pupil's day, were considered deserving of close study and possible imitation. This subject is dealt with in detail by Mr S. V. Utechin in *The Soviet Cultural Scene*, edited by W. Z. Laqueur and G. Lichtheim, Atlantic Books, 1958.

I have mentioned these innovations in Soviet educational policy because I think they throw some light on the state of mind of a section of Soviet youth, on that evident mood of apathy and cynicism of a good many young people, in spite of the education which they have received, against which the Soviet press constantly inveighs. The problem which the Soviet authorities now face in trying to combat this mood is a very real one, real in the West, too. What sort of education shall we give in our affluent society to those who must necessarily perform jobs that are monotonous and of no distinction, and what sort of social life can such young people demand?

From the nature of Communist society, this question remains very much unsolved in the Soviet Union. It is true that Soviet education is technically excellent. The old target of academic education for everybody has been dropped, but the official policy still aims at providing some kind of full-time education for *all* children up to the age of 17—an aim which could well be emulated in a country like Britain. The current Soviet programme for the polytechnization of secondary schools probably also contains valuable ideas for training boys and girls to face our technological age. But it is *after* school, after the competitive examinations, that the real competition for a much smaller number of prizes begins for Soviet teenagers—and deep disappointment often sets in.

There is, first, the sharp disillusion in store for those who do not make the grade. About 70 per cent. of the students of Moscow University at the present day are themselves the sons and daughters of the intelligentsia. If, as is common knowledge, they are often scared by their parents with the phrase "If you don't work hard, you'll become a simple worker", this throws light on the plight of those who are condemned to precisely that. For in the Soviet Union, as much as in the United States, failure to rise is like an offence against the national myth. "I was a shepherd, a shepherd's son, and now I am a cultured man." Such personal advance has for long been a constant theme of Soviet literature and propaganda. Mr Khrushchev himself has liked to stress it again and again, citing himself personally as an example. But in the more developed Soviet society of today, where ruthless competition forces many an adolescent to feel "I have been through school, but I have not risen socially, I'm an also-ran", it appears that Mr

Khrushchev may soon be untypical. At any rate, the failure of many youngsters to achieve that particular social status to which constant propaganda had made them feel entitled is certainly a cause of youthful disaffection, especially as Soviet life offers so few other social and cultural compensations for those who do not rise. It is this mood of pervasive disillusion among a large section of Soviet youth which Mr Khrushchev has sought to counter by his tirades against idle intellectuals, by his sponsored schemes for pushing the young into raw new territories, by trying in general to revive the idea that all work for the Soviet Union which is economically useful is thereby noble—"therefore be happy, though frustrated". The new boarding schools are probably conceived as instruments for inculcating this patriotism.

Since the 20th Communist Party Congress, the slogan under which Mr Khrushchev has gathered the threads of power in his own hands and those of the Party Leaders has been one of "Back to Leninism". In education, too, it appears his evident intention to raise a new Soviet generation in the spirit of some sort of revived militancy.

THE MISSING TEENAGE CULTURE

As in talking about American youth of today one always comes back to the problem of commercialized culture, so in Soviet life it is the Government's education policy which is always in the foreground when one talks about young people. Some observers think that Khrushchev will succeed in arousing a new militancy. To my mind this is highly doubtful. Today Soviet society has clearly reached a stage where it can do without this coercion. The managerial and technical know-how, the industrial power are all there. If mere affluence is the goal, revolutionary militancy and discipline are simply no longer necessary. And Soviet young people have also changed. They have become more demanding. And one of the difficulties in reconciling those who have to perform lesser jobs to their fate is the lack of teenage culture which the system offers.

One simple reason for this lack is that outside the centres of the main cities Soviet life is, by any reasonable Western standards, still outstandingly drab. With some exceptions: for instance, many facilities have been provided for sport. But, speaking generally, the demand of the young generation for bright clothes, a more relaxed social life, for such an innocent pastime as listening to jazz (which holds an enormous attraction) has simply not yet been met, and Soviet young people of all classes seem aware of this deficiency. Miss Sally Belfrage relates in her entertaining account of life among young people in Moscow[1] how Soviet students talked with no hesitation about the limitations which the housing shortage imposed on their sex life, the tiresome stratagems it made necessary. Lower down the social scale, it is this same general drabness of life which evidently drives so many adolescents to the one main outlet of Soviet life—getting well and properly drunk. Mr Khrushchev himself took up the problem in his speech to the last Komsomol Congress, saying: "It is necessary to combat the *intolerable* phenomena of drunkenness among young people."[2] Western Prime Ministers have not yet had to make such an exhortation.

The absence of a real youth culture, by which I mean the chance for Soviet young people to have some independent social life and entertainment, has also become a more urgent problem in Soviet life because one gets the feeling that by today the Communist system of organizing and regimenting all young people within centralized State youth organizations has very much seen its day, at least as far as adolescents from the age of 14 or 15 upwards are concerned. It is at this age-level that the Soviet system has been failing. For example, it is noteworthy that while the official children's literature is generally well edited and often brilliantly imaginative, for years the books and journals produced for adolescents have been unbearably empty and dull. This is not really surprising. Children recognize and respond to authority. But it is difficult to stimulate the imagination of adolescents while at the same time ordering them to remain rigidly conformist, in line with the ideas of a past generation.

This dilemma is today met above all inside the official Soviet State youth organizations, through which out-of-school, holiday and free-time activities are organized. The Pioneer Movement probably still works well enough, though there is evidence that even young children get bored with having their holidays and play

[1] Sally Belfrage, *A Room in Moscow*. André Deutsch, 1958.
[2] *Pravda*, 15th April 1958.

activities always organized from above, instead of being able to arrange some of them for themselves. However, of more significance for the future of Soviet life is the fact that the Komsomol, the official young Communist organization and the régime's principal instrument for controlling the activities of *adolescents*, has by general admission lost its drive and its appeal to youth. Again, this is not surprising. The Komsomol organization was created during the revolutionary days to function as a small voluntary body of young Communist enthusiasts. Today, with practically the entire adolescent age-group enrolled, the Komsomol has become something utterly different: a rigid, centralized State youth organization, in which social life is linked with sluggish political indoctrination, but in which the Soviet young people of today feel, above all, profoundly bored. At any rate, complaints that modern Soviet youth in the Komsomol is apathetic, that the young show no altruism, are unwilling to engage in political duties and find political discussions a bore, form a constant refrain in the Soviet press. Mr Khrushchev himself has also tried to attack this idea of boredom:

> Life in Komsomol organizations should literally seethe and initiate overflow. Then everyone will find something to do and young people will not complain that life is boring in Komsomol organizations, whereas today you hear such complaints frequently.[1]

It looks more likely, however, that in the changing Soviet society of today this whole system of politically controlled State youth organization, with instructions always passed from top to bottom, has outlived its usefulness. What emerges from the public discussion about the Komsomol is that an air of hypocrisy has in the eyes of the young attached itself to the organization—the usual accusation is that the Komsomol secretary in private behaves quite differently from what he preaches in public. By way of countering this youthful opposition to regimentation, it is interesting that the Komsomol book and magazine publishers have in the last two or three years taken some hesitant but probably significant steps to give ordinary adolescents a chance to express their genuine individual views on "human interest" topics. Usually this is done

[1] *Pravda*, 19th April, 1958.

by getting a letter-writer to raise a problem and to invite comment from readers. The story is as a rule a simple one, in the style of "true confessions". For instance, a girl, who is a good Communist, may have been going out with a boy who is the son of some local high official, who rides in his father's car, who looks down on her poor but honest parents, and whose only interest is in dancing and flirting. Though it made her unhappy, was she right to break off the relationship? In spite of their careful selection, the young readers' comments on such questions seem to reveal one thing: a powerful, underlying desire by Soviet adolescents to argue out their own views on "human interest" questions, to arrive at their own decisions—to have their own youth culture.

What results these stirrings can have in the strait-jacketed, censored Soviet society in creating a more spontaneous youth culture is hard to say. But there is another aspect of this issue on which we should keep our attention. In the few contacts between West and East which the Soviet leadership has not been able to avoid, it is always Western youth culture which has exerted the fascination: it is always Soviet adolescents who are fascinated by Western art, by nylons, jeans and jazz, by free Western ways—the attraction never works vice versa. In other words, the Soviet education system may be exemplary in its technical standards, but in almost all other sides of life which interest young people it is the doctrinaire Soviet leaders who are trying to hold back the inter-national *Zeitgeist*, who are out of step with the questing outlook of youth of today.

Not that Soviet leaders like Mr Khrushchev show any sign of giving way. One can only guess how they will manœuvre to meet the general dissatisfaction of Soviet youth with its too narrowly limited life. Among the majority of Soviet young people, this general dissatisfaction is probably still no more than a vague emotion, but in the meantime some actual groups of young rebels against Soviet authority have become more defined.

WHO ARE THE REBELS?

They can be divided into four groups. Starting at the top, there are the students who are *politically* openly dissatisfied with Soviet censorship, with the lack of free expression and the dreary rigidity of Marxist-Leninist dogma; students of the type of the small groups who at the time of the Hungarian revolution formed private discussion circles and who today urgently seek more contact with Western art and literature. These young dissidents certainly exist—in brief encounters they can be found in Moscow and Leningrad. Many of them are among the best young people in the Soviet Union and one can only wish them well for the future.

Below these are what journalists have called the "jet-set"; the members of this set, as Mr Edward Crankshaw has said, are what the name conveys,

> the sons and daughters of the very rich and very privileged, who have no intention of working, believe in nothing at all (not even in revolt), and do their best to turn their fathers' Sochi villas into imitations of Palm Beach. They dress in imported European clothes; they drink themselves silly; they philander and fornicate; they gamble and dance. Regarding the mass of the people as cattle and the intelligentsia as prigs and bores, they live almost entirely to themselves, in and out of each other's houses, and are thus rarely seen.[1]

The "jet-set" are only a minority phenomenon. So, though more numerous, are the next group below them, the *stilyagi*, or "style-boys". These bright young rebels of the Soviet big cities have perhaps been given more publicity than their numbers merit. Their speciality was that they faithfully copied the flashy clothes, the haircuts, the mannerisms of British Teddy boys and American zoot suiters; they evidently managed to do this through glimpses of Western films and magazines—and through all kinds of other strange loopholes in the Iron Curtain. They were intent, above all, as an act of deliberate adolescent rebellion, to copy everything they thought Western; their dominant craze was for jazz, rock and jive; they eagerly created a black market in smuggled jazz records, often home-made and copied from foreign broadcasts. The *stilyagi* were jeered at by the Soviet press, and written up with some excitement in the Western press. The main interest of the *stilyagi* phenomenon was in showing that such a rebellious fashion could burst out in the Soviet Union at all—the movement appeared, however, to have passed its peak in 1959-60.

[1] Edward Crankshaw, *Khrushchev's Russia*. Penguin Books, 1959.

None of these groups was numerically large. They were all minority phenomena of the new Soviet middle class, and the great majority of young people in this class, like their counterparts in the West, are today too preoccupied with the expanding professional opportunities before them to stray far from the conformist path.

A much more serious and persistent problem is posed by the "young hooligans", as they are always called in the Soviet press, lawless youths mostly belonging well down the social scale, some of them moving about in defiant gangs, who are found in most parts of the Soviet Union. In the immediate post-war period, this hooliganism was largely linked with the poverty and disruption which the war had brought to Soviet Russia. It is interesting, however, that such gangs of "hooligans" have been produced in apparently undiminished numbers during the recent, more settled period in Soviet life. There does seem to be something international here, some basic trend of our age. For, in fact, most Soviet accounts of the "hooligans" reveal them as very ordinary young criminals, as juvenile delinquents, or simply as cynical young members of mutinous gangs, numerous enough to form a recognizable stereotype in Soviet life.

Individually, they seem to have drifted into this life for the usual reasons, such as an inadequate home background. What is interesting is that Soviet society, in spite of the disciplined school system, the Pioneers and the Komsomol, and in spite of the general passion for education, should have produced these young delinquents in such numbers that their gang activities have rendered districts of Soviet towns and cities unsafe. Exactly how large the problem is cannot be stated—comprehensive crime statistics are not published in the Soviet Union, which is probably significant. However, according to the *Leningrad Pravda* (14th March 1959), "until recently, about 62·5 per cent. of all disturbance of the peace in Leningrad were committed by young persons below 25 years of age". That the problem is, however, pretty large can be gathered by the usual sign—the frequency with which reports of criminal cases involving youths are referred to in the Soviet press, not in ordinary news reports but in carefully worded, didactic editorials designed to focus attention on an urgent public problem.

The likely reasons for this extent of juvenile crime or "hooligan-ism" are the deficiencies of Soviet society mentioned earlier. There is, first, the general drabness, the acute lack of teenage culture especially for those in the submerged quarter or third of Soviet youth who still get little out of life. There is the resentment of the "also-rans", the adolescents for whom education has brought no advancement in a society where, even more than in the United States, the official myth has it that everyone must rise in status. Thirdly, "hooliganism" seems also a straight reaction against the rigid regimentation in Soviet life. The answer of a section of Soviet youth to constant, arid indoctrination lies evidently in complete cynicism.

SOVIET PENAL METHODS

Like other aspects of the Soviet system, Soviet penal methods are in many ways contradictory, with progressive and brutal methods of treatment intermingled. Up to the time of the penal reforms enacted in 1958, the Soviet code towards juveniles under 18 was by Western standards extremely harsh. Young offenders could be thrown into prison on long sentences or sent to labour colonies for stretches of many years. With the death of Stalin and the slowly changing mood in Soviet society in the 'fifties, came legal reform. By and large, the new Soviet juvenile penal system is in practice no longer markedly different from that of Britain and other Western countries. A fair proportion of young offenders are convicted only conditionally and remain at home under super-vision, though this is not carried out by a special probation officer, but by the young person's teachers, employers, or Komsomol leaders. More serious teenage offenders can be sent for several years to corrective work colonies, which are in effect farm-and-workshop schools where the stress is not on punishment but on the re-education of the young offenders within a reassuring framework of discipline and authority, really very much as in Britain's Approved Schools and Open Borstals. Western visitors to such Soviet work colonies have found them sympathetically and efficiently conducted—like most Soviet educational establishments.

This is as one might expect. But equally noteworthy is the other Soviet offensive against the army of the young hooligans, which stems straight from the autocrats in the Kremlin and betrays their anger at any defiance of their will. This offensive is essentially political. It is not easy to get the precise facts, just as the Soviet authorities publish no overall juvenile crime statistics which would show the size of the problem. However, it is instructive since this is a new development, that in many places squads of young Communists have recently been issued with arms and detailed to go on patrol with the militia, to guard streets and public places against dangerous gangs of hooligans. Press reports, warning against abuse of power, showed that some of these groups of zealous young Communists rather too quickly became moral disapprobation squads, beating up youths they did not like, e.g. as one press report had it, "merely because they wore drainpipe trousers". Another step was the institution, under the banner of "collective responsibility", of mob courts in places where young people were employed, with powers to impose fines and to shame offenders by ostracizing them. Together with these measures went angry outbursts in the press, making the point that young delinquents, by opposing the purposes of Soviet society, were in effect political enemies and so liable to far heavier penalties. Thus, a certain V. Soloukhin wrote in the *Literary Gazette* (13th January 1959) that young criminals were getting off quite undeservedly with light sentences under the new criminal code.

We should understand that criminals are our *political* enemies. We are progressing to communism, but they are getting in our way and hindering our advance. They draw honest young workers into their orbit. It is appropriate to recall that during the counter-revolutionary rising in Hungary, not the least important part was played by criminal elements. If a criminal murders or robs, if he corrupts a young Soviet lad, in what way is he not a *saboteur*?

LIGHT AND SHADE

How serious is this trend? "Saboteurs"—the word as applied to young delinquents, or even to adolescents who are merely anti-social, has an old-fashioned Communist ring. However, the signs that the tide of Soviet life is moving in the opposite direction are more numerous. On 11th June 1960, the Young Communist newspaper, *Komsomol Pravda*, actually published a letter to the editor whose author bluntly said: "To hell with the moon-rocket—I'd rather have a square meal." The author, a young worker who signed himself simply "Aleksei", said that before the moon-rocket went up he had been 300 roubles in debt—and he still was. Elaborating his point, he said that if one told any worker that without the rockets his kid would be able to go to a kindergarten, that a metre of worsted cloth would cost half what it did and that he could buy the electric iron for which he had been waiting, such a worker would answer: "For God's sake, stop sending those rockets up." While the editors of the Young Communist newspaper in their reply tried to demolish Aleksei's ideas, the fact that they published his letter showed, first, that his views were widespread, which one knew, but also greater readiness to let them be expressed publicly—another small move towards greater normality and freedom in Soviet life.

Light and shade: at what rate the life of Soviet youth will change so that it more closely resembles the life of youth in the West is hard to forecast. But in the meantime, it is fairly evident where valuable lessons can be learned from Soviet education, and where not. To sum up, for me the most interesting side of Soviet education remains the way in which, through political accident, the bourgeois ideals of fifty years ago have somehow been preserved in Soviet schools, so that a visitor from the West who enters a Russian classroom seems to be carried back to a simpler world. "Be patriotic: work hard for your country's sake. Learning gives you status: work hard for your own sake. Always be respectful, polite. . . ." Perhaps it is the main Soviet advantage that these old commands of yesterday are still valid in the Soviet classroom of today, without any intervention from the siren voices of our commercial culture. In the West, we cannot return to this past, but what we can learn from Soviet practice is the benefit of combining stimulus with unhesitating authority and discipline in education, and of passing on this benefit to the largest possible number of young people.

On the other hand, there is little, if anything, to be learned from the Soviet practice of organizing the leisure of the young—from the whole system of regimenting adolescents within a centralized State youth organization, like the Komsomol. Not merely because our whole Western outlook is opposed to the idea of a "State youth". All the signs are that even in the Soviet Union this sort of rigid youth organization, in which orders are handed down to the young from above, has become ossified and out of date. One probably saw this most unmistakably illustrated in Poland after the October Revolution of 1956. The moment the young Poles could choose, they could not get out of the Communist youth organizations fast enough. In this one clear instance of competition between a Western and a Communist way of life for youth, between personal freedom and regimentation, the West won hands down.

CHAPTER XXIII

Resisting the Mass Attack

EXPANSION VERSUS PURPOSELESSNESS

BACK to Britain—to these small and crowded islands, to the British affluent society, which is, however, also a welfare state society and where the problems of youth and education should like other social problems be of manageable proportions.

Some of the topics on which I have touched in preceding chapters may seem a far cry from the starting-point of this book, namely the plight of a little group of Teds on a London housing estate. Yet I feel it is not too far-fetched to regard their plight as throwing a special light on the major social changes which affect us all today. For the rise of delinquency has to be seen as one among many similar symptoms of the growing social unbalance in the affluent society.

Looking at the development in Britain of the last ten years, one can distinguish something which seems like a built-in conflict in this society—a conflict between, on one side, a growing sense of widening opportunities, of expansion, and opposed to it, an alarming drive towards purposelessness. Perhaps the lines of this conflict are already more sharply drawn in Britain with its particularly powerful mass entertainment industry than in the other countries of Europe.

To start with the sense of expansion: it cannot be said too often that the affluent society holds out tremendous possibilities of a freer life for the ordinary man. In the mid-'fifties, even in an over-crowded island like Britain, the pace of technological progress had become breathtaking, and not merely in such headline fields as nuclear energy, rockets and jets, computers, miracle drugs and the advance of mass motoring. In its farewell to the 'fifties, *The Economist* declared that in the middle of this roaring decade something began to happen in the field of consumer goods which could only be called a breakthrough. "Ten years ago the ordinary working woman—nearly one-half of the nation—was a slave in an antiquated kitchen; today mechanical slaves on the hire-purchase have sprung up around her as she works in the non-telly hours."[1]

A sense of accelerated purposefulness was especially noticeable among the young. By almost any index of actual measurement, the boys and girls of 1955-60 were a more self-reliant, ambitious and active generation than their predecessors. A somewhat greater proportion went to Grammar Schools. More boys and girls stayed on voluntarily at Secondary Modern Schools for extra terms after the age of 15 and more went to Technical Colleges. Owing to past neglect, the lag in British education was not made up for even now, but one could readily get an impression that the most interesting things going on in the country were those which concerned the young. At the University Grants Committee, early in 1960, I was told of plans to raise the total of university students from 80,000 to 170,000 within ten years; at the Ministry of Education, of a drive to double the annual output of technologists by 1965. The young seemed also strikingly more energetic and enterprising in the way they conducted their own affairs. They matured earlier, they married earlier; they participated in greater numbers in the arts and sports. Many of them, indeed, looked to be far more at home in the affluent society than their elders, and again not only in coping with new scientific knowledge and techniques. Teenage singers with dubious voices earned vast incomes; dramatists under 21 had plays put on in the West End; in sports like swimming, mere schoolboys and schoolgirls were national champions. (At the European Swimming Championships of 1958 a Scottish schoolboy of 17, Ian Black, won three gold medals, while a London schoolboy, Brian Phelps, won the high diving medal at the age of 14!). Even more than their parents, the young "had never had it so good". In many working-class families, the difference between the generations was that the adolescents of today, with full employment taken for granted, could not even imagine the anxieties felt by their parents during the high unemployment days of the 'thirties.[2]

[1] *The Economist*, 26th December 1959.

[2] An informant in the North put this to me as follows: "In the 'thirties, if you didn't work hard, you were threatened with unemployment, of being without the right references. Right through life, that first reference, that piece of paper, could be important. What the new factor is, is this full (and it is often over-full) employment for the young. For many families, this is a wholly new experience, and this makes for the great schism between the generations. The young men (and girls,

However, this was clearly only one of several conflicting trends in the affluent society. Against this picture of bustling youth and a sense of expansion and purpose in British life, one could also, in looking at Britain in 1960, set its precise opposite. There was undeniable evidence that a fairly large section of British youth felt frustrated, angry, bored and adrift without firm moral guidance. Employers complained more frequently about the indifference of the young towards their work. Complaints from teachers spoke of a bored or disaffected generation of teenagers in many secondary schools, and the number of young delinquents went up year by year. All these things seemed symptoms of another side of the affluent society—of a new and disturbing drift into purposelessness. This drift was, of course, not confined to the young. Over the whole of society it was reflected by the growing subordination of other sides of life to the advertisement and sale of consumer goods. In the United States the dangers of this drift have already been the subject of warning studies. In Britain they are well illustrated by the significant changes over the last years in the character of the British press.

THE MASS ATTACK

The British popular press is far from being, as someone said, the worst in the world—newspapers in many countries are far less scrupulous and politically far more vicious—but it could well lay claim to the title of being the most trivial. Like many others who have come to this country after receiving their first education abroad, I have never really become reconciled to the mixture of crime, sex and triviality which is day by day served up by the Press Lords to the British people. Fleet Street has always seemed to me an industry unnatural and accidental in its size and outlook, an unnecessary burden upon the long-suffering British people, who deserved something better. For instance, during the recent

too) don't care about this job or that, they aren't worried about references. . . . This is even true of serious student apprentices. They may be serious, but they aren't worried about their chance of jobs; there's not the same respect for and fear of the employer. That's the great schism, from which all kinds of new youth phenomena have appeared."

difficult period of readjustment to the country's position of a power of the second rank, the relentless sensationalism of British popular newspapers in search of headline stories has made it even harder for their readers ever to know where their country stood. I am here not concerned with the whole peculiar structure of the London popular press, which has been admirably dealt with by writers like Richard Hoggart. My relevant point is that the British press has undergone some distinct changes with the arrival of the affluent society—the break-through year might be put at 1955, when the advertising industry also broke into television. The change was that the popular newspapers became much more clearly subordinated to the basic dynamic of the new society, the drive to increase the volume of personal consumption, with all other functions dropping behind. To quote a few of the new developments:

(*a*) Through mergers and take-over bids, ownership of newspapers became concentrated in the hands of still fewer and still larger financial combines.

(*b*) The most rapid expansion of circulation, soaring into millions, was that of the women's weekly magazines which specialized in advertising clothes, cosmetics and all types of family consumer goods.

(*c*) In the popular daily newspapers, political comment tended to be projected in terms of sensational "stories", and at the same time the total columns devoted to British and international politics were noticeably cut down. From the viewpoint of the popular press, Britain seemed to be withdrawing from the international stage. Political features were replaced by pages written by women journalists for women about fashions, furniture, food and parties; by special supplements shading into direct advertising; and above all by expanded personality gossip columns, chronicling the lives of celebrities and the rich. Especially the rich: it was significant to note how in Britain, in 1960, millionaires were given far more attention by the press than had been accorded to them in 1950.

(*d*) The tone and appearance of the newspapers changed, too. There were more headlines and pictures; there was more disjointedness, more name-dropping, less ordinary text. The language of this text also became more artificial and more stylised—i.e. when a person was mentioned, it also became the rule to mention his age, hair-colour, height, occupation or income, whether they had relevance or not. With the artificiality, a note of malice also crept in, especially in gossip columns—in fact, the note of psychopathic malice in these columns is one of the disturbing signs of spiritual disruption in the British affluent society.[1]

(e) As fewer and larger financial interests were involved in the competition for circulation and advertising revenue, this competition became more intensive (and ruthless). To obtain their gossip information, the larger papers developed the technique of saturation coverage, whereby reporters were sent swarming into every aspect of the private lives of people involved in a story. The practice was not new, but made more systematic and impersonal.

(f) A telling example of this is provided by the change which has come over the sporting pages of British popular newspapers since the war. Twenty years ago, sporting events were still regarded as part of the traditional ritual of British life, to be described as such. In 1960, description of actual matches was very much reduced, even in the League Football season. What instead made the headlines were "stories", preferably "sensations"—a row, a sacking, a record transfer fee, a squabble over a manager's salary. During the 1959-60 season, a famous football manager told me that he was beginning to look upon the whole flock of sporting journalists as scavengers. Instead of reporting matches, journalists were now hanging round the homes of his players, calling on them or, in their absence, on their wives, trying to extract scraps of information about the dissatisfaction of players, possible jealousy, offers from rival clubs; in fact, scandal. That is, the sports pages of the British popular newspapers were being brought into line with their other pages. The new sensationalism was presumably considered a better accompaniment to the adjacent advertisements, mostly connected with betting and the Pools, which provided the financial revenue for these pages. In a country which first originated both organized amateur sport and sporting journalism, how swift the deterioration!

I have often thought that one could see this trend well illustrated at a big athletics meeting, say one of the major championships at the White City Stadium in London. Amateur athletics is a sport

[1] For an illuminating analysis on this subject, see Brian Inglis, "The Psychopaths", *Encounter*, September 1960.

which has since the war seen an enormous expansion in England. It has been taken up enthusiastically by the young, from schoolboys and schoolgirls upwards; it is an amateur sport, giving equal pleasure to participants and spectators; it has its beauty of motion —to watch a big meeting at the White City can be a rare aesthetic experience. It is, however, also instructive to listen to the paperboys, selling the London evening newspapers, who at such a meeting make their way through the spectators, like interlopers from outside. Their regular cry is always "Two-thirty winner" or "Australian Football Results". That is, the raucously repeated message of the London evening newspapers to those watching at the White City is that they should take their eyes from the spectacle of amateur sport before them—no money in that!—and turn their attention to mass-manufactured opportunities for betting, an objective in line with the betting advertisements in their sports pages and the accompanying sport-as-sensation headlines. This clash between two views of sport seems to me a neat example of the conflict between purpose and purposelessness inherent in the affluent society. Because the sports pages of newspapers are those to which many young people turn first, their deterioration must have a special impact on youth.

THE NEED FOR INTERVENTION

Of course, to give the affluent society its due, this deterioration is not the only trend among its mass media. If television advertisements can be described as representing a new form of brainwashing, the broad impact of television has certainly been educational. It can also be argued that the popular women's weeklies, *Woman*, *Woman's Own*, *Woman's Realm* and the rest, have played a valuable rôle in helping working-class girls and housewives with sensible, practical advice, even though their general output of romance, glamour and hedonism, to fit the advertising, is dangerously feather-brained. It would also be wrong to suggest that British popular newspapers do not *still* contain excellent features, even though the number of trained political journalists on their staff has fallen sharply in the last few years. But what matters is the dominant trend in the mass media. It is, I believe, Mr Arthur Miller who has described the popular press as primarily an industry for the manufacture of fantasy; and the pertinent fact is that since the early 'fifties, the financial pressures in the British newspaper industry have worked steadily in the direction of increasing and standardizing such fantasy. That is, if it is the explicit commercial aim of mass journalism in the affluent society to reduce all news, serious or trivial, to fragments in a single, disjointed, gossipy passing show, a technique so well described by Mr Richard Hoggart in *The Uses of Literacy*, then the British popular press has, in the three years since the publication of his book, advanced already further towards this ideal.[1]

Such an advance must also have its influence on the constant tug-of-war over the direction in which the affluent society is developing. One could perhaps put it as follows. If, through the medium of television, millions of ordinary British viewers have been given a clearer picture of the issues of the day, as has certainly been the case—on such questions as the emergence of Africa, the colour bar in Britain, difficulties over rail and road traffic, the problems of hospitals, of schools—then this represents a genuine widening of knowledge, in keeping with the progress in schools and universities: one might say, an advance towards a greater sense of national purpose in British life.

Conversely, if the advertising of consumption goods becomes more and more dominant on television, and if the popular press, in trying to compete for advertising revenue, steps up its emphasis on crime, sex, sensation and gossip, this means a redoubled mass attack against such a sense of national purpose.

Perhaps one should not exaggerate the influence even of Fleet Street newspapers with gigantic circulations upon national life. Their more sensational and gossipy tone since the advent of the affluent society is only a symptom of the economic unbalance of this society and its overstress on personal consumption. But the new note of purposelessness in turn exaggerates this unbalance

[1] Writing about the demise of most British "middlebrow" periodicals in the 'fifties (*Encounter*, August 1960), Mr Robert Holles remarked: "We are left with a magazine and Sunday newspaper coverage which presupposes that the population is composed of ten per cent. articulate eggheads and sixty per cent. sniggering halfwits, with a balance of women who are obsessed with frustrated romance and the latest knitting patterns."

of society. Looking at British life in the 'fifties, it seems evident that this sort of mass attack has its socially harmful results, especially on the minds of the rising generation. It tends to counter the sense of purpose and expansiveness in the affluent society. It creates an atmosphere in which a large part of the young make no use of their educational opportunities—the rise in delinquency is only one rather dramatic illustration of this mood.

Whatever the outcome of this tug-of-war, it seems obvious what is desirable: to encourage the forces of progress, of social emancipation in the British affluent society and to discourage the drive towards purposelessness. *But this cannot come about by itself.* It clearly demands purposeful action, public action, in fact State action. Writing in 1960, after a decade in which Britain has steadily lost ground in industry and trade relative to other countries, I have no doubt of the need for such intervention. What is required is in itself quite simple—namely for a few more per cent. of the national income to be diverted from personal consumption and transferred to investment for the future. First, greater investment to modernize plant and equipment, in technology and research—this often-reiterated need is not my subject. The second increased investment for the future ought to be in education—to bring British State education in the broadest sense up to quite a different level from that prevailing today. This step, again, seems to me required for two reasons. The need to strengthen Britain's competitive position in a technological age is an argument few would quarrel with. But I also think this educational reform should also be carried out quite explicitly for another reason—in order to keep the country's adolescents until a much later age right out of the racket of the commercial youth market, to protect them against the influence of the mass media, in fact in order to place them under more purposeful educational authority which can prepare them for life in the affluent society rather better than is the case today.

Educational reform on such lines is to my mind an essential British task for the 'sixties, just as it could also provide an answer to the marginal problem of delinquency. The fact that this task is mentioned at least in outline seemed to me to lend unusual interest to two official reports of 1959-60, the Crowther Report on the education of adolescents and the Albemarle Report on the reform of the Youth Services, from which I have quoted before.

CHAPTER XXIV

Conclusion: New Angles

CORRECTING THE UNBALANCE

CAN an affluent society *afford* to finance essential public services on an adequate scale? One has only to turn the question round, to ask whether an affluent country can afford *not* to make such provision, to see that this question is not fiscal but political—a question of deliberate choice of priorities.

For example, could a rich country like Britain not *afford* an adequate pay scale for its police force? The question seems absurd, yet when the Metropolitan Police Commissioner, Sir Joseph Simpson, announced that London's police force was in the spring of 1960 (and in the midst of a sharp crime wave) one man in four under strength, he added that there was not a man in his force who did not consider himself underpaid: "A good many claim, no doubt with good cause, that their wives earn as much as they do, under much more agreeable conditions."[1]

In fact, by 1960 the shortage had reached a stage where one could be sure that, whatever happened, steps would be taken to attract more men into the force through drastically improved pay conditions.

The same rhetorical questions could be asked about other social services. Could Britain not afford the insignificant sums needed to give reasonable salaries to such key workers as probation officers, or prison and Borstal officers, or to house adult prisoners otherwise than three to a cell in mid-Victorian edifices? Or to turn to more general provision for the young—could Britain not well afford to spend more than 3 per cent. of the gross national income on education, even though poorer countries were spending pro-portionately much more? Or to raise the school-leaving age beyond 15? Or to reform the system whereby youth clubs were run on shoestring finance with the aid of voluntary donations, while trained youth leaders were asked to make do on an unskilled worker's pay?

[1] Reported in *Daily Telegraph*, 13th May 1960.

In themselves, these questions seem surely absurd—as absurd as it would be to ask whether Britain could genuinely not afford to build the roads for the million motor-cars it turns out each year. In what follows I have based myself on the assumption that it is perfectly possible for any British Government to allocate the division of the national income so that far more is spent on essential public services. In a country like Britain, where purchase tax is already well established, the fiscal mechanism for transferring further funds to public use may not even be so difficult to find, if only the will is there. In any case, in the field of education this is something that just has to be done. It was the clear recognition of this need, I felt, which lent special interest to the Crowther and Albemarle Reports of 1960. Neither document, it is true, recommended immediate spectacular Government action. Yet here were the reports of two major committees of enquiry which, for the first time, accepted the arrival of the British affluent society as a fact, pointed to the dislocation it had caused in the lives of young people, and called for conscious public intervention to correct this. From this standpoint, both documents may be remembered as landmarks.

The Crowther Report[1] was produced by the Central Advisory Council for Education (England), which at the request of the Minister of Education had for three years examined the English system of State education for boys and girls between 15 and 18 "in relation to changing social and industrial needs". In 1960 this system still had its archaic features even in the case of the most privileged and talented boys and girls who passed on with ease to university. However, the decisive conclusion of the Crowther Report was its recognition of the needs of the majority of adolescents, far too large a majority, who were *not* being educated at all after fifteen. The report underlined that at the age of 17 only one boy and girl in eight was still receiving full-time education; between 15 and 17, only one boy in five and one girl in fifteen received any part-time education. That is, at the most suggestible stage of their lives, most boys and girls were pushed into a complex adult society without really adequate education or guidance.

The authors of the Crowther Report saw this not only as a waste of ability, which the country could ill afford, but as a moral

[1] *15 to 18*   H. M. Stationery Office, 1959.

wrong inflicted on youth: "There seems to us to be no social injustice in our community more loudly crying out for reform than the condition in which scores of thousands of our children are released into the labour market." To counteract this, the Report proposed that the leaving age should in the 1960s be raised from 15 to 16 (a somewhat conservative and limited increase, but in the right direction); that part-time education, especially technical, should be substantially increased; that, following this, County Colleges for further education should be established; and that the State should pay generously for these extensions of the school system.

The Albemarle Report was a slighter document, and rather more literary in its style. The Albemarle Committee had been appointed in 1959 to enquire into the Youth Services in England and Wales. These included a great variety of organizations, uniformed and non-uniformed, serving young people of all ages. But in practice the real subject of enquiry was the provision of leisure-time facilities for adolescents, that is, the state of the country's network of youth clubs, mainly boys' clubs and mixed clubs. What was right and what was wrong about these institutions in England was not really in very much doubt—they had the advantages and defects of their history. Most of them had been started back in the bourgeois age in a spirit of middle-class charity to keep working-class boys and girls "off the street", a function they retained until well into the depression days of the 'thirties. Some of the most famous (and best-run) clubs for boys and girls had been established by bodies like Public Schools and Oxford and Cambridge Colleges in places like the old East End of London. Since that time, the youth clubs had, indeed, changed. They had become efficiently organized by bodies like the National Federation of Boys' Clubs and the National Association of Mixed and Girls' Clubs. Some grants from local authorities supplemented their private funds. Even so, and in spite of much dedicated effort and local success, it was felt that the whole organization of the youth clubs had itself become a problem. The traditional spirit of charitable effort, often reflected in the very look of the club premises, seemed as hard to shake off as it was unsuitable for the new age.

At any rate, the Albemarle Committee noted that in the 'fifties the majority of adolescents who had left school at 15 to go into jobs were not members of any youth club at all. The authors of the Report stated that it was wrong—indeed socially harmful—to leave so much of the leisure time of these more affluent but often bewildered youngsters of today to exploitation by purely commercial interests. In somewhat general terms, the Report therefore proposed a ten-year plan by which the youth clubs were to be gradually remodelled. A national youth council was to be set up, better premises built, more youth leaders trained; and, again, the State was to make the main financial provision for these reforms.

WANTED: A SENSE OF NATIONAL PURPOSE

All this made good sense. However, the British tradition of approaching problems through government-appointed committees of enquiry also has the drawback that the terms of reference of the enquiry are often limited to fit with the way official minds are already thinking, and a well-chosen committee is also not anxious to propose what its Minister is likely to reject. At any rate, in both the Crowther Report and in the Albemarle Report, the analysis of the defects of the affluent society went much further than the corrective steps which the committees thought it fit to suggest to a Conservative Government.

This was true especially of the Crowther Report. In fact, its main proposal, to raise the school-leaving age from 15 to 16, had already been put forward by Sir Will Spens in 1938 and actually included in the 1944 Education Act, though never enforced. Moreover, had the Crowther Committee been simply bold enough to state that an affluent Britain could afford to spend not 3 per cent., but, like many other countries, nearer to 5 per cent. of the national income on education, it could have done without some of its elaborate recommendations on the problems of educational finance. Even so, when one reads the pages of both these intelligently written reports, one common theme stands out. In Britain in 1960, the majority of middle-class boys and girls, plus those who were trained to become middle-class, were educated up to the age of 18 or beyond, while their social life during this period was also strenuously organized. By contrast, the majority of working-class boys and girls left school hardly educated at 15, to proceed at once into a pseudo-adult life of earning and spending, the majority without membership of any leisure-time organization.

It is interesting that both the Crowther and the Albemarle Reports held that in the new British society this class contrast was socially harmful and no longer justifiable. It led to an undoubted waste of ability, to renewed class distinctions, it engendered youthful malaise and played its part in spreading juvenile delinquency. To lessen this discrepancy, both Reports—and this is the crucial point—proposed State intervention to arrest some of the dangerous trends of the affluent society. The basic recommendation was that the outlook of the country's teenagers should be shaped much more directly through the conscious endeavours of the community and not merely left to the combined persuasions of the advertisers, the press, and the "pop" record industry.

Within the English tradition of *laisser-faire*, this was quite an innovation in official thinking. One might have imagined that in a world grown so highly competitive as that of the present day, any proposals to raise the standards of British State education would have aroused special interest. In fact, almost the opposite was the case. Though both the Crowther and the Albemarle Reports had a good press, the general public interest in their recommendations was not profound. Not even at Westminster. When the Government in April 1960 rejected the Crowther Committee's proposals for raising the school-leaving age during the 'sixties—a bad and timid decision, though fortunately not irretrievable—less than one-tenth of the Members of Parliament attended the debate in the Chamber.

To go into the specific reasons for this indifference would bring me into the field of party politics, which is here outside my subject. But I think one generalization is relevant, that in Britain in 1960 what one might call the sense of national purpose had become unusually dimmed. Perhaps I should define this generalization. As a democratic country with a *laissez-faire* tradition, Britain can, of course, have no officially imposed philosophy, like a Communist country, and it would also have been too much to expect British life in the 'fifties to have that overall sense of purpose, in which every citizen is aware of over-riding national aims, which one can find today in new countries like Israel, Ghana, Egypt or Cuba; nor even that same purposefulness one met in Britain during the war

But instead, Britain, more than most countries, has something which can be called a national way of life, something very insular and liberal and unique; to the extent that maintaining this British way of life and developing it and building on it could be called the national purpose: and my point is that the active sense of such purpose had in the 1950s noticeably waned. Democracies can grow tired, as was shown in the U.S.A. after Roosevelt. Similarly, in Britain, the 'forties had been a time for greatness and creativeness: the decade saw Churchill, the R.A.F., the convoys going through, the Grand Alliance, the Attlee Labour Government, the Health Service, the new pattern of public housing, the achievement of independence within the Commonwealth for India, Pakistan, Ceylon. By reaction, the 'fifties looked like a decade of dull fatigue. British leadership of Europe fell apart; the Conservatives cut a sorry figure over Suez; at home, the Labour Party floundered, exhausted. The welfare state became prosaic, the ideal of Commonwealth a shadow; political issues grew remote from the ordinary man and especially from the young. All in all, the sense of national purpose, any national purpose beyond material consumption, receded into the background.

I think this intellectual confusion was linked not only to the relative decline of Britain in terms of world power and a consequent loss of political direction. For the ordinary man, another cause was the suddenly accelerated shift towards the new life of the affluent society, the increase in the consumption drive, the more strident note one could notice in popular newspapers, in magazines, in television advertisements. Even if the politicians did not know what to make of it, the advertisers, the magazine publishers, the gossip writers and publicity agents, who went from strength to strength in the new society, knew well what its dominant forces were.

For that matter, so did any secondary school teacher, struggling with a class of indifferent adolescents in trying to compete with the lure of commercial youth culture. It was the acknowledgment of these new trends, and of the general need for counter-measures to create a new sense of purpose, which made the Crowther Report and Albemarle Report significant documents of the new age—even if the government actions they recommended are to my mind inadequate and likely soon to be superseded.

SOCIAL ADVANCE AND EDUCATION

To look ahead in terms of education. Since British society is for better or worse considerably stratified, already something of a "meritocracy", any movement for educational reform will have to take place on two levels. There are the organization men and women: to compete today, Britain must have a class of administrators, scientists and technicians who will be as efficient and purposeful as their equivalents anywhere else; and, as the unceasing newspaper advertisements of situations vacant show, this is going to be a considerably larger class than the old middle class. How this class will be recruited from Public Schools, Grammar Schools and Technical Colleges does not belong to the subject of this book. It does, however, touch on it indirectly, because for one thing the doors through which working-class boys and girls can rise into this new middle class should clearly be as wide open as possible; and furthermore, provided these doors are open wide enough, because a more purposeful educational drive at the higher levels must affect the tone of the British education system all the way down.

Even so, the more important task is that of giving the 70-80 per cent. majority of British boys and girls who are early school leavers a more appropriate and modern education than many of them are getting today. Indeed, it may well be the most important task of social reform facing the country. After all, the really revolutionary social change in the British scene of today is the steady *embourgoise-ment* of the working class. In material terms, in such things as housing, cars and television, this is easy to see. But public opinion has not yet caught up with the educational and other changes which must surely go with this social revolution. Here I come back to the picture at the starting-point of this book—that of my little group of confused Teds, hanging about aimlessly on their new London Council Estate, defiant of society, not knowing what to do with themselves. Their confusion may represent an extreme pre-dicament, but I think it throws light on a general and urgent British educational need of today, which is simply this: that the material advance of British working-class youth should be accompanied by an equivalent cultural advance. Just as in the mid-'fifties there was a "break-through" in material consumption, so there has now to be a "break-through" in education, because it is evident that the present secondary modern school system is not adequate as preparation for the new society.

There is already an extensive literature on its inadequacies. For present-day needs, the system falls short in that the majority of boys and girls leave far too early. A good many of the jobs into which they are drawn are from their nature tedious, mechanical, monotonous, offering little outlet for natural adolescent emotions and so creating a sense of frustration—this phenomenon has been noted in German and American studies as well as in this country. Perhaps much of this emotional frustration during the working day cannot be helped: all the more reason, therefore, for not exposing adolescents to it at the immature age of 15.

In the second place, there is a fair measure of agreement among teachers that the secondary modern school system with its present-day curriculum is inadequate as a "bridge" to working life. The shock when young teenagers encounter the different morality and temptations of working life is often an acute one.

However, to my mind the main defect of the present State school system lies in the way in which it still perpetuates outworn class distinctions. Under the tripartite secondary school structure set up in 1944, by which abler boys and girls are "creamed off" at 11, not merely to go to different schools, but, in effect, into a different social life, cultural class distinctions are being preserved and even intensified which are inappropriate to the affluent society. And this is not merely a matter of different education within the school walls. The exaggerated difference in school-leaving age plays an equal part. The authors of the Albemarle Report noted that those teenagers who at 15 had gone into easy jobs with good money, were spending most of their earnings on a surprisingly narrow range of mass-produced consumption goods and entertainments; for instance, not merely on pop records in general, but each month on a very few records which the industry plugs as top-of-the-month hits. In view of the increased power and skill of advertising techniques, this need surprise nobody. The trouble is, however, that the whole outlook of such teenagers also becomes shaped and narrowed by the advertisers' culture which is projected at them in order to promote the sale of the products. A working-class girl who is induced to spend a pound a week on "pop" records and another pound a week on hairstyling and cosmetics—which is common enough—is through her very preoccupation with this expenditure isolated in class terms from other girls of her age who at grammar school and technical colleges are being taught quite different cultural values.

This excessively class-orientated system of education, whereby the majority of boys and girls are pushed (or lured) far too early into the racket of the teenage market, is harmful in a number of ways. There is little need to stress the waste of abilities among early leavers which is involved. There is, however, one special piece of evidence of a sort of cultural "downward pull" at work in the affluent society which ought to receive attention.

To judge from the regular complaints of certain teachers, something like a genuine breakdown of discipline has in recent years occurred in a number of the more difficult secondary modern schools in various parts of the country. In most cases, these schools are found in areas like the traffic-filled inner working-class districts of London, where the population tends to be unorganized and shifting and there is little, if any, local community spirit. Often enough, these are also among the schools worst affected by the persistent shortage of teaching staff. But the problem goes further than this. As teachers see it, many boys and girls of 13 or 14 in these schools have their minds already so firmly fixed on the world of jobs and money and the glittering attractions of the commercial youth culture that they regard their last years at school as a mere senseless waste of time, and react accordingly. Conversely, a good many unhappy teachers have been made to feel it to be a complete waste of time and effort to keep such teenage and worldly-wise boys and girls, who contemptuously refuse to be taught, at school at all. It was significant that the publication of the Crowther Report, advocating raising the school age to 16, led to a number of letters to the press from secondary modern school teachers who opposed this move, and mostly they were teachers who, after entering the profession as idealists, had simply thrown in their hand. Now, even if this breakdown in discipline is marginal, the significant thing is that, as far as I know, it has no parallel in any country on the Continent, where the authority of secondary schools has nowhere declined so sharply. Since one cannot assume innate mental characteristics which make British teenagers more unteachable, the reason for the difference, it seems to me, is that in Britain the teenage market is more developed, while the commercial mass attack directed against youthful minds has also been going on for a rather longer time.

This breakdown of discipline in schools is one danger sign of a sort of cultural "downward pull" as one of the trends of the affluent society. The other is, of course, the rise in actual juvenile delinquency—it is noteworthy that in 1959 this was already so marked that both the Crowther Report on secondary education and the Albemarle Report on the youth services mentioned it definitely as a problem to be attacked by educational and recreational reform. And quite rightly—this is the heart of the matter.

SCHOOLS FOR THE AFFLUENT SOCIETY

What then, should be done?

The ideas put forward below should not be regarded as cut-and-dried proposals for educational reform—this would not be within my competence. My approach throughout has been to treat the rise of juvenile delinquency in Britain in the 'fifties as a danger signal throwing light on much broader changes in the social life of today. But what these changes in turn suggest is that a much stronger "upward pull" has somehow to be infused into the whole British State education system, to counter the opposite pulls of the new affluent life. Both for social reasons and other obvious reasons, such as Britain's competitive future in a technological age, the drive for British boys and girls to "get on" has to be given a new moral force—larger numbers than hitherto have to be enrolled in it. And since the old bourgeois values to which one could formerly appeal have lost impact, this means that a new educational framework for such a drive to "get on" has to be provided. If this reasoning stands, a number of practical measures appear to me to follow.

(1) In order that the level of the majority of secondary school boys and girls should be raised, not only in classroom attainment, but by enlarging their whole range of interests, the State school system must be less class-divided. That is, the 1944 Education Act with its tripartite system of social as well as educational separation of children at the age of 11 should by now be seen as reflecting the superseded class differences of the bourgeois age—

and relegated to the past as such. The top stream of boys and girls, who should be the natural leaders in secondary schools, must no longer be so quickly separated from the majority, to leave the latter leaderless. It is perfectly true that the country has to train its specialist class of organization men and technicians, and from this standpoint it would probably be all wrong to tamper with such traditions as Manchester Grammar School's capacity to turn out a hundred efficient young scientists every year. But without going into such questions as the pros and cons of the comprehensive school (which straightaway introduces such further complicated questions as the size of the "university sixth form"), I feel that, in looking to the future, the problem of specialist education for a new administrative-technical middle class can be solved without introducing *social* separation in the secondary school system at a time when children are no more than 11—as in other countries, the educational separation could well take place only at the age of 14, 15 or 16 years.

(2) This could be achieved more easily if the age of compulsory school attendance were to be substantially raised throughout the country—not merely to the age of 16 *after* 1970, as the present Conservative Government proposes, but at a much earlier date to the age of 17. Perhaps one might qualify—not for *every* boy and girl but, say, for all *except* those in the lowest streams for whom prolonged schooling is judged unsuitable. Even if this is not clearly seen today, I believe it will rapidly become apparent that a much longer secondary school period is needed to train youngsters to cope with the demands of our technological age, and one argument is compelling: if other countries, and especially Soviet Russia, are aiming at far more ambitious educational targets, Britain cannot afford to remain out of step. In fact, here the Soviet challenge may become a decisive factor. This challenge has been talked about in terms of export trade, or of arms, but one feels inclined to say: "Forget this, the primary Soviet challenge is in education." That is, if the Russians establish a strenuous polytechnic type of education for the majority of their children to the age of 17, as they probably will do in the course of the 'sixties, Britain cannot continue with her present class-divided and old-fashioned education system, by which training after 15 is only for the minority, and still hope to compete. While this may soon become clear, I believe

the social argument for raising the school-leaving age is equally strong—namely simply to enable all boys and girls to grow up more naturally within an organized life appropriate to their age-group (as middle-class children already do) instead of being thrust out as pseudo-adults—to sink or swim in the affluent society.

(3) Such a decisive expansion of secondary school life would naturally pose major problems. It might create difficulties for industries which at present rely very much on juvenile labour, but automation may in any case take care of this. It would also be a blow to the various cruder commercial interests which at present exploit the teenage market, but as for them, *tant pis*. A more serious objection against a substantial raising of the school age is that it would involve vast new expenditure on school buildings and equipment and an even greater increase on teachers' training facilities. So it would, of course, but greater than the nation could afford? Even a crash programme to step up education could only mean that instead of an adequate 3 to 4 per cent., as now, Britain could devote perhaps 5 to 6 per cent. of the national income to education, which some other countries are already doing. Basically, the question is not one of the means but of the will.

A more important objection has sometimes come from the teaching profession, namely that at present a large number of boys and girls in the lower intelligence groups seem unable to profit from being kept at school, even up to the age of 14 or 15: trying to teach them only drives teachers to despair and they would therefore be much better off if put earlier to some practical work. From time to time this argument has been advanced forcefully by teachers from bad schools who, term after term, have struggled in vain to inject pitiful fragments of an academic curriculum into classes of hostile, unresponsive but already fully fashion-conscious and sex-conscious louts and hussies—or so the dismal picture looks. For the schools and the teachers concerned, the problem of such apparently unteachable 14-year-olds is today serious enough, but I suspect strongly that the resistance of these particular working-class boys and girls to school is due far less to inbred low intelligence, as is often alleged, than it is a cultural problem; if one likes, a peculiarly English class problem. The resistance seems like a survival of historic class differences, a hangover from past generations of degraded English working-class life, in which these boys and girls still display the defensive hostility of the old slums against a middle-class institution like secondary school. The lure of the crude commercial youth culture, whose standards are so much more easily attained than school knowledge, has now evidently helped to increase this resistance. But, just because I believe the problem posed by these obstructive teenagers to be largely cultural, I also feel that it is one which longer compulsory school attendance, more individual attention in teaching and a keener sense of purpose in school life could go far to solve, especially in more democratic schools where the natural leaders are not "creamed off" but are present to set the tone.

(4) At this point one also touches on the problem of the young delinquents. "Delinquency starts not at school but in the home"— true enough. But there is one important point to be made. If we have to accept that in the changed climate of the affluent society adolescents will tend to have weaker family ties, it is important that this should be compensated by a school life in which there is a stronger sense of guidance and where a youngster can feel that he belongs to a purposeful group of his own age, which is not that of the street corner. Altogether, I feel that if it becomes possible by means of a longer period at school and more stimulating teaching, to infuse a new outlook into the schools with greater emphasis on "getting on", this sort of *embourgeoisement* would be a powerful means of drawing adolescents away from the Teddy boy society and its haunts, and so of reducing the delinquency figures. *Better and more purposeful education may mean less need for purposeful re-education.* This may sound a prosaic answer to the problem on which I have in this book spent so much time, but I am sure the answer is in this direction.

To make another minor but not unimportant point, the raising of the compulsory school age to 17 would also make it easier to effect long-envisaged reforms of the present system of juvenile courts and Approved Schools. The treatment, or rather the re-education, of young offenders under 17 could simply be integrated into the structure of general education. The juvenile courts could be transferred into juvenile welfare tribunals on which headmasters and teachers would be represented, while the Approved Schools could also be brought into line, as State schools with special disciplinary features but part of the general school system, just as the E.S.N. schools, the schools for educationally sub-normal children, form such a part today. After all, where is the basic difference?

(5) However, these are subsidiary issues. The main purpose of raising the school-leaving age would be to raise the whole level of knowledge and attainment of the working-class majority of boys and girls in English State schools, to give them new interests and a better view of the world they live in, and for this a good many changes would also be required in the curriculum. Some of these one can already see being introduced here and there. A significant passage in the Crowther Report stated that a boy leaving school in the 'sixties was likely in his lifetime to witness at least one complete technological revolution in his occupation. The job he worked in as a youth might not exist any more by the time he reached 40, when he might be working on processes and with machinery not even devised today; and this might well be the case not only in new industries but in transport, in agriculture or in distributive retail trade. "To cope with such a world," said the Report, "the first quality that is needed is adaptability." And the new fact is that this no longer applies only to a minority trained in special skill. After remarking that the rapidity of technological changes requires the production of a larger number of qualified scientists, technologists and technicians from the schools, the Crowther Report goes on to say that though these will remain a minority, for the great mass of ordinary boys and girls, too, the advent of a new technological age has created altered needs:

> To be able to comprehend something of the language of science and technology; to be at home in a world of machines; and to be able to adjust to a rapidly changing environment. There will be less need in the future for "skill" in the old-fashioned sense of the word; what will be needed in ever-growing volume will be the quality that can perhaps be described as "general mechanical intelligence". . . .

One can go further. What is needed is education much more purposefully designed to produce not only technological adaptability but also social adaptability—to prepare young people both for their working life and their social life in the new affluent society that lies ahead of them. This sort of purposeful education for every pupil is the aim of the Soviet school system, in theory, at least, though in practice very much distorted by Communist dogma: but there are useful lessons to be learned from the theory.

Of course, with due differences. In a free country like Britain, if boys and girls are to appreciate an extended school period, they could not be forced to do this, nor subjected to mass propaganda. They would, above all, themselves have to feel that the extra school years made sense as profitable preparation for their own adult life. Without going into detail, I believe this would mean fairly drastic changes in the curriculum. The burden of the likely change is that the slant of the later secondary school years would have to be made more deliberately vocational. To my thinking, the weight of argument in the current educational debate lies with those who maintain that as British boys and girls are growing up in a highly industrialized country which must export in order to live, this fact should somehow already be brought home to them at school—for instance, industry ought to be brought nearer to the schools and the schools into closer contact with industry. To this end, the practice of visits to industrial and commercial firms, already introduced by enterprising secondary modern schools, could be made more regular and systematic. Youth Employment Officers, whose numbers should be increased, could be brought into contact with school life at an earlier stage. The actual school curriculum during the additional years could also without much harm be made more directly practical. For instance, adolescent girls could learn domestic science or take typing and secretarial courses while still taking part in the organized social life of school. In the same way, for boys, pre-apprenticeship courses could be made part of the secondary school life, though this would depend on the much-needed extension of the individual apprenticeship system itself.

THE FUTURE SCHOOLS

Something like this trend towards adjusting education to new realities of a changing society can already be observed in certain secondary modern schools where the majority of pupils are working-class boys or girls, but the atmosphere of the school is distinctly more middle class than ten years ago. I saw a good illustration of this at a big secondary modern school for boys in Middlesex, on the very outermost fringe of London. True, this was a new school, a showpiece of the Middlesex County Council, with everything in favour of experiment. The school was equipped with facilities for handicraft and machine workshops which an expensive Public School might envy. Its spread-out, functional buildings stood in an expanse of open green space, large enough for several association and rugby football pitches. Most of the boys were the sons of artisans and skilled and semi-skilled workers who were earning high wages in the new modern factories west of London and who were living on new modern housing estates—a working-class population rapidly going up in the world (and which, in fact, in 1959 elected a Conservative for Parliament).

This naturally made experiment easier. I was interested to learn from the headmaster that special arrangements had been made with some of the large firms in the area for boys to start on actual apprenticeship courses while still remaining at school, and a good proportion of the boys were in fact staying on a voluntary extra year or more for this purpose. And their continued presence as a school leadership, said the headmaster, had led to something like a general up-grading. I saw, for instance, boys in the C and D streams (apt to be neglected in bad schools) who were performing a task such as running the lending library. Outwardly, too, the school had a middle-class look. Boys wore blazers with school badges; I saw some of them going out to play rugby football on well-prepared pitches; for all I knew, England being England, there might already be a school song. Perhaps all this up-grading was a shade self-conscious, but, as the headmaster said, the most important aim was that boys should be able to start on their technical training while still at school, while playing team games and playing a rôle in the organized social life of the school, instead of spending their free time in standing about aimlessly at street corners, as many of them would otherwise have done. And this seemed to me the essence of the matter.

True, this particular local authority school, standing among green fields and brand-new housing estates, looked specially favoured for this sort of social upgrading. One could not quite expect this atmosphere to be reproduced amidst the traffic din and temptations of inner London. Yet I felt that this particular school did point to the desirable pattern of English education of the future. The addition of another two years of obligatory school attendance could probably make it easier to make the pattern universal. At any rate, as I wandered through this new secondary modern school in Middlesex, which seemed so expressly designed to turn out the technicians of today, I felt that it was much more like a Soviet school than any English school would have looked fifteen or twenty years ago. Reflecting on this as I drove back to London past new factories, traffic roundabouts with a background of occasional fields, advertising posters for soft drinks, shopping arcades, suburban cinemas, through the raw emergent landscape of a new England, it came to me that the point of resemblance was not that both in the school I had just seen and in a Soviet school the stress was on technical training. It was rather that in this school in Middlesex, too, rather as in a Soviet school, one had the feeling that a whole stratum of the population had put "lower-class" status aside and was advancing into a new life.

Can the example of such a leading school be followed fairly rapidly throughout the secondary school system? A group of young teachers I talked to told me that I need not worry. Under the pressure from the teaching staff, or from parents who felt that they had made good in life, and because there was really no other possibility, the whole spontaneous trend in the secondary modern schools was in the direction of middle-class values, ways and speech—the effect was already especially noticeable among the girls. My young informants felt that in this process something was also lost—a traditional quality of working-class spontaneity in speech and manner, a directness and lack of emotional inhibitions, which could be very attractive.

Perhaps there is this loss. But since there is no alternative, could this advance towards middle-class standards in the State school system not be made altogether more *dynamic*, so that boys and girls again felt conscious of direction and authority in the society they lived in, and so that their imaginations were stirred? At any rate, I feel that the secondary school system, more than anywhere else, is the place where a greater sense of purpose and drive can be brought into British life. A greater sense of national purpose, too. There should be no doubt that if what is today fashionably called a "crash programme" could be introduced to step up British State education, not only the actual standards of attainment in secondary schools would be transformed, but the consequent social "upward pull" would be felt among adolescents throughout society—all the way down to the groups of Teds and Drifters in their juke-box cafés.

WHAT SORT OF YOUTH SERVICES?

Much the same could be said about the Youth Services. Their chief need is to provide far better social and recreation facilities for the majority of working-class 15- to 18-year-olds, who are in this respect still badly underprivileged.

Here, too, there is a class barrier to be breached. To anyone from abroad, English class distinctions still appear as sharply drawn in leisure time as in schools. Middle-class teenagers have sports and social life organized for them at schools and colleges. Working-class teenagers have little of the sort. This statement has to be qualified. There are also the youth clubs, available to early school-leavers in most parts of England at least on one or two evenings a week, yet here a problem of outdated class outlook has to be solved. The youth clubs have changed since the time when they were started as moral rescue efforts in the slums, yet many of them have not changed enough—they are still only *half-modern*. My own composite impression left from visits to many London youth clubs is of strenuous activity in a gym; of rather dressed-up youths playing billiards or ping-pong; of rather self-conscious teenage girls; of a frequent undertone of defiance contrasting with the middle-class voices of club leaders and student helpers; and, nearly always, the picture of one particular room where a gramophone was turned on to top volume and scores of younger boys and girls crowded the floor, a few jiving, the majority just standing and listening to the appalling blare.

This is not meant disparagingly. Some clubs, with devoted and selfless workers, have done admirable work for difficult youngsters. Other clubs, rather more numerous, where the youngsters are not at all difficult, but only keen, can show the visitor an impressive and expanding range of activities—sports, amateur dramatics, motor-cycle clubs, foreign holidays. But the one thing I felt was wrong with the whole club structure (and this view was shared by many youth workers) was that most youth clubs have remained segregated class institutions. It was really extraordinary that in 1960 one might not find a single middle-class youngster in a typical youth club in the London area. (In the outer suburbs, the reverse might be the case. The members of a youth club would all be from grammar schools or the "A" stream from secondary modern schools, with those lower down somehow excluded.) Consequently, the ordinary urban youth clubs do not give their young people enough of a chance to meet their contemporaries from different walks of life, to rise socially, to "get on".

This may be a reason for the feeling that the youth clubs, as they are, have been left far behind by the changes in the affluent society. The proof, at any rate, is that the majority, and when one reaches the age of 16 to 17 age-groups the great majority, of early school-leavers are today not regular members of any youth organization. Instead, they are drawn away into the world of the commercial youth culture, even though this often means frustration, insecurity and drift.

It was this problem of the untouched majority that the Albemarle Report tried to resolve. The authors were aware of something old-fashioned in the whole structure of the youth clubs. Implicit in their recommendations for a National Youth Council, for better club premises, for training professional youth leaders and paying them proper salaries and for generous grants from public funds, was the idea that the clubs should be re-modelled in order somehow to be brought up to date, to catch the elusive mood of the young of today, to overcome their resistance and meet their real desires.

And here, no doubt, lies a great difficulty. It is never easy to find the right form of organization for the young, and the result is often quite unexpected. As example one can take the Boy Scout movement, which was surely one of the oddest and yet subtlest inventions of the twentieth century. Baden-Powell took certain ceremonials from primitive societies, the Zulus, the Iroquois, blended them with late-Victorian morality, added some elements from merchant marine and sailing-ship life, discovered intuitively a good deal of what we know of group dynamics and provided the uniform of the Boer War heroes—and the result became a major invention. Through the international scout movement, millions of young people made a better adjustment to life. By now, the scout movement has probably had its day among boys and girls over 13 or 14. Yet, at the time when it was launched, who could have foreseen in turn that the esoteric jazz from a corner of New Orleans would one day provide youth with one of its main preoccupations, with a new international language—almost a new youth world of its own?

Still, if it is accepted that large numbers of young people are today more active than ever before (more sailing, rowing, jazz, dancing, motor-cycling, etc.) and many more want in a confused way to be active but do not know how, the preliminary proposals of the Albemarle Committee to re-equip the youth clubs made good sense, especially the financial recommendations for proper State aid. It seems anomalous, to put it mildly, that in 1959 the sum total of Government and Local Authority grants to the entire Youth Services was less than the cost of the Approved Schools. If the Albemarle Committee's recommendations for multiplying this total several times over, for a "generous and imaginative" building programme, for doubling the force of trained youth leaders, and so on, are implemented, no doubt this could give the Youth Services at least emergency aid.

CENTRES OF ANIMATION

However, on a long-term view one can go much further. The demand of the teenagers of today for a social life all of their own and for places where they can lead this social life undisturbed may be nothing novel. What is quite new, however, is the scale, the intensity of this demand, clearly connected with the present changes in family life and the earlier maturity of adolescents. In this respect, I found the same views on the Continent. The complaints by and about adolescents who were too much "in the street" because they had "nowhere to go" sounded exactly alike. As in England, I found also that current ideas of town planning had not yet caught up with the needs of youth. The usual standardized design of blocks of labour-saving flats (or small houses) with shopping streets, perhaps a playground for small children, and nothing much else, reflected the fact that the average family had grown smaller, its ties looser, while its members looked for more of their entertainment outside: but within this design, the special needs of adolescents were simply left out.

One could see this deficiency perhaps most directly—and visually—on the average London housing estate, as a rule consisting of rows of blocks of flats and nothing else. For the adolescents who have been moved to such estates, home has become a smaller and more impersonal place; at the same time, the old familiar meeting places on doorsteps and under the lights at street corners have gone, with nothing put in their place. A good example of this could be seen at the L.C.C. estate at Woodberry Down, in North London. Here, in what was practically a self-contained area, impressively designed complexes of flats housed upwards of 7,000 people, or the population of a small town, yet for years after the estate had gone up, the youth club provision still consisted only of a temporary hut. Something in this state of affairs is surely wrong. It is not surprising that many new estates have become breeding-grounds for groups of adolescent Teds and Drifters. It is also significant that several of the New Towns around London, where the combination of elaborate planning and financial stringency has produced a rather arid landscape of monotonous rows of small houses and gardens—arid, that is, when seen through the eager eyes of youth—should already have produced sizeable "youth problems".

These problems may well continue to grow. If, as looks likely, the majority of the population will from now on live in this rather "classless" new landscape of blocks of flats, sprawling suburban estates, New Towns, arterial roads, with cars and television aerials everywhere, we must realize that to the young this new landscape can seem something of a wilderness, with few landmarks to which they can feel emotionally attached. To this new landscape one new amenity must therefore be added. Each locality should by design include properly planned provision for the leisure time of its adolescents. This might be a well-organized local youth club, or on a larger scale a real centre for sport, music, dancing, or in a smaller area even a properly run café—but above all a place where the young can meet, preferably with adult guidance well in the background. How such places should be run, whether, as may be best, by the remodelled existing youth organizations, is something experience would show.

A second point is equally important. Just as in the interest of a more balanced society the remodelled English secondary schools of the future should display much less class divisions, so I think it essential that the Youth Services should at least to some extent (one mustn't be Utopian) break through the existing class barriers. As far as future major ventures go, my inclination is therefore for the larger type of youth centre, on the Scandinavian model. In one respect, namely the important visual one, I think the architecture of the new secondary school already provides a basic design for the future. Just as a traveller returning to England in 1960 would certainly be struck by one change—the architecturally dominant and often striking-looking school in each new area, so I believe that in 1970, say, each medium-sized town should have its equally prominent youth centre; also an essentially modern building, with imaginative facilities for music, dancing and play; for more elaborate hobbies like a ciné-photography club, real jazz, amateur acting or boat-building; the complex might be geographically linked with the local public library or swimming pool, it might be administratively run by the local youth clubs—these are details. In France, a chief organizer of the new youth movement of the *Maisons de la Culture et de la Jeunesse* told me that he liked to see each such centre (of which there are some excellent ones in France, but, of course, still far too few) as a true *centre d'animation*—a busy recognized meeting-place for the young which would bring new animation to the social life of its whole area, and this seems to me just the right definition.

New animation to what end? In England today one hears much talk about the need for the Youth Services to present a new "challenge to youth". The nature of this challenge is sometimes still oddly looked for in such things as mountaineering; there is nothing wrong in introducing working-class boys to mountaineering, or for that matter to sailing, ski-ing or other such sports, but to equate this with a major challenge to youth seems curiously old-fashioned, as though we were still at the day when Mallory and Irvine stood on the North Ridge of Everest. The Albemarle report comes nearer when saying that the Youth Services should encourage and challenge boys and girls to run their own activities as much as possible by themselves. But I think one can be much more precise. First of all, when people speak of "presenting a challenge to youth", the reference is, in fact, to working-class youth, the great mass of early school leavers who today go into dull yet well-paid routine jobs. (Nobody, for instance, worries much about finding a "challenge" for the students at Colleges of Advanced Technology!) And this defines the real challenge, not to youth, but to the Youth Services themselves. In material terms, the young people they are concerned with have been caught up in a rapid process of *embourgeoisement*—they have plenty of money in their pockets—but this is not enough. Indeed, culturally many of these boys and girls are today being exploited and downgraded. They are subjected to the mass attack of the advertisers and mass-entertainers, involved in the drift towards a purposelessness which is a feature of the affluent society. And the main task of the Youth Services is, quite simply, to oppose this drift; to help the majority of newly affluent young people to lead a fuller social life, to widen their interests and activities, to acquire greater urbanity, take keener interest in further education, in short, to "get on".

It is, in fact, the same urgent task which faces the secondary school system and which should be pursued by the Youth Services in close co-operation.

POSTSCRIPT

There is a time to end. As the reader who has borne patiently with me to this point in my book may feel, after all the various topics upon which I have touched, these concluding proposals for expanding British secondary education and Youth Services may not amount to much (and some are directed at specifically British youth problems only). Yet my basic point—and the justification for this book—is my belief that all these problems of educational reform have today taken on a new urgency, paradoxically, perhaps, because of the multitude of other social problems with which the affluent society has faced us. For the essence of so many of these problems is their novelty. The affluent society—perhaps it has been the first virtue of Professor Galbraith's invention of this compelling term to accustom us to the idea that, following upon the contemporary break-through in mass consumption, in advertising and mass-entertainment, we have indeed already entered into a new age.

As far as the young are concerned, their widened opportunities in this new age are obvious. But as I have tried to outline in earlier chapters, the onset of the affluent society has brought other social changes in its train, some far-reaching. It has begun suddenly to weaken the traditions of bourgeois society. It has transformed and loosened family relationships. Impelled towards independence at a much earlier stage, the adolescents of today are exposed to an influence quite new in scale in the shape of the commercial youth culture. It was the starting-point of my argument that the wave of juvenile delinquency in these post-war years should be seen as sign of strains in this revolution in the life of youth—and of new problems for society. How intensively should we educate our youth—I am here referring not to any élite but to the mass of the ordinary young who are stepping into the affluent society; how deliberately should we watch and guide their social life and protect them against the destructive influences of our time? These are questions which, I feel, are still unsolved in Britain and Western Europe, in the United States and in their different way in the Soviet Union. Set against this background, the particular suggestions I have put forward for educational reform in Britain may not look very imposing. Yet about the need for such reform there is this to be said: if we have to accept that the affluent society is with us as inevitably as is the nuclear age, the first task surely is to try to enable the young generation to cope better with the difficulties of this society than many of them can do now. And this task of devising a better framework of educational and social discipline for the young is also important because the new society does not look as stable as its advertisers make out—the young rebels have a point here. As the authors of the Albemarle Report said (the reference is to Britain, but the implications are wider):

Today's adolescents live within a world sharply divided into two immense blocks of power; and a world under con-stant threat of nuclear catastrophe. In addition, their own country's power and international status, once so great and indisputable, are now less easily assured. These issues may only be made articulate by a few. We are persuaded, neverthe-less, that they are felt to lie immediately behind the small stage of many an adolescent's activities, like a massive and belittling backcloth.

It is the young of today who face these complications and since it is essential for the young to feel that the future belongs to them, this may be the best hope for the way ahead.

As I was writing the concluding pages of this book, I was talking to an expert who had been selecting top-level student apprentices for further training and who said of them:

> What impressed me about these young men, and I've felt this increasingly, is that they were so strikingly autonomous. . . . They already seemed to have a rocklike philosophy of life. They had an affectionate toleration for their parents but did not accept guidance from them—they were trying to adjust their relationship to their parents so as to maintain this affection, while organizing their lives in their own way. They were pretty clear what sort of career they wanted—they seemed also to want to marry early and have relatively large families. . . . Outlook always changes over the generations, but I have seen nothing to compare to the accelerated rate of change in the last ten years, in the way these matter-of-fact young men simply accept the disorders of our age which so confuse us.

But there is every reason to help this young generation by providing a greater sense of order.

Index